CURRENCY POWER

CURRENCY POWER

Understanding Monetary Rivalry

BENJAMIN J. COHEN

PRINCETON UNIVERSITY PRESS

PRINCETON AND OXFORD

FOR RAE AND ABE,

EVER PRESENT

Contents

Tables and Figures

Acknowledgments

I have been a student of the international political economy of money for more than half a century. Over that long span of time, my work has benefitted enormously from the insight and advice of literally scores of friends and colleagues—far more than I can properly acknowledge here. I can only hope to assure them all of the deep debt of gratitude that I feel toward them. This book, drawing on a lifetime of research and reflection, could never have been written without their help.

I offer special thanks to Eric Helleiner, Jonathan Kirshner, and two anonymous readers for their very helpful comments during the preparation of this manuscript, and to my students Geoff Allen and Tristin Beckman for their tireless assistance. Thanks also to Chuck Myers, formerly political science editor at Princeton University Press, for his enthusiastic encouragement when this project was first getting under way, and to Eric Crahan, Chuck's successor, for his unwavering support as the manuscript moved forward.

The book is dedicated to the memory of my parents, Abraham and Rachel Cohen, immigrants from "the old country" who lived long enough to see their dreams for their first son fulfilled in the New World. It was they who instilled in me a life-long respect for study. They set the high intellectual and ethical standards by which I try to live to this day. Long gone, they are ever present.

Abbreviations and Acronyms

BIS	Bank for International Settlements
BRICS	Brazil, Russia, India, China, South Africa
CCI	Contemporary Capabilities Index
CFA	Communauté Financière Africaine (African Financial Community)
CINC	Composite Index of National Capabilities
CNH	offshore yuan (China)
CNP	Comprehensive National Power (China)
CNY	onshore yuan (China)
COFER	Currency Composition of Official Foreign Exchange Reserves (IMF)
COW	Correlates of War
DM	Deutsche mark
ECB	European Central Bank
ECCU	East Caribbean Currency Union
ECU	European Currency Unit
EDP	excessive deficits procedure (Europe)
EFSF	European Financial Stability Facility
EGPI	Elcano Global Presence Index (Spain)
EMS	European Monetary System
EMU	Economic and Monetary Union (Europe)
ERM	Exchange Rate Mechanism (Europe)
ESM	European Stability Mechanism

EU	European Union
GDP	gross domestic product
GPI	Global Power Index
HHI	Herfendahl-Hirschman Index
HKMA	Hong Kong Monetary Authority
IMF	International Monetary Fund
IPE	international political economy
IR	international relations
NATO	North Atlantic Treaty Organization
NSI	National Security Index (India)
OMT	Outright Monetary Transactions (Europe)
PIGS	Portugal, Ireland, Greece, Spain
PBOC	People's Bank of China
QFII	Qualified Foreign Institutional Investor (China)
RMB	renminbi, "people's currency" (China)
SDR	Special Drawing Right (IMF)
SGP	Stability and Growth Pact (Europe)
SNA	social network analysis

CURRENCY POWER

Introduction

Great powers have great currencies.
– *Robert Mundell*[1]

A Nobel laureate in economics, Robert Mundell knows currencies. On matters of money, he is a master. But what does his clever aphorism actually mean? What precisely is the relationship between currency and power? What is cause, what is effect, and what are the implications for the distribution of wealth and authority around the world? The aim of this book is to answer these critical questions.

The global economy lacks a global currency. Instead, we are forced to work with a potpourri of "state" currencies issued by individual national governments or by groups of governments in a monetary union. That is unfortunate. In terms of efficiency, one single supranational money would make much more sense, since transactions costs would then be minimized. No one would have to worry about the cost of currency conversions or the risk of exchange-rate changes. As Mundell once quipped, the optimum number of currencies is like the optimum number of gods—"an odd number, preferably less than three."[2] But does anyone seriously believe that in a fragmented world of nearly two hundred sovereign states, credible agreement can be reached on terms for the creation and management of a genuine global money? From a political point of view the option seems unattainable, even risible. Much more realistic is the prospect that the world will continue in the future, as it has in the past, to rely mainly on a limited selection of national currencies to play vital international roles.

Historically, a pronounced hierarchy has always existed among the world's diverse moneys. I have previously characterized that hierarchy as the Currency Pyramid.[3] From the days of the earliest coins in ancient Asia Minor, competition among currencies has always thrown up one or a few market favorites—*great currencies* that, for shorter or longer periods of time, predominate in use for cross-border trade and finance and set a standard for all other moneys. Though issued by national governments, we call them international currencies or international money. The process by which they acquire cross-border roles is termed *internationalization*. Historical examples in the Western world include the silver drachma of early Athens, the gold solidus of the Byzantine Empire, the Florentine florin and Venetian ducat of Renaissance Italy, the Dutch guilder in the seventeenth century, the Spanish-Mexican silver peso of the eighteenth century, the pound sterling in the nineteenth century, and the US dollar in the twentieth and (so far) twenty-first centuries.

Not insignificant is the fact that in every case the great currency's issuer, at least at the start, was also a *great power*—in its own day a major, if not dominant, player in the great game of global politics. The gains for the world economy are clear. An international currency supplies the lubricant needed to keep the wheels of commerce turning. But what of the political implications? There would also seem to be every reason to believe that currency internationalization can have a considerable impact on the distribution of capabilities and influence among states. If not, why would we hear so many complaints about the "exorbitant privilege" long enjoyed by the United States owing to the widespread popularity of its greenback? As a practical matter, currency internationalization is unavoidably associated with state power in broad political terms. My goal in this book is to advance our conceptual and analytical understanding of the political dimensions of international money.

There can be no doubt of the practical stakes involved. Currency internationalization is the product of intense competition. At first glance the process might seem mostly technical, best left to economists. But in reality monetary rivalry is profoundly political, going to the heart of what political scientists mean by the global balance of power. At this particular moment of history the US dollar remains supreme among international currencies, as it has since World War II, both reflecting and reinforcing America's position as world superpower. But increasingly the greenback's dominance is said to be under threat from challengers such as the euro, Europe's common currency, or possibly the Chinese yuan. As the race is run, questions abound. Will the dollar be surpassed by its rivals? Is the greenback's perceived weakness a symptom of broader US geopolitical decline, or could it be a contributing factor? Would decline of the currency's competitiveness mean decline of the United States as a great power? Or conversely, could the greenback successfully fight off its challengers, including the yuan, to remain the dominant world currency in a second "American Century"?

Regrettably, we have little systematic theory to help us understand monetary rivalry. The modern field of international political economy (IPE) has had remarkably little to say about the concept of power in currency relations. Well into the 1990s—apart from some early discussions by Charles Kindleberger, Susan Strange, and myself[4]—monetary power languished, in the words of Jonathan Kirshner, as "a neglected area of study."[5] Interest was revived by Kirshner's oft-quoted *Currency and Coercion*, leading, most prominently, to two substantial collections of essays edited by Thomas Lawton et al. and David Andrews.[6] But to this day the extant literature remains thin at best. Scholars like to talk about monetary power, but relatively few have taken the time to seriously analyze the concept, its meaning or sources, in formal theoretical terms.

Many questions, therefore, remain unanswered. Is state power necessary or sufficient for a money to gain international status, besting competitive rivals? Conversely, does currency internationalization add to or subtract from a state's power in relation to other states? Does a loss of state power necessarily reduce international use of its money? Or does a loss of a currency's competitive status diminish the power of the issuing state? These are the central questions to be addressed in this book. My focus is on the causal links connecting currency and power—the structural sources and consequences of power in international monetary affairs.

The book begins with two chapters of introductory material that are needed to set the stage for the discussion to follow—chapter 1 on the essentials of currency internationalization and chapter 2 on the basics of power analysis. Together, these two chapters form a critically important prelude for the drama to follow. Chapters 3 to 5 focus on the development of theory, building on insights from chapters 1 and 2 to frame a series of ideas about the causal links between currency and power. Chapters 6 to 9, in turn, make use of those ideas to analyze the currency race today, in order to gain a better understanding of the nature of monetary rivalry at present and its implications for the balance of power among states in the future. Chapter 10 concludes.

Chapter 1 offers a primer on the nature and implications of international money and currency internationalization as generally understood by scholars today. Most of this material is known to economists but may be less familiar to political scientists or others. Several critical questions are addressed. What drives the process of currency internationalization, what determines which currencies manage to become internationalized, and what does the universe of international currencies look like? Most importantly, what are the presumed implications of the process for the countries that issue an international currency? The chapter draws from several previous publications of mine.[7]

Chapter 2, in parallel fashion, offers a primer on the analysis of power, expanding on insights from the formal literature of international relations (IR). This material will be more familiar to political scientists but may be less known by economists or others. Power is ubiquitous in the study of world politics. Yet the concept itself is remarkably underdeveloped in formal theoretical terms. Indeed, IR scholars find it difficult to concur even on a basic definition of the term. Taking cues from a variety of sources, the chapter outlines a core agenda for the study of power encompassing four key clusters of questions. These questions concern, respectively, the meaning, sources, uses, and limits of power. The chapter is adapted from an essay originally co-authored with Eric Chiu.[8]

With these vital preliminaries in mind, chapter 3 opens the theoretical part of the book with a broad discussion of power in the general setting of international monetary relations. Expanding on a paper of mine first published in 2006 and harking back to another essay that appeared decades earlier,[9] the chapter establishes an understanding of the concept of international monetary power, with particular emphasis on its meaning, sources, uses, and limits. The specific role of an international currency as a source of power is carefully distinguished from the broader, more generic concept of monetary power in general.

Building on that discussion, chapters 4 and 5 then narrow the focus to address the book's central question: What is the relationship between currency and power? These two chapters constitute the conceptual heart of the book. In thinking about the relationship between currency and power, it is not always obvious which way the arrow of causation runs. The working premise of this pair of chapters is that currency and power are mutually endogenous. Currency internationalization influences state power; state power influences currency internationalization. The arrow, I submit, simultaneously points in both directions.

In chapter 4 the emphasis is on state power as a *dependent* variable, driven by competitive currency choice. For analytical purposes, a state's initial endowment of power, broadly defined, is assumed to be given. The core issue is: What happens to that endowment of power once the national money comes into widespread use across borders? In short, what is the value added of currency internationalization? International currencies, the chapter stresses, vary considerably in terms of both domain (geographic reach) and scope (range of roles). Power implications, therefore, vary considerably as well. The key contribution of the chapter is to disaggregate the concept of currency internationalization into the several separate roles that an international money may play. Attention is focused on four specific questions: What is the effect on overall state power of each individual role, considered on its own? Are there interdependencies among the various roles? What are their relative or cumulative impacts? And what happens to state power if a currency begins to lose its appeal as international money? An earlier version of the chapter appeared in 2013.[10]

Complementing chapter 4, chapter 5 then reverses the arrow of causation, now treating state power as an *independent* variable driving competitive currency choice. What role does broader state power play in the internationalization of a currency? Can an international money be "manufactured" by deliberate government strategy? And what is the effect of geopolitical decline on cross-border use of a currency? Again, the concept of internationalization is disaggregated into a currency's several possible roles. Drawing in part on a paper published in 2014,[11] the chapter puts particular emphasis on the role of national security considerations in both the rise and the fall of currencies. International moneys appear to exhibit a characteristic life cycle consisting of a succession of two broadly self-reinforcing processes—first a "virtuous circle" in which power resources promote internationalization while internationalization simultaneously promotes state power; and then a "vicious circle" in which the reverse is true, geopolitical decline sapping the appeal of a currency that in turn further erodes economic and political capabilities.

Following these theoretical chapters, the book turns to praxis, offering an applied analysis of monetary rivalry today and, prospectively, in the future. Chapter 6 begins with a sketch of the contours of competition among international currencies at present, updating an earlier analysis co-authored with Tabitha Benney.[12] Many sources argue that the global currency system is moving from unipolarity (centered on the dollar) toward a multicurrency system, with several poles (such as the euro and the yuan). Polarity, however, is a notoriously crude measure of the level of competition in any system, since it takes no account of any inequalities among the poles. A better approach is encompassed by the notion of *concentration*, borrowed from the discipline of economics, which integrates inequalities and polarity into a single measure of competitive structure. An empirical analysis of concentration in the currency system, again disaggregated by individual roles, shows that the competitive structure of the system has changed little over a period stretching back a quarter of a century. The dollar still dominates, its power seemingly undiminished. The euro remains a distant second, its power unrealized. And all the rest, including China's yuan, are also-rans, though many regard the putative rise of the Chinese currency to be virtually unstoppable.

Chapter 7 looks more closely at the dollar in an attempt to understand why the greenback still dominates. Madeleine Albright, secretary of state under President Bill Clinton, once described the United States as the "indispensable nation." This chapter argues that, similarly, there is reason to believe that the dollar is the *indispensable currency*—the one money that the world cannot do without. Building on the theory developed in chapters 4 and 5, this chapter seeks to explain why, despite more than half a century of persistent foreign deficits, and mounting external debt, the greenback remains the top international currency. Particular emphasis is placed on the depth of US financial markets, along with such considerations as network externalities in trade, extensive foreign-policy ties, national security considerations, and the absence of credible alternatives.

Chapter 8, in turn, looks at the euro, for a long time considered the greenback's most potent challenger. The question here is: Why has the euro's potential remained unrealized? At the time of the euro's birth back in 1999, expectations were high. Europe's new joint money appeared to enjoy many of the attributes needed for competitive success as an international currency, including a large economic base, political stability, and an enviably low rate of inflation, all backed by a joint monetary authority, the European Central Bank (ECB), that was fully committed to preserving confidence in the currency's future value. Yet in practice the euro has disappointed. After a fast early start, international use for most purposes leveled off and, under the pressure of Europe's sovereign debt crisis, has even begun to slip back a bit. Moreover, it is well known that while the dollar continues to be used virtually everywhere, the euro's domain remains confined to a limited number of countries with close geographical and/or institutional links to the European Union. This chapter explains why none of this should have come as a surprise. The euro was flawed from the start, owing to structural defects in the design of its governance mechanisms, and these defects, in turn, have exacerbated other weaknesses, hampering Europe's ability to compete with the United States in projecting financial, political, or military power. Chapters 7 and 8 draw from several recent publications of mine.[13]

Chapter 9 then turns to the yuan, also known as the renminbi (RMB, the "people's currency") or, more colloquially, the "redback." Here we ask: Is the rise of China's currency unstoppable? After long hesitation, Beijing appears to have made internationalization of the RMB an official policy goal, and a concerted strategy is now being implemented with that lofty ambition in mind. Extending two previously published papers,[14] the chapter argues that while China's strategy is soundly conceived, its chosen means will almost certainly prove inadequate owing to a range of practical limitations in the realms of both finance and politics. Progress of the RMB as an international currency will not come easily, if at all.

Chapter 10, finally, pulls all the strings together to summarize the contents of the book. In analytical terms, the preceding chapters make three key contributions—first, to move the political dimensions of international money to center stage; second, to explore systematically the causal links between currency internationalization and state power; and third, to disaggregate the separate roles of international money. Chapter 10 spells out the book's primary findings regarding both the theory and praxis of currency internationalization.

1

International Currency

International hierarchies are pervasive.
—*David Lake*[1]

This book is about currency and power. But before we can explore the details of their relationship, we must first establish a clear understanding of each of the two concepts considered separately. What do we know about currency internationalization? What do we know about international power? These are the essential building blocks for the discussion to follow.

Power analysis will be the subject of chapter 2. This chapter focuses on currency, outlining the nature and implications of international money as generally understood by social scientists today. The aim is to provide a baseline and context for the analysis to follow: a consensus perspective on the basics of currency internationalization. Several critical questions are addressed. What drives the process of currency internationalization, what determines which currencies will become internationalized, and what does the universe of international currencies look like? Elsewhere I have referred to this last question as the "geography of money."[2] Most importantly, what are the presumed implications of the process for the countries that issue an international currency?

MOTIVATIONS

Currencies, if attractive enough, may be employed outside their country of origin for any of a number of monetary purposes. The standard taxonomy for characterizing the roles of international money, which I can

TABLE 1.1. The roles of international money

Levels of analysis	Functions		
	Medium of exchange	Unit of account	Store of value
Private	Foreign exchange trading, trade settlement	Trade invoicing	Investment
Official	Intervention	Anchor	Reserve

take pride in originating,[3] separates out the three familiar functions of money—medium of exchange, unit of account, store of value—at two levels of analysis—the private market and official policy—adding up to six roles in all. Specialists today generally speak of the separate roles of an international currency at the private level in foreign-exchange trading (medium of exchange), trade invoicing and settlement (unit of account and medium of exchange), and financial markets (store of value). At the official level, we speak of a money's roles as an exchange-rate anchor (unit of account), intervention currency (medium of exchange), or reserve currency (store of value). Each of the six roles is distinct in practical as well as analytical terms. The taxonomy is summarized in table 1.1.

Currency internationalization alters monetary geography by accentuating the hierarchical relationship among currencies, expanding the domains of a few popular moneys well beyond the jurisdictions of the countries that issue them. The outcome is produced by a sort of a Darwinian process of natural selection, driven above all by the force of competition—much like Gresham's Law, except in reverse. Instead of "bad" money driving out "good," as Gresham's Law traditionally holds, the good money drives out bad. There is nothing irrational about the process. On the contrary, internationalization may be regarded as a quite natural demand response to prevailing market structures and incentives.

Analytically, the motivations for internationalization can be easily appreciated. The incentive derives from the economies of scale, or reduced transactions costs, to be gained from concentrating cross-border activities in just one or at most a few currencies with broad transactional networks. To do business in each country in a separate money is analogous to barter and clearly inefficient. Within any single economy, monetary exchange—rather than barter—reduces the expenses associated with search and bargaining. So too between states. The costs of transactions are narrowed by making use of one or just a few currencies rather than many. In the words of one study: "The necessity of 'double coincidence of wants' in a decentralized foreign exchange market may be overcome by using indirect exchange, through a generally acceptable medium of exchange instead of direct exchange of currencies."[4] The greater the volume of transactions that can be done via a single currency, the smaller are the costs of gathering information and converting from one money to another. Monetary theorists describe these gains as money's "network externalities" or, simply, the network value of money. Network externalities may be understood as a form of interdependence in which the practices of any one actor depend strategically on the practices adopted by others in the same network of agents.

In fact, currency internationalization improves the usefulness of money in all its roles. International standing enhances a currency's value both as a commercial medium of exchange and as a unit of account for the invoicing and settlement of trade; and these effects in turn also broaden its appeal as a store of value, by facilitating accumulation of wealth in assets of more universal purchasing power. At a minimum, it will pay market agents to hold some level of working balances in a popular international currency. Depending on cross-border variations of interest rates and exchange-rate expectations, it will pay them to use it for longer-term investment purposes as well.

Moreover, once a money comes to be widely used by private actors, it is more likely to be employed by governments too, as a reserve currency, intervention medium, and anchor for exchange rates. Public actors too can benefit from the economies of scale offered by a broad transactional network. Historically, the typical pattern of internationalization is adoption first by the private sector, with the public sector then following.

CHOICES

Why are there so few international currencies? Within individual countries, the role of a single money can be promoted by the coercive powers of the state. Sovereign governments can deploy legal-tender laws, exchange controls, and related regulatory measures to force residents to make use of the national currency for all legitimate monetary purposes. Inside their borders, states enjoy a *de jure* monopoly on the creation and management of money. But at the international level, the capacity for coercion is more limited. Compulsion is of course possible in colonial or quasi-imperial clientalistic relationships. But in the more normal case, in relations among independent nations, monopoly is replaced by competition, and actors must be *persuaded* rather than compelled to make use of one currency rather than another. Rivalry for market share, as a rule, is the essence of the process of internationalization. Typically, to gain standing, a money must be *competitive*.

And what makes a money competitive? What determines which currencies will prevail in the Darwinian struggle? The principal qualities required for competitive success are familiar to specialists and hardly controversial. Both economic and political factors appear to be involved.

On the economic side, demand seems to be shaped most by three essential attributes. First, at least during the initial stages of a currency's cross-border use, is widespread confidence in the money's future value. The historian Carlo Cipolla, in his magisterial survey of the early moneys of the Mediterranean world,[5] laid particular emphasis on "high unitary value and intrinsic stability" as essential conditions for the emergence of a dominant international currency—in other words, a proven track record of relatively low inflation and inflation variability. High and fluctuating inflation rates increase the cost of acquiring information and performing price calculations. No currency is apt to be willingly adopted for cross-border purposes if its purchasing power cannot be forecast with some degree of assurance.

Second are the qualities of *exchange convenience* and *capital certainty*—a high degree of transactional liquidity and reasonable predictability of asset value. The key to both is a set of well-developed financial markets, sufficiently open to ensure access by outsiders. Markets must not be encumbered by high transactions costs or formal or informal barriers to entry. They must also offer considerable depth, breadth, and resiliency—the three most fundamental characteristics of an efficient financial sector. *Depth* means the ability to sustain relatively large market orders without impacting significantly on an individual asset's price. *Breadth* means trading volumes and enough market competition to ensure that the spread between ask (sell) and bid (buy) prices is small. And *resilience* means the ability of market prices to recover quickly from unusually large sell or buy orders. Secondary markets must be fully operational for most if not all financial claims.

Finally, a money must promise a broad transactional network, since nothing enhances a currency's acceptability more than the prospect of acceptability by others. Historically, this factor has usually meant an economy that is large in absolute size and well integrated into world markets. A big economy creates a naturally ample constituency for a currency; the potential for network externalities is further enhanced if the issuing state is also a major player in trade. As economist Jeffrey Frankel has suggested, "the currency of a country that bulks large in the world economy has a natural advantage."[6] No money has ever risen to a position of international preeminence that was not initially backed by a leading economy. The greater the issuer's weight in global commerce, the stronger will be the "gravitational pull" of its currency.

On the political side, both domestic and international considerations may play a role. Domestically, political stability and effective governance in the country of origin would seem critical. Potential users are unlikely to be attracted to a currency that is not backed by adequate protection of property rights and genuine respect for the rule of law. Nor will they be drawn to a regime that lacks a demonstrated capacity for successful policy management. As Andrew Sobel points out in an important historical study, success in the Darwinian struggle among currencies rests heavily on the key microfoundations of political stability and accountable government.[7] In past episodes of currency internationalization, from Britain's pound sterling to the US dollar and today's euro, there was never any doubt about the durability of these key attributes. Issuing governments could be counted upon to faithfully enforce contractual obligations. Had circumstances been otherwise, it is hard to imagine that any of these currencies would have gained much traction in international markets. Why would actors deliberately expose themselves to serious political risk if they do not have to do so?

Internationally, the experiences of the pound and dollar suggest that security considerations may also be of considerable importance. At the private level, a militarily powerful nation can provide a "safe haven" for nervous investors. A strong defense ensures a more secure investment climate. At the official level, currency preferences of governments may be influenced by broader foreign-policy ties—traditional patron-client linkages, informal security guarantees, or formal military alliances. Could the timing of sterling's ascendance in the nineteenth century, paralleling the emergence of the formidable British Empire—the empire on which the sun never set—have been a mere coincidence? Can it be an accident today that with the conspicuous exceptions of China and Russia, most big dollar holders around the world are formal or informal allies of the United States? The greater the ability of an issuing state to project power beyond its borders, the more likely it is that friends and allies will feel comfortable using its money.

None of these attributes is a constant, however, as history amply demonstrates. Quite the contrary, in fact. Every one of a currency's attractions is subject to erosion with time, particularly if an issuing authority imprudently abuses the privileges derived from internationalization. Market preferences, which determine the outcome of the competitive process, may well change substantially from one period to the next. Shakespeare's words are as apt for money as they are for monarchs: "Uneasy lies the head that wears the crown." No currency has ever enjoyed a permanent dominance for international use.

Candidates

Few currencies are able to meet all the demanding economic and political qualifications for internationalization. That is not pessimism but realism. Given the substantial stakes involved, the competition that is at the core of the process of internationalization is bound to be unforgiving.

In some cases, currencies are effectively disqualified because they fail to perform all three of the standard functions of money. They are not *full-bodied* moneys. That is especially true of so-called artificial currency units like the Special Drawing Right (SDR) of the International Monetary Fund (IMF) or Europe's old European Currency Unit (ECU), which have existed primarily as notional units of account. Neither the SDR nor the ECU was ever available for use as a medium of exchange. The same was also true of the "transfer ruble" created by the former Soviet Union for denominating trade within the Soviet-led bloc of "socialist" nations before the end of the Cold War. Trade among bloc members was based on strict bilateral balancing. Monetary values were expressed in transfer rubles, but these existed solely for accounting purposes. Trade with non-bloc members was done entirely in dollars or other Western currencies. The ruble that was used inside the Soviet Union was tightly regulated and rarely adopted for transactions abroad. Despite the Soviet Union's geopolitical importance at the time, its national currency never had any real international standing.

In other cases, currencies are disbarred in practical terms by inconvertibility. Technically, Article VIII of the Charter of the IMF imposes a convertibility obligation on all Fund members. To this day, however, a majority of the Fund's membership—mostly the least developed economies—still take advantage of a legal loophole afforded by the Charter's Article XIV to prolong rigid exchange and capital controls. No one would ever consider any of their currencies credible candidates for internationalization. A money need not be fully convertible to attain some measure of use by at least a few market actors or governments. But some minimal measure of transferability is essential if a currency is to go far in the Darwinian struggle.

Among more fully convertible currencies, many fail to appeal internationally because they lack one or more essential attributes. Some issuing states may have a poor record on inflation or lack sufficient depth and liquidity in their financial markets. Others may simply not be big enough to offer a broad transactional network or to project power effectively. And others may lack the requisite political stability or rule of law.

Incumbency also matters. International currency use is highly path dependent. The playing field is by no means a *tabula rasa*; at any given moment, market actors and governments are already locked into established patterns of behavior. Newcomers, therefore, start at a distinct competitive disadvantage that may be difficult to overcome. As the late Ronald McKinnon noted, "there is a tremendous first-mover advantage to the national currency already ensconced as international money."[8]

In fact, currency choice is notoriously subject to inertia owing to the often high cost of switching from one money to another. The same network externalities that promote the use of a first mover can long delay the rise of other currencies. Why would market actors go to the trouble of adapting financial practice to a different money unless they can be sure that others will make use of it, too? A challenger must not just match at least some of the qualities of existing international currencies. It must somehow also offer advantages sufficient to persuade agents to risk making a potentially costly change. As we shall see in later chapters, lags are an inevitable part of the process, though scholars debate over how long (or short) the delay might actually turn out to be.[9]

In practical terms, it is not easy to compete with a money that is already as well established as the US dollar has been since World War II. America's greenback enjoys undoubted incumbency advantages. Not least is the fact that the language of its issuing country, English, happens as well to be the universal language of international business. The idea of converting from one money to another is less appealing if it also means switching from one language to another.

In recent experience, the currencies that have managed to achieve even marginal acceptance for cross-border purposes can be counted on the fingers of two hands. Over the post–World War II period, the dollar has dominated. Among all the world's other currencies, only West Germany's old Deutsche mark (DM), Japan's yen, and the euro have for a time been competitive enough to also gain a significant share of the market for international money. Others have exhibited lesser degrees of market appeal.

THE CURRENCY PYRAMID

How, then, can we best visualize money's geography? International relations have always been characterized by a degree of hierarchy, as David Lake has usefully reminded us—a "rich tapestry," as he describes it, with "varying hues and textures."[10] There is no reason why the same should not also be true of international currencies. Cross-border competition naturally gives rise to a rich tapestry of hierarchy in the world of money. The use and influence of a few popular currencies can reach far beyond the legal jurisdictions of their issuing authorities, spanning large parts of the globe, while the effective domains of other currencies are sharply shrunk, sometimes dramatically.[11] The persistence of hierarchy among moneys has long been recognized by monetary historians.[12] In the modern era, elevated status has been affirmed by such labels as "key currencies" or even "dream currencies"—the moneys that investors dream in.[13]

Nearly half a century ago the noted British scholar Susan Strange introduced the first systematic taxonomy of the world's most widely used currencies.[14] Strange distinguished four types of international money: neutral currencies, top currencies, master currencies, and negotiated currencies. *Neutral currencies* are moneys that appeal to market actors for strictly economic reasons (stable value, network externalities, and the like). Add dominance by the issuing country in related structures and issue-areas, and a money may be described as a *top currency*. *Master*

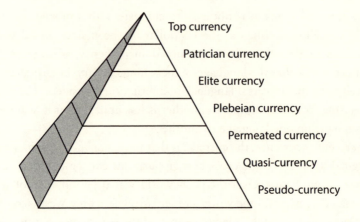

Figure 1.1. The Currency Pyramid.

currencies derive from formal dependency relationships, such as colonial ties, and rely on a degree of coercion. *Negotiated currencies,* by contrast, rely more on persuasion and result from diplomatic bargaining or informal understandings to promote or sustain foreign use.

More recently, I sought to build on Strange's foundation by introducing the image of a Currency Pyramid to more fully represent the hierarchy of moneys around the world (figure 1.1).[15] The Currency Pyramid is narrow at the peak, where one or a few moneys dominate, and increasingly broad below, reflecting varying degrees of competitive inferiority. The moneys at the top includes the four currency types that Strange identifies in her taxonomy. The advantage of the pyramid image is that it reaches further down to take account of other, lower rungs in the hierarchy as well.

Though difficult to operationalize for analytical purposes, the image of the Currency Pyramid is nonetheless useful to convey the colorful diversity of money's competitive relationships while at the same time not exaggerating the degree of refinement that we can bring to the exercise. In all, seven categories of money are identified. The labels for each stratum, though slightly tongue-in-cheek, are meant to accentuate the steeply vertical imagery appropriate to an accurate mapping of monetary geography.

The seven categories are as follows:

Top Currency. With a nod to Strange's use of the same label and with the same meaning in mind, this rarified rank is reserved only for the most esteemed of international currencies—those whose use dominates for most if not all types of cross-border purposes and whose popularity is more or less universal, not limited to any particular geographic region. In the modern era just two currencies could truly be said to have qualified for this exalted status: Britain's pound sterling before World War I and the US dollar after World War II. In principle more than one top currency might be in favor simultaneously, as were the pound and dollar together during the interwar period, before sterling went into what proved to be a long and irreversible decline.[16] Today, however, the greenback alone occupies the highest stratum of the Currency Pyramid. No other money comes close. Though doubts about the dollar's future are widespread, generating heated debate, the currency's global preeminence, for now, remains undiminished.[17]

Patrician Currency. Just below the top rank we find currencies whose use for various cross-border purposes, while substantial, is something less than dominant and/or whose popularity, while widespread, is something less than universal. Historically, some of the moneys in this category, corresponding to Strange's category of neutral currency, have appealed simply because of their inherent economic qualities; others have resembled more her remaining categories of master currency or negotiated currency. Today the patrician category obviously includes the euro, which stands second to the greenback in most categories of cross-border use. Following its creation in 1999, many observers predicted that the euro was destined to achieve parity with the greenback, or perhaps even surpass it, in a relatively short period of time.[18] In practice, however, the euro's early promise as a rival to the dollar has remained unrealized. After a fast start, cross-border use of the currency soon leveled off and, especially after Europe's sovereign-debt problems that began in the spring of 2010, has come to be largely confined to the EU's immediate hinterland around the European periphery and in parts of the Mediterranean littoral and Africa. The only other patrician currency of note these days is the Japanese yen, despite some recent loss of popularity. Many observers expect the ranks of patrician currencies to be joined soon by China's yuan. Some even expect the RMB one day to eclipse the dollar, describing its ascent as "unstoppable."[19]

Elite Currency. In this category belong currencies of sufficient attractiveness to qualify for some degree of international use but of insufficient weight to carry much direct influence beyond their own national frontiers. Here we find the more peripheral of the international currencies, little more than bit players on the currency stage. These moneys too may be considered to correspond to what Strange meant by neutral currencies. Today the list of elite currencies would include inter alia Britain's pound (sadly, no longer a top currency or even a patrician currency), the Swiss franc, and the Australian and Canadian dollars. All of these currencies are used to some extent in global currency and financial markets because of their inherent economic qualities. In addition, the Australian dollar and South African rand play significant roles as exchange-rate anchor and reserve currency in their respective neighborhoods in the southern Pacific and southern Africa.

Plebeian Currency. One step further down from the elite category are plebeian currencies—more modest moneys of very limited international use. Here we find the currencies of the smaller industrial states, such as Norway or Sweden, along with some middle-income emerging-market economies (for example, Singapore, South Korea, and Taiwan) and the wealthier oil-exporters (for example, Kuwait, Saudi Arabia, and United Arab Emirates). Internally, plebeian currencies retain a more or less exclusive claim to all the traditional functions of money, but externally they carry little weight (like the plebs, or common folk, of ancient Rome). They tend to attract little cross-border use except perhaps for a certain amount of trade invoicing.

Permeated Currency. Included in this category are moneys whose competitiveness is effectively compromised even at home, through what economists call *currency substitution*—adoption by residents of a popular foreign currency as a preferred alternative to the national currency. Although nominal monetary sovereignty continues to reside with the issuing government, foreign money supersedes the domestic alternative, particularly as a store of value, thus accentuating the local currency's degree of inferiority. Permeated currencies confront what amounts to a competitive invasion from abroad. Judging from available evidence, it appears that the range of permeated currencies today is in fact quite broad, encompassing many economies of the developing world, particularly in Latin America and Southeast Asia.

Quasi-Currency. One step further down are currencies that are superseded not only as a store of value but, to a significant extent, as a unit of account and medium of exchange as well. Quasi-currencies are moneys that retain nominal sovereignty but are largely rejected in practice for most purposes. Their domain is more juridical than empirical. Available

TABLE 1.2. Benefits and risks of an international currency

Benefits	Risks
Reduced transactions costs	Currency appreciation
International seigniorage	External constraint
Macroeconomic flexibility	Policy responsibility
Political leverage (hard power)	
Reputation (soft power)	

evidence suggests that some approximation of this more radical degree of inferiority has indeed been reached in a number of fragile economies around the globe.

Pseudo-Currency. Finally, we come to the bottom rank of the pyramid, where currencies exist in name only—pseudo-currencies. The most obvious examples of pseudo-currencies are token moneys like the Panamanian balboa, found in countries where a stronger foreign currency such as the dollar is the preferred legal tender. Along with the many small permeated currencies and quasi-currencies, pseudo-currencies have sometimes been scornfully dismissed as no more than "junk currencies."[20]

BENEFITS AND COSTS

Finally, what are the benefits and costs of an international currency? To approach an understanding of the relationship between currency and power, we must first have a firm grasp of all possible implications for the country of origin, whether positive or negative.

In a diverse literature stretching back decades, drawing from political science as well as economics, we should not be surprised to find wide variation in lists of possible gains and risks compiled by different analysts. From these many sources we can distill a consolidated catalog that may be regarded as reasonably inclusive. A comprehensive list would include a total of some five broad classes of gain and three major risks, as summarized in table 1.2. Benefits stressed by economists include a cluster of favorable impacts at the microeconomic level, subsumed under the rubric of *transactions costs*, as well as, at a more aggregate level, two forms of gain labeled *international seigniorage* and *macroeconomic flexibility*. Political scientists are inclined to add two effects that are more overtly political in nature: *leverage* and *reputation*. Risks of internationalization include the possibility of undue *currency appreciation*, an unwelcome *external constraint* on domestic monetary autonomy, and a burden of *policy responsibility* that could go with the privilege of currency leadership.

Transactions Costs

At the microeconomic level, several benefits accrue to residents of any country that provides an international currency. Perhaps most prominent is the boost to profits in the banking sector, long ago characterized by economist Alexander Swoboda as "denomination rents."[21] Since home banks enjoy privileged access to the resources of the issuing country's central bank, enabling them to more easily create monetary liabilities denominated in the national currency, a distinct competitive advantage is gained as compared with financial institutions elsewhere. Business can be expanded abroad at lower cost, generating greater earnings than would otherwise be possible. In Swoboda's words, "the average level of profits of the banking system of an issuing country will tend, other things equal, to be higher [due to the extension of the market] than that of the banking systems of other countries."[22] Included in these extra earnings may be commissions charged for an increased volume of foreign-exchange transactions as well as fees for loans, investment services, or other ancillary activities.

Nonfinancial enterprises in the issuing country also benefit in at least two ways. First, internationalization enhances their ability to do business abroad in home currency, thus lowering exchange risk. Though the gain for firms may be less substantial than typically assumed,[23] it can nonetheless be significant, particularly in the case of trade contracts where payment are due long after goods are initially ordered. And second, access to international financial markets is broadened, enabling select firms to borrow more cheaply and on a larger scale than they normally could at home. Ordinary citizens also benefit to the extent that they are able to use their own money when traveling abroad—a notable convenience.

Not all residents gain, of course. Most of an international currency's benefits at the microeconomic level accrue to the more externally oriented sectors of the economy, implying potentially significant distributional consequences. But while some are favored by lower transactions costs, few if any residents experience any direct increase of costs so long as the currency remains competitive. The gains of "winners" come mainly at the expense of actors abroad rather than at home. For the issuing country as a whole, relative to the outside world, the net impact is positive.

Seigniorage

Technically defined as the excess of the nominal value of a currency over its cost of production, seigniorage at the international level is generated whenever foreigners acquire and hold some amount of domestic money in exchange for traded goods, services, or foreign investment assets. Cross-border accumulations of the national money represent an implicit economic transfer that constitutes a real-resource gain for the economy as a whole.

Two components are involved. One results from foreign accumulations of actual cash—bank notes and coins. Since no interest is paid on the cash liabilities of a central bank, holdings of its notes and coins abroad represent the equivalent of an interest-free loan to the issuing country. In the case of the United States, as much as 60 percent of the outstanding stock of Federal Reserve notes is estimated to be in circulation outside the country, amounting at end-2011 to perhaps $650 billion.[24] Even at today's low borrowing costs, that translates into an interest saving for the US government of as much as $15 billion to $20 billion a year—in absolute terms a not negligible sum, though little more than a modest one-tenth of one percent of America's gross domestic product (GDP).

The second component, rather more substantial, derives from foreign accumulations of financial claims denominated in the home money, an increase of effective demand for assets that has the effect of driving the cost of borrowing below what it might be otherwise. Effectively, an interest-rate subsidy is generated. Economic theory would suggest that acquisitions are most likely motivated by liquidity considerations. The gain is often referred to as a "liquidity premium." Political science would add a second motivation, a desire for a safe haven for investments, which can generate a further "security premium,"[25] sometimes also called a "security tax."[26] In practice, the two motivations are difficult to disentangle. Overall, for the United States the total subsidy has been estimated to amount to as much as 80 basis points, producing an annual saving of at least

$150 billion for the federal government and other domestic borrowers.[27] A comparable estimate for Europe suggests a gain of as much as 0.5 percent of GDP for the members of the euro zone.[28]

Alternatively, the value of the second component can be estimated by calculating the difference between the (higher) returns on foreign assets of an issuing country and the (lower) cost of foreign liabilities. For the United States as a whole, studies put the excess return on net foreign claims at 300 or more basis points per year.[29] At anywhere from 1 percent to 3 percent of GDP, these figures are anything but negligible.

Macroeconomic Flexibility

Cross-border use of a currency can also loosen the constraint of external payments imbalances, enhancing policy autonomy. The greater the ability to pay for foreign goods and services with a country's own money, the easier it is for the authorities to sustain public policy objectives both at home and abroad. In effect, external market discipline is relaxed. For a resentful Valéry Giscard d'Estaing, French finance minister back in the 1960s, this was an "exorbitant privilege" that set the United States, with its dominant dollar, apart from other nations. Many outsiders still complain about America's presumed exorbitant privilege.

Here too, as at the microeconomic level, there are potentially significant distributional consequences. Not all domestic residents may benefit from the exorbitant privilege. As Jeffry Frieden long ago reminded us,[30] some sectors of an economy—particularly those sensitive to the risk of inflation—might actually prefer more rather than less discipline on potentially spendthrift politicians. But from the point of view of the state as a whole, engaged as a sovereign actor in relation to other states, there seems little doubt that the greater degree of freedom for monetary and fiscal policy may be regarded as a net plus.

Leverage

Foreign influence is a fourth possible benefit of an international currency. An element of dependence is created when outsiders come to rely on some national money for a variety of international roles. That dependence puts the issuer in a position to exercise leverage through its control of access to a vital financial resource. The more others rely on a currency, the greater is the issuer's potential capacity for pressure or control.

Leverage can be exercised either directly or indirectly. Most familiar is direct political action in selective circumstances, deployed through the calculated use of available policy instruments, including side payments (bribery) or sanctions (coercion)—in other words, carrots or sticks. In *Currency and Coercion*, Jonathan Kirshner labeled such policies "enforcement" or "expulsion."[31] Friendly countries may be granted loans or privileged access to its currency in the midst of a monetary or financial crisis; conversely, adversaries may be deprived of access to essential clearing networks when political tensions run high. Less familiar is a form of leverage that operates more indirectly by favorably altering material incentive structures—what Kirshner called "entrapment." Because of an established currency's importance, foreign users develop a stake in its continued success and hence may more or less willingly adapt to the issuing country's preferences and requirements without even being asked.

Reputation

Finally, at the symbolic level, widespread international use of a currency can promote the issuer's overall reputation in world affairs. Broad circulation may become a source of status and prestige, a visible sign of elevated rank in the community of nations. Internationalization of a money can provide a potent symbol of international primacy, working through co-option and attraction to shape the preferences of others. Economists may scoff at such psychological notions, which are certainly difficult to pin down empirically. But the importance of cognition and culture in monetary affairs has by now been well established by historical and contemporary research.[32]

Appreciation

On the cost side, one frequently mentioned risk of internationalization is the exchange-rate appreciation that could result from increased foreign demand for a currency. The more a money gains in popularity, the greater is the likelihood that some degree of overvaluation could result, at least initially. For home consumers appreciation actually represents a benefit, since purchasing power is increased. But for producers the effect is distinctly negative, since the competitiveness of exports and import-competing output will be impaired. Both sales and employment will be adversely affected. In the case of the United States, one source estimates a net financial cost that rises by as much as $30 billion a year for each 5 percent movement upward of the dollar's exchange rate.[33] Another source estimates a net loss of as many as six million jobs in the United States in a typical recent year.[34] Again, these are by no means negligible amounts.

External Constraint

Even more serious is the possible constraint that could be imposed on domestic policy autonomy by an excessive accumulation of liquid foreign liabilities. Macroeconomic flexibility could be compromised by a growing "overhang" of highly mobile debt, whether held abroad as cash or in the form of liquid claims denominated in the home money. To persuade foreigners to hold onto their accumulated holdings, interest rates may have to be raised, reducing or even eliminating seigniorage gains[35] and constraining domestic policy. Eventually both leverage and reputation could also be adversely affected.

Two specific dangers are posed for the issuer's central bank. One is the risk of volatile movements into or out of the currency, which could make the demand for money less stable in aggregate terms. Policy makers, at any given time, may find it more difficult to target interest rates or an appropriate growth rate for money supply. The other is the risk that over time domestic policy may become increasingly hostage to external factors, especially if doubts begin to mount regarding the currency's future value or usefulness. Ultimately, to persuade actors abroad to hold onto their accumulated balances, priorities at home may have to be compromised or sacrificed. Though neither danger is easy to quantify, both must be regarded as real and could be potentially significant.

Policy Responsibility

Even more difficult to quantify is one last risk of internationalization—the possibility that in return for the benefits it receives, an issuing country will find itself obliged to assume greater responsibility for management of broad regional or global monetary structures. Quite apart from market-driven pressures on its central bank, the issuer may find itself called upon to accommodate systemic needs or fragilities should conditions warrant. Monetary policy may have to be modified to contain a crisis, or subsidized credits may have to be provided to rescue economies in distress. A complete catalog of the benefits and costs of an international currency cannot ignore the contingent political claim that goes with monetary leadership. One source calls it the leader's "exorbitant duty"[36]—effectively, the flip-side of currency internationalization's "exorbitant privilege." The idea was well expressed by Timothy Geitner, then president of the Federal Reserve Bank of New York, in the midst of the financial crisis of 2008:

> Another way to think about this is that the privilege of being the reserve currency of the world comes with some burdens. Not that we have an obligation in this sense, but we have an interest in helping these guys mitigate the problems they face.[37]

To paraphrase Robert Mundell: Great powers may not only have great currencies, they may also have great responsibilities.

MISPLACED CONCRETENESS

In principle, all of these five classes of gains and three major risks should be included in any systematic analysis of the benefits and costs of an international currency. In practice, however, that is not usually the case. Indeed, much of the extant literature tends to suffer from what the philosopher Alfred North Whitehead called the "Fallacy of Misplaced Concreteness"—essentially, the error of mistaking the abstract for the concrete. The problem has long plagued mainstream economics. More than a half century ago, the distinguished economist Fritz Machlup highlighted the issue, berating his colleagues for "the general fallacy involved in jumping the distance between a useful fiction and particular data of observation."[38] Regrettably, though, his warnings have long been forgotten. Contemporary analyses of currency internationalization too often overlook the degree of abstraction in their models and draw unwarranted conclusions about material reality.

Typical was a study not long ago by McKinsey Global Institute,[39] which posed the question: What are the benefits and costs of being an international currency? The study purported to offer a firm empirical calculus for the US dollar, concluding bluntly that "Today, it is not clear that the United States enjoys much of a privilege at all. . . . [At best] the United States derives a relatively modest net financial benefit."[40] But was that dismissive conclusion warranted? McKinsey's calculus included quantitative estimates for just two of the several effects of currency internationalization—specifically, seigniorage benefits and the cost of exchange-rate appreciation. A few other considerations were mentioned, but only in passing. The distance between the narrow empirical content of the study and the broad inferences drawn by its authors was clearly too great to be persuasive. Concrete reality was egregiously distorted by an undue reliance on a limited range of data.

Even more egregious is a recent polemic from Jared Bernstein,[41] formerly chief economist for Vice President Joe Biden. According to Bernstein, the United States should act decisively to terminate the internationalization of the greenback—in his words, to "dethrone king dollar"—as soon as possible. The reason, he argues, is that foreign demand for America's currency costs millions of US jobs due to exchange-rate appreciation. No other effect of internationalization merits any notice. The possibility that there might be some offsetting benefits is never even considered.

Nor are commentaries like these by any means atypical. Economist Hans Genberg, to cite another example, bases a "calculus of international currency use" on just two specific considerations—seigniorage gains and impacts on transactions costs.[42] C. Fred Bergsten, a well-known commentator, concludes that the United States "would benefit from a reduction of the international role of the dollar" after focusing on just two costs—an increased external constraint on domestic policy and the risk of currency appreciation.[43] Elias Papaioannou and Richard Portes, assessing prospective benefits and costs for the euro, quite explicitly downplay political aspects in order to concentrate on empirical specifications of economic effects.[44] Similarly, two Chinese economists, Wen Hai and Hongxin Yao, evaluating the pros and cons of internationalization of the yuan, rely on estimates of just three possible factors—seigniorage, reduced transactions costs, and impacts on domestic monetary policy.[45] In all these cases, the concreteness attributed to reality seems seriously misplaced.

Why, then, does the fallacy persist? It could be because of the value that has long been attached to parsimony in mainstream economic research.

Typically, a reductionist style is favored that seeks to pare messy reality down to its bare essentials—aiming "to predict something large from something small," as the economist Harry Johnson once put it.[46] In the social sciences we are always faced with a basic trade-off between parsimony and detail—between the refined abstractions required for theoretical generalization and the elaborate descriptions required to ensure external validity. The most prized work on currency internationalization today clearly follows contemporary fashion, tilting toward simplicity rather than complexity.

But it is also tempting to see more: an unfortunate inclination to permit analysis to be driven by data availability, even at the risk of distorting reality. Clearly, some of the effects of internationalization defy easy quantification—particularly the more political benefits and risks involved. How do we put a number on leverage or reputation? What metric do we use for flexibility or responsibility? It is so much more convenient simply to concentrate on factors that can putatively be estimated, however crudely, and just wave a hand at the rest. One is reminded of the old joke about the man seen late one night under a lamp post, down on his knees searching for a set of keys. Is that where you lost them?, he is asked. No, they were lost down the street, but the light here is better. Too much of the literature just goes where the light is.

CONCLUSION

Overall, then, much is understood about currency internationalization—its motivations, choices, and presumed implications. Driven by the force of competition, the process of internationalization produces a distinct hierarchy among currencies. For the nations whose currencies come to play cross-border roles, benefits as well as costs may be considerable. But how does this all translate into power? Is state power necessary or sufficient for a currency to gain international status, besting competitive rivals? Conversely, does currency internationalization add to or subtract from a state's power in relation to other states? Does a loss of state power necessarily reduce international use of its currency? Or does a loss of a currency's competitive status diminish the power of the issuing state? About these questions we have remarkably little theory to guide us. The following chapters seek to provide some answers.

2

Power Analysis

The more we look into the question of power,
the murkier the concept becomes.
—*Simon Reich and Richard Ned Lebow*[1]

Chapter 1 summarized the essentials of what we know about currency internationalization. In parallel fashion, this chapter explores what we know about power in international relations. Again, the purpose is to provide a baseline and context for the discussion to follow. Such a background discussion is imperative if subsequent chapters are not to get lost in a welter of conflicting terminologies and interpretations. The central questions addressed in this book cannot be answered without some clarity about the basics of power analysis.

Power is of course ubiquitous in the study of international relations. Actors of all kinds—individuals, enterprises, governments, multilateral organizations—are said to have power (or not); to use power; to be affected by power; to submit to power. Power across the globe is said to be concentrated or dispersed; the distribution of power is said to be stable or changing; the exercise of power is said to be effective or ineffective. Power is everywhere. Yet for all its ubiquity, the concept is remarkably underdeveloped in formal theoretical terms—a "somewhat mysterious notion," in the words of a recently published *Encyclopedia of Power*.[2] Though power analysis has attracted enormous interest over the years, consensus remains elusive across a range of issues. In place of any sort of common understandings, we find nothing but "theoretical confusion and cacophony."[3]

Indeed, scholars find it difficult to concur even on a basic definition of the term. What are the essential properties of power? What are its sources? How does it operate? And what are its limits? Words like capability, force, and influence are thrown about, but with little clarity concerning their precise meaning or connections. Robert Gilpin once described the idea of power as "one of the most troublesome in the field of international relations."[4] The only true point of agreement, quips David Baldwin, is on the "unsatisfactory state of knowledge about this topic."[5] The frustration expressed by Simon Reich and Richard Ned Lebow is understandable. The concept of power remains highly contested.

In the absence of consensus, we have no choice but to settle for pragmatism in our analysis. We must accept that power is a slippery concept that comes in many forms—a complex and multifaceted phenomenon, almost chameleon-like in character. There is no single formula that will serve for all purposes.[6] We must be prepared to choose among multiple dimensions and interpretations of power, depending on the circumstances at hand. Whatever the issue we propose to study, we must assume that the characteristics and implications of power are all highly contingent. As Michael Barnett and Raymond Duvall advise, scholars "must work with multiple conceptions of power, suggest how they can accomplish this task, and demonstrate how a consideration of power's polymorphous character will enhance and deepen theoretic understanding of international politics."[7] Or as Joseph Nye puts it, more bluntly: "Power always depends on context."[8]

In practical terms, pragmatism means that power analysis must contend with four key clusters of questions. These concern, respectively, the meaning, sources, uses, and limits of power. For all four clusters, context clearly matters. For any particular issue, how do we define power? Where does power come from? How are capabilities converted into action? And what determines the limits of power? Together, these four questions define the core agenda for any serious study of the role of power in international affairs—including monetary affairs.

MEANING

First, what do we mean by power? The focus of this book is on *state* power: the resources and capabilities of sovereign governments. More often than not, IR scholars casually equate the power of states with *influence*: the ability to alter the behavior of others. Formally, the approach goes back to the early work of Robert Dahl, who argued that "A has power over B to the extent that he can get B to do something that B would not otherwise do."[9] Power is understood simply as a capacity to control outcomes—"letting others have your way," as diplomacy has jokingly been defined. A state, in this sense, is powerful to the extent that it can effectively pressure or coerce others; in short, to the extent that it can exercise leverage or enforce compliance. Typical is a recent survey of the subject by Baldwin, in which he explicitly equates power with influence or control.[10] Baldwin is widely respected as a key pioneer in the development of power analysis over the years.[11]

Influence, however, is not the only possible meaning of power. There is also a vital second meaning, as peace researcher Berenice Carroll long ago reminded us.[12] That second meaning corresponds to the generic dictionary definition of power as a capacity for action (going back to the Latin root for power, *potere*—"to be able"). In IR and IPE, this is a matter of policy independence or what some call "policy space." A state is also powerful to the extent that it can act unilaterally—that is, to the extent that it is able to operate freely, insulated from outside pressures, and to deflect the influence of others. In this sense, power does not mean influencing others; rather, it means not allowing others to influence *you*—others letting *you* have your way. A useful synonym for this meaning of power is *autonomy*.

Conceptually, influence and autonomy may be understood as two distinct (albeit interrelated) dimensions of power. We may label them, respectively, the *external* and *internal* dimension. Roughly analogous is the familiar distinction between the notions of "power over" and "power to," increasingly found in the IR and IPE literatures.[13] Scholars who focus on one actor's power *over* others are speaking of influence, the external dimension. Those who, by contrast, concentrate on what actors can achieve (power *to*) are speaking of autonomy, the internal dimension. In practical terms, it is evident that power has two dimensions, not just one. As Dahl notes: "The logical complement of influence is autonomy."[14]

For the most part, regrettably, the extant literature tends to downplay the dimension of autonomy, focusing attention primarily on questions of influence. Only rarely does the "power to" take center stage. One recent example is offered by the "realist structural theory" of Richard Harknett and Hasan Yalcin, which places core emphasis on the "struggle for autonomy."[15] I would submit, however, that the distinction between the two dimensions is critical. Both are based in social relationships and can be observed in behavioral terms; the two are also unavoidably interrelated. Real value is added by bringing autonomy formally into the picture alongside influence.

Not everyone agrees. For many, this may be a distinction without a difference—a conceptual redundancy. Influence arguably is inherent in the notion of autonomy, inseparable in practice. Start with the fact that international relations are inescapably reciprocal. A potential for leverage, therefore, is automatically created whenever policy independence is attained. By definition, a capacity to act unilaterally may generate repercussions or ripple effects—in technical language, "externalities"—that compel others to react in one way or another. In that sense, a measure of influence is necessarily generated as an inescapable corollary of autonomy. The two, it might be said, are not really complements at all. Rather, they could be seen merely as two parts of the same whole.

That kind of argument, however, overlooks a key additional distinction. We may also speak of two distinct *modes* of influence: passive and active. Both modes are implied by a capacity for independent action. But the ways in which they relate to the traditional notion of influence are quite different from one another.

The mode of influence that derives inherently from autonomy is *passive*, representing at best an incidental by-product of power; it can be said to operate at all only because of the exercise of autonomy. Moreover, the impacts involved are diffuse and undirected. There is no agency (action) or intentionality involved. The passive mode is very different from what is conventionally meant by influence in power analysis, which most often is understood to imply some degree of targeting or intent—"purposeful acts," in the words of David Andrews.[16] Autonomy translates into influence in the accepted sense of the term—a dimension of power deliberately aiming to shape the behavior of others—only when the potential for leverage is *activated*, self-consciously applied to attain economic or political goals. Otherwise, when the potential is not activated, autonomy remains distinct from influence in the accepted sense.

Why is the distinction between autonomy and influence important? It matters because, as a practical matter, the difference can have profound implications for the way we understand the balance of power among states. There is in fact a critical organic relationship between the external and internal dimensions. Though not all scholars agree, logic suggests that power must begin with autonomy, which generates a *potential* for leverage; influence—the deliberate *activation* of leverage—should then be best thought of as functionally derivative. In practice, an ability to target behavior abroad would seem inconceivable without first attaining and sustaining a relatively high degree of policy independence at home. First and foremost, actors must be free to pursue their goals without outside constraint. Only then would they be in a position, *in addition*, to exercise authority elsewhere. As the saying goes in American football, the best offense starts with a good defense.

That does not mean that autonomy must be enjoyed in *all* aspects of international affairs or in *all* geographic relationships in order to be able to exercise influence in any single context. States can successfully apply leverage in selected issue areas or relationships even while themselves being subject to pressure or coercion in others. But it does mean that in a *given* context, power would seem to begin at home. First and foremost, policy makers must be free to pursue national objectives in the specific issue area or relationship without outside constraint—to avoid compromises or sacrifices adopted in order to accommodate the interests of others. Only then would a state be in a position, *in addition*, to enforce compliance elsewhere. Autonomy, the internal dimension, may not be *sufficient* to ensure a degree of foreign influence. But it would certainly appear to be *necessary*—the essential foundation of influence. In any given context it is possible to think of autonomy without influence; it is very difficult to think of influence without autonomy.

The material consequences of this understanding may be considerable. Consider, for example, the extraordinary growth of nations like China in recent decades, which is thought to have dramatically broadened the global distribution of power. It may be argued, however, that the diffusion of power has been mainly in the dimension of autonomy rather than influence. That would mean that while some emerging economies have gained a degree of insulation from outside pressures, few as yet are able to exercise greater authority to shape events or outcomes. As a result, leadership in the system may well have been dispersed rather than relocated—a pattern of change that could generate greater, not less, ambiguity in prevailing structures of economic governance. My term for this is *leaderless diffu-sion.*[17] In that context, the distinction between the two dimensions does obviously matter—though in practical terms, clearly, the issue is empirical and can be settled only by careful analysis of the facts.

The first question for power analysis, therefore, is: How useful is the distinction between the two dimensions of power? Given the subject matter at hand, is a focus on influence sufficient? Or is analysis misleading without a comparable emphasis on the dimension of autonomy? Clearly, we cannot expect to make much progress in the study of power if we cannot even agree on the starting point: what we mean by the term.

SOURCES

Next, what are the sources of power? Here consensus is especially elusive. At issue are the capabilities of states—their *ability* to operate autonomously or exercise influence. At one level of analysis, scholars disagree on where those capabilities come from: what we may term the *roots* of power. At another level, debates rage over how those capabilities manifest themselves: what have come to be called the *faces* of power. Nowhere in the analysis of power is the cacophony greater.

The Roots of Power

Whether power is understood in terms of influence or autonomy, two contrasting approaches have traditionally competed to explain where state capabilities come from. One, drawing inspiration from early realist theory, is the *elements-of-power* approach (or *power-as-resources* approach), identifying power with tangible resources of one kind or another. In this view, power is rooted in specific properties or possessions of a state such as territory, population, armed forces, or natural resources. The other, of more recent origin, is the *relational power* approach (or *social power* approach), associated more with a liberal perspective on IR theory. In this view, power is identified as a type of causation derived from the structure of relations between states.

The elements-of-power approach is embodied in a number of popular indicators of state power built from diverse lists of material attributes. Perhaps best known is the Composite Index of National Capabilities (CINC) developed by the long-standing Correlates of War (COW) project.[18] CINC is comprised of six objective metrics considered to be particularly relevant to the ability to wage war—military expenditure, military personnel, energy consumption, iron and steel production, urban population, and total population. Another example is the Global Power Index (GPI) developed by the US government's National Intelligence Council.[19] The GPI is based on gross domestic product (GDP), population size, military spending, and technology, recently supplemented with additional variables for health, education, and governance. And a third example is the Audit of Major Powers published by the Web-based magazine *European Geostrategy*,[20] which includes variables drawn from four different categories—cultural pull, diplomatic influence, economic strength, and military reach.

On the other side of the globe, Chinese strategic thinkers, working in the same tradition, have developed an indicator of their own called Comprehensive National Power (CNP, *zonghe guoli*), constructed from some eight state properties, including natural resources, military strength, and indices for other political, social, and technological factors. The approach, according to China scholar David Shambaugh, is integral to the country's geopolitical ambitions.[21] The Chinese leadership, Shambaugh suggests, has "wisely learned one key lesson from studying the experiences of other previous powers: genuine global powers possess multidimensional strength. . . . The Chinese grasp the idea that power is comprehensive and integrative."[22] The CNP is meant to provide an indigenous and scientific measure for comparing China's capabilities against other major powers.[23]

Similarly, in India a National Security Index (NSI) has been developed combining six sets of attributes, including economic capability, military capability, population capability, technological capability, foreign affairs capability, and energy security.[24] Here too the intention is to compare the country's capabilities against other major powers. And closely related is the Elcano Global Presence Index (EGPI), created by Spain's Royal Elcano Institute,[25] which seeks to measure the effective positioning of nations outside their own borders. By comparing its own index for each nation's "presence" with more conventional indices of power, the Elcano Institute aims to measure the extent to which any individual country may be "punching above or below its weight."

The appeal of the elements-of-power approach is obvious. Scholars naturally are attracted to quantitative measures that appear useful for empirical analysis. But the downsides are equally evident, as numerous sources have noted.[26] First, there is the question of what variables to include for the purpose of estimating power. As the multiplicity of indicators demonstrates, from the CINC to the EGPI, serious analysts can sincerely disagree on what properties matter most for determining state capabilities. The choice of components in an index is subjective at best, at times even arbitrary. Hence any single index may actually turn out to be quite misleading. And second, more substantively, there is the question of how the capabilities of different agents interact: the strategic dimension of power. Indicators like the CINC and its various counterparts simply compare one country's capabilities with others. They say nothing about how these capabilities relate. Put bluntly, they say nothing about the *politics* involved. Summarizes Nye: "Any attempt to develop a single index of power is doomed to fail because power depends upon human relationships that vary in different contexts."[27]

In the alternative relational power approach, by contrast, politics is central. Power is assumed to be a function of actual or potential interactions—a social characteristic—rather than derived simply from the material attributes of any one actor. What matters is not an accumulation of "power resources," no matter how intuitively appealing that may seem. Rather, it is the strategic dimension that takes center stage. Capabilities are understood in terms of who depends on whom and for what.

From its beginnings some half century ago, the modern field of IPE has relied heavily on the relational power approach. Inspiration came first and foremost from the early insights of economist Albert Hirschman in his World War II–era *National Power and the Structure of Foreign Trade*, a book long neglected until it was rediscovered in the 1960s.[28] Looking at Nazi Germany's trade relations with neighboring countries in East-Central Europe and the Balkans, Hirschman highlighted the hidden politics of international trade: how conditions of dominance and dependence among states may arise naturally from the asymmetries of foreign commerce, and how import and export policies may be used opportunistically to exert political pressure and leverage.

Subsequently, the relational power approach was more fully developed by Robert Keohane and Joseph Nye in the 1970s in their landmark work on the implications of growing interdependence in the post–World War II global economy.[29] States, Keohane and Nye noted, were becoming increasingly intertwined. Hence each was becoming more and more dependent on others in all sorts of issue areas. But since mutual dependence was rarely symmetrical, advantages were created for less dependent states that could more easily dispense with the relationship. In the global system as a whole, Keohane and Nye concluded, it is possible "to regard power as deriving from patterns of asymmetrical interdependence between actors in the issue-areas in which they are involved with one another."[30] The basic question, in simplest terms, was: Who needs whom more? Power, in general, could be understood to consist of a state's control over that for which others are dependent on it.

Most recently, the relational power approach has been formalized with the introduction of social network analysis (SNA) into the mainstream of IR and IPE scholarship.[31] Borrowed from sociology, SNA focuses not on the specific attributes of individual actors but rather on the ways in which diverse actors relate to one another. Interactions in a given issue area take place within a structure called a network, defined as "a set of units . . . and a rule that defines whether, how, and to what extent any two units are tied to each other."[32] Individual units are termed nodes; the connections between them are known as ties, links, or paths. The links among the nodes create a persistent pattern of relations—a network— that in turn serves to constrain or enable actors. The capabilities of any particular node derive not from its material properties but rather from the nature of its links with other nodes, which define its position within the network. As one source summarizes, power is directly related "to network position, to persistent relationships . . . rather than individual attributes. . . . Capabilities in the networked view rely on connections to other members of the network."[33]

In SNA, the dimension of position that matters most for power analysis is *centrality*: how much others rely on a particular node to maintain the structure of relations. The more central is the position of a node, the greater is its power. Both autonomy and influence are enhanced. In formal terms, centrality is measured by the number and strength of paths in the network that must pass through that particular node. The more links there are through the node and the greater is the asymmetry of those ties, the more central is the actor. In plain language, centrality is a measure of dependence, just as emphasized in the relational power approach.

Even today, though, the earlier elements-of-power approach continues to be widely used, mainly because of its seeming advantage for purposes of empirical study. Objective measurement of capabilities derived from relational asymmetries is inherently difficult. How can we accurately quantify degrees of dependence or control? How do we estimate the number and strength of links among nodes in a network? By comparison, it is much easier to construct an index comprising some number of tangible possessions and attributes. But such efforts also have their limits, as already noted. The property concept of power may at times be arbitrary; considered outside a specific strategic and political setting, any one inventory of power resources could even be quite misleading. Purely quantitative measures obviously have their value, but mainly as a supplement to analysis based more in the alternative social power tradition. Effectively, the two approaches are complementary and are best used in tandem.

Two Faces of Power

Beyond the question of roots lies an even more challenging issue: How do capabilities manifest themselves? Must power necessarily be proactive, involving deliberate intent, or might some forms of power simply be "structural," a product of circumstance rather than purpose? Here as well two contrasting approaches have traditionally competed.

For many scholars, direct purposive action would appear to be essential to the manifestation of capabilities. Given the widespread popularity of Dahl's early definition of power, it is understandable that much of the literature would persistently equate the concept with some kind of overt act deliberately intended to alter behavior. Power is equated with a logic of consequence determined by bilateral relations. The goal is assumed to be influence—to get others to do something contrary to their underlying preferences (here equated with interests). Achievement of the goal is assumed to require a calculated use of available policy instruments, including various forms of side payments (bribery) or sanctions (coercion). Proactive application of carrots and sticks is seen as essential.

Others, however, disagree. Even before the rediscovery of Hirschman's early book, US political scientists Peter Bachrach and Morton Baratz had usefully pointed out that direct purposive action represented just one "face" of power, and perhaps not even the most important.[34] Power may also have a *second* face that operates more indirectly through the constraints and opportunities created by systemic infrastructure, which determines the payoffs available to individual actors. Behavior may be driven, despite actors' preferences, by a logic of consequence determined at the *systemic* level. For the second face of power, influence derives not from individual properties or specific interdependencies but rather from the overall *structure* of relations. What matters is not conscious intent but simply the force of circumstance. The second face of power might be exploited proactively, but it need not be. Its impact might be felt even if the "powerful" actor is entirely passive.

Closely related to these ideas is the approach popularized by Britain's Susan Strange, initially in a 1988 book titled *States and Markets*.[35] Like Bachrach and Baratz, Strange drew a clear distinction between two forms of influence in the global economy, which for her purposes she labeled, respectively, "relational" power and "structural" power. Relational power, like Bachrach and Baratz's first face (and echoing Dahl), was the familiar power of A to get B to do something that B would not otherwise do—a capacity to extract advantage within the established framework of activity. Structural power, by contrast, was "the power to shape and determine the structures of the global political economy . . . the power to decide how things will be done, the power to shape frameworks within which states relate to each other"[36]—a capacity to extract advantage by favorably modifying the existing structure of incentives and payoffs. Four key structures were identified: security, production, finance, and knowledge. If relational power could be said to refer to the ability to gain under the prevailing rules of the game, she said, structural power should be understood to represent an ability to gain by rewriting the rules of the game. In other words, structural power was the power to set the agenda that defined the choice set available to others.

Over the years, Strange's approach has proved extraordinarily popular, owing no doubt to its seeming clarity and insight. For generations of scholars in Britain and elsewhere, her concept of structural power has been a core inspiration—a central tenet of what I have elsewhere described as the British school of IPE.[37] Even the most inspired thoughts, however, are apt to have their limitations—and Strange's ideas about power are no exception. By no stretch of the imagination could her musings be described as genuine theory in the accepted sense of the term. As Keohane has pointed out,[38] Strange had a "disdain for theory" and offered little in terms of causal analysis. Her approach was essentially descriptive, lacking any kind of formal conceptualization of the origins or evolution of power structures. Her approach thus left a number of loose ends to be tied up by others.[39] Acknowledges one of Strange's most devoted followers, her "famous four structures" were really no more than "a mere organising framework, a heuristic typology in place of a theory."[40]

Moreover, with the wisdom of hindsight, it is clear that Strange's notion of structural power was less original than many have imagined. That, by itself, is no crime. But it does dim some of the luster of her historical legacy. Clearly, Bachrach and Baratz got there first. Similarly, in a study of my own that I published in 1977[41]—a book that Strange reviewed, not unkindly[42]—I tried to make the same distinction that Strange did later, labeling the two levels as "process power" and "structure power." The genealogy of the distinction between the two forms of power has more recently been spelled out by Eric Helleiner and Carla Norrlof.[43] In some of her last writings, Strange showed an awareness of earlier contributions—most explicitly in an article published in 1994,[44] where she cited previous theorizing about separate "levels" of power by inter alia Steven Lukes and Robert Dahl.[45] Lukes and Dahl are also listed, albeit without discussion, among the references in her penultimate book, *The Retreat of the State*.[46] But nowhere is there any acknowledgment of what role, if any, these precedents might have played in inspiring her own work or of what contrasts there might have been between their perspectives and hers. Today it is clear that Strange was by no means the first to think along these lines.

Structural Power

In most respects, Strange's concept of structural power corresponds closely to Bachrach and Baratz's second face of power, which can also be understood as a form of structural power. Both approaches place primary emphasis on the role of circumstance—structure—in determining outcomes. But there is also a major difference between them, which goes back to the distinction between the two modes of influence, passive and active. At issue, once again, is the question of agency. And that issue in turn raises an even more critical question: Is structural power necessarily beneficial? These are important questions, as we shall see in later chapters.

For Bachrach and Baratz, the second face of power—their version of structural power—was essentially passive. The capacity to shape constraints and opportunities was not necessarily sought—for the most part, it was simply the incidental by-product of a major actor's autonomy. The idea is captured well by Lloyd Gruber, who coined the term "go-it-alone" power: the ability to unintentionally influence the choice sets available to others simply by acting independently.[47] By going it alone, he writes, some actors "can have the effect of restricting the options available to another group (the losers), altering the rules of the game such that members of the latter group are better off playing by the new rules despite their strong preference for the original . . . status quo."[48] The causal mechanism works along the lines of the sequential Stackelberg leadership model of game theory. One actor (the leader) moves unilaterally, establishing a payoff structure. Though no intentionality may be involved, others (the followers) are nonetheless compelled to decide how to respond.

For Strange, by contrast, much more agency was typically involved. It is true, she conceded, that structural power "need not be . . . consciously or deliberately sought. . . . Power can be effectively exercised [simply] by 'being there.'"[49] But for her that was the least interesting aspect of the concept. In her view, the whole point of structural power was the ability to extract advantage—to favorably control outcomes. Even if it was not sought, once a capacity to set the agenda became manifest it was bound to be used purposively by the leader to promote self-interest at the expense of others. What good is an ability to bend the rules in your favor if it is not used? Targeted exploitation of privilege was the name of the game. In *States and Markets* and elsewhere, Strange's illustrations of structural power largely involved proactive policies by dominant actors—most prominently, the United States, whose global hegemony she seemed at pains to demonstrate was at the time as great as ever. "Using this model or analytical framework," she wrote, "the conclusion seems inevitable that the United States government . . . [has] not in fact lost structural power in and over the system."[50] In an insightful analysis, Stefano Guzzini labels this aspect of the concept "indirect institutional power"—the deliberate manipulation of the rules of the game.[51] The contrast with Bachrach and Baratz could not be greater.

Clearly, if Strange is right, structural power must be good for the leader. That would certainly not seem an unreasonable premise. Indeed, it would almost surely hold true for the kind of structural power that is exercised purposively. Why deliberately manipulate the rules of the game, after all, if no gain is to be expected? But it would not necessarily hold true for the kind of structural power that emerges without conscious intent—"go-it-alone" power that simply results from "being there." At times, in such circumstances, agenda setting may actually operate not to the leader's benefit but rather to its disadvantage.

To illustrate, consider the newly dominant role of China today in global commodity markets. Overall, the proverbial Middle Kingdom has become a market leader—indeed, the world's biggest importer of a wide variety of foodstuffs, agricultural raw materials, minerals, and fuels. China's ability to move primary product prices, therefore, is unparalleled. Stronger growth in the Middle Kingdom translates directly into higher prices worldwide. This may certainly be regarded as an example of structural power. But it is difficult to see it as advantageous to the Chinese. For all its size, China lacks true monopsonistic power. It is still largely a price taker, not a price maker. Hence if commodity prices rise, the Chinese too must pay more for their imports. As one recent analysis observes, "China may have the ability to increase global prices, but as Chinese importers have to pay these higher prices, it's hardly a beneficial power."[52]

In short, structural power may also have a downside. That is a point that we will have to keep in mind when we get to the structural power of an international currency.

More Faces

The possibility of at least two faces of power—relational power and structural power—is now commonly accepted in the literature of IR and IPE. But in the words of late-night television ads: Just wait, there's more! Even more faces of power are now recognized as part of the picture.

Both the first and second faces of power assume that preferences are given and invariant. What changes are the constraints and opportunities for achieving those preferences. Further complexities arise, however, if we add the possibility that preferences themselves, not just incentive structures, may be altered, inducing behavior to be guided by a logic of appropriateness rather than a logic of consequence. The idea of preference shaping was broached early on by Steven Lukes in what has since come to be called the *third* face of power—a capacity to influence the thoughts of actors in ways that persuades them to desire things that they might otherwise have ignored or opposed.[53] In Lukes's words: "A may exercise power over B by getting him to do what he does not want to do, but he also exercises power over him by influencing, shaping, or determining his very wants."[54] The third face of power is essentially cognitive in nature, working through constitutive impacts on identity and interests along lines suggested by constructivist theory.

Closely related is the now familiar distinction between "hard" power and "soft" power first introduced by Nye.[55] Hard power derives from the material capabilities of a state and is manifest in both the first and second faces of power. Soft power, by contrast, involves more intangible forms of influence derived from the attraction of a state's culture and ideologies, working at the cognitive level to shape perceptions, beliefs, and values. With its emphasis on co-option and identity, soft power corresponds most closely to the third face of power. As Nye himself put it recently, "Soft power rests on the ability to shape the preferences of others to get them to want what you want."[56] The third face of power is also roughly analogous to Antonio Gramsci's idea of hegemony, which the well known Marxist theorist identified as one of the central control mechanisms of global capitalism. Through a hegemonic culture, Gramsci argued, the values of capitalism become the "common sense" values of all, thus helping to maintain the status quo. The three faces of power have been summarized by Colin Hay under the headings of *decision-making*, *agenda-setting*, and *preference-shaping*.[57]

Today we even have a newer taxonomy, proposed by Barnett and Duvall,[58] that suggests not three but *four* types of power, defined by varying combinations of two analytical dimensions—the kinds of social relations through which power works (specific actors or social relations of constitution) and the specificity of social relations through which effects on actors' capacities are produced (direct or diffuse). The four types of power are: (1) *compulsory power*, consisting of direct control of one actor over another; (2), *institutional power*, where control is exercised indirectly through diverse relations of interaction; (3) *structural power*, involving the constitution of actors' identity and preferences in direct structural relation to one another; and (4) *productive power*, comprising the socially diffuse production of subjectivity in systems of meaning and signification. Compulsory power corresponds roughly to the first face of power; institutional power, to the second face; and structural power (in this taxonomy), to the third face. The real novelty of the approach lies in the fourth type, productive power, which was not explicitly anticipated in previous literature.

According to Stephen Krasner,[59] the Barnett-Duvall taxonomy effectively summarizes several decades of discussion about power. In his words, the approach "allows power to escape from the clutches of realism. Scholars working from different perspectives, notably constructivism, can invoke power as well; it is just not materially based power."[60] But one could also argue that an escape from realism had already been promoted by the prior work of the likes of Lukes, Nye, and Gramsci. The neat two-by-two matrix suggested by Barnett and Duvall has an intuitive appeal. However, by inserting a fourth type of power into the mix, based on diffuse social relations, the approach actually has the effect of distracting attention from the direct state-to-state relations that are of most concern to IR theorists. Productive power, effectively a fourth face of power, may be useful for some analytical purposes—in particular, for the study of emergent social norms and intersubjective understandings—but it adds little to state-centric analysis.

Questions

Thus the questions here are many. First is the contrast between the power-as-resources approach and the social-power approach. Does the topic at hand affirm the greater relevance of the relational concept of power, as generally assumed in most scholarship, or is a reconsideration of the property concept of power warranted? Second, there is the contrast between relational and structural power. Does the topic signify a form of structural power, or is power still derived primarily from specific instruments and interdependencies? If structural power is in evidence, is it exploited proactively or does it operate passively? And if it does operate passively, is it beneficial to the leader or disadvantageous? Third is the contrast between hard and soft power. In context, how useful is the distinction between a logic of consequence and a logic of appropriateness? And fourth is the contrast between the classic three-faces typology of Barach and Baratz combined with Lukes and the additional fourth type of power highlighted by Barnett and Duvall. Does the notion of productive power add anything of value for the particular issue under study?

USES

Next is a cluster of questions relating specifically to the external dimension of power: the deliberate and calculated *use* of power, whatever its source, to exercise influence—what Andrews calls "influence attempts."[61] As Reich and Lebow have suggested, "capabilities are only one component of power. Power also depends on the nature of a state's capabilities, how they developed, and how they are used."[62] The central issue here is statecraft: the challenge of translating capabilities into action.

For observers of world affairs, it seems evident that quite often statecraft falls short of potential. Seemingly powerful states do not always make use of all the power resources at their disposal. That suggests a need to distinguish clearly between capabilities and agency. Even if central decision makers know their preferences, they may not always act on them. As Nye suggests, "Power conversion—getting from resources to behavioral outcomes—is a crucial intervening variable."[63] The issue was captured long ago by James March in his distinction between "basic force models" and "force activation models."[64] Putative capabilities are one thing, actual implementation quite another. Force may not in fact be activated. Baldwin calls this the "potential power problem."[65]

What explains the potential power problem? Why might force not be activated? At least three explanations are possible. First, there is the issue of costs. Governments cannot think just about the potential benefits of an influence attempt. There may be significant costs involved as well. For rational policy makers, relying on a logic of consequence, the question is: Would the potential gain from an influence attempt be substantial enough to outweigh possible downside risks, either at home or abroad?

Second is the issue of domestic politics, which may shrink a government's room for maneuver in its foreign relations. As Robert Putnam long ago reminded us,[66] statecraft is a "two-level game" where initiatives abroad can be severely hampered if they do not accord with the configuration of preferences at home. Central decision makers may be stymied by resistance from key interest groups or by the complexities of the country's political institutions. Put differently, they may lack the internal "political capacity" needed to formulate, implement, and enforce policy in external relations.

And third is what Baldwin calls the "fungibility problem"[67]—a question of finding the most effective policy instruments for the task at hand. The purposeful exercise of power requires not only intention but also means—practical tools by which leverage can be actively applied to shape behavior. Influence can be exerted through multiple pathways. Power, as such, is useless unless it can be made manifest and applied through specific means.

Standard IR theory, going back to classic works of Harold Lasswell and Baldwin,[68] distinguishes four broad categories of statecraft: (1) public diplomacy: manipulation of information ; (2) formal diplomacy: representation and negotiation; (3) economic statecraft: managing the availability of goods, services, or money; and (4) military statecraft: actual or threatened use of violence, weapons, or force.

For governments wishing to engage in influence attempts, the challenge is find the instruments that best harness a country's generic power to achieve specific ends. That is by no means an easy task. Power, clearly, is not an undifferentiated mass, equally effective in all circumstances. Dahl castigated this idea as the "lump" concept of power. In practice, individual means of influence may differ greatly along a variety of relevant vectors, including most critically scope, domain, and weight.[69] *Scope* refers to the range of issues affected by a state's actions; *domain*, to the number of other actors subject to its influence; *weight*, to the probability that the behavior of other actors will in fact be altered. Distinctions like these are important because it is evident that what works for a government in one set of circumstances may not work in another or with the same degree of effectiveness. In other words, power resources may not be interchangeable—that is, fungible. Can available instruments be mutually substituted without losing much of their value? States may enjoy substantial power resources yet lack the means needed to achieve success in a chosen context.

The questions here, therefore, are twofold. First, is the potential power problem a serious issue? In context, are there any clear examples of seemingly powerful states that have failed to seek influence to the extent that might be expected? And second, what are the most salient explanations? What accounts for observed failures to convert capabilities into action?

LIMITS

Finally, we come to the *limits* of power. A capacity to exercise influence can be described in many ways: the three or four faces of power; relational or structural power; hard or soft power. But even if capacity is purposefully activated and practical means are found to apply leverage, there is no assurance that compliance can actually be enforced. Power is not absolute.

In practice, the limits of power are elastic and likely to vary considerably, depending on circumstances. Perhaps the most critical variable is the *degree* of asymmetry in the pattern of relevant interdependencies. These help to determine the "weight" of a state's power. Does the less dependent state enjoy something close to monopoly control over that for which others are dependent on it, or must it contend with rivals? In the absence of an effective monopoly, even the most determined influence attempts could encounter resistance from targeted actors, leading to outcomes falling short of a sender's aspirations. Faced with overt attempts to exploit power resources, targeted actors may respond strategically, seeking to make use of alternative power resources of their own or perhaps aligning with other similarly situated partners ("balancing"). Intention and means both may be necessary for the effective use of power, but they are hardly sufficient.

Worse, over time the exercise of power may become its own worse enemy, leading to a gradual erosion of leverage and possibly even to a net loss of influence. This is what Giulio Gallarotti means by the "power curse"[70]—the risk that the accumulation of power may, in time, actually act to diminish a state's control over outcomes or the behavior of others. In Gallarotti's words, "the quest for power often creates the seeds of its own destruction."[71] Countries may become victims of "power illusion"—a growing misperception of how strong they really are. Vulnerabilities may come to be underestimated; capabilities may be wasted; countervailing actions and other negative feedbacks may be discounted. Power breeds its own demise.

The questions here are threefold. First, is there strong evidence of limitations on the exercise of power? To the extent that influence attempts have been actively pursued, have targets tended to resist or acquiesce? Second, what explains observed outcomes? In context, what accounts for the "weight" of the leverage of individual states? And third, are there signs of a power curse? Is the exploitation of power becoming self-defeating?

Conclusion

Overall, then, the agenda for power analysis is long. Whatever the topic at hand, four issues define the proper focus of discussion: meaning, sources, uses, and limits. Each issue, in turn, is multifaceted, spawning a cluster of separate questions. Pragmatism demands that all four clusters must be considered in any given context. Anything less would leave the concept of power as highly contested as ever.

3

Monetary Power

*Money can't buy love, but it improves
your bargaining position.*
—*Christopher Marlowe (1564–1593)*

W̶e have looked at currency and power separately. Now it is time to
start bringing the two together. Analysis begins here at the broad-
est level, with the general concept of international monetary power. What
are the sources of power in international monetary relations? Where does
monetary power come from? How does it manifest itself? And what role
does currency play in this specific context?

This chapter argues that in the context of monetary affairs, power is all
about autonomy. The central issue confronting states, first and foremost,
is the distribution of the burden of adjustment to external imbalance.
The ultimate foundation of monetary power lies in a capacity to avoid
the costs of payments adjustment—to maintain the state's policy space,
as free as possible from foreign constraint. From these roots grow diverse
instruments and opportunities for the exercise of influence abroad.

Ceteris paribus, the greater a state's capacity to avoid adjustment costs,
relative to that of other countries, the greater is its monetary power. But the
devil, of course, is in the details. What do we mean by adjustments costs?
What are the sources of the capacity to avoid adjustment costs? What are
its limits? And what is the specific role of a nation's currency as a source of
power? The aim of this chapter is to address these critical questions.

In brief, I argue that adjustment costs can be said to come in two
forms—a *continuing* cost of adjustment and a *transitional* cost of

adjustment. Corresponding to each of these costs, in turn, is a specific form of monetary power—respectively, a power to *delay* adjustment and a power to *deflect* adjustment. The sources of the power to deflect lie in the structural characteristics of national economies. The power to delay, by contrast, is derived more from financial variables, including especially central bank reserves and external borrowing capacity. Currency internationalization enters the picture as a significant enhancement of access to external credit. For the privileged few states whose national currencies play international roles, the power to delay is amplified.

Previous Discussions

As indicated in the introduction, the modern field of IPE has had remarkably little to say about the concept of power in monetary relations. There is no generally accepted theory of monetary power. All we have is a fractured and scattered literature that shares barely any consensus at all. As in the wider IR field's approach to power analysis, we find theoretical confusion and cacophony.

Broadly, comments on monetary power tend to fall into some four loose clusters. First are the many discussions that simply take the concept of monetary power for granted. The very familiarity of the notion seems to obviate any need for explication. Illustrative is an early article by the noted scholar Joanne Gowa on an important monetary negotiation that took place back in the 1970s.[1] The article is often cited for its pioneering incorporation of power considerations. At issue was a proposal to create a so-called substitution account at the International Monetary Fund to absorb excess reserve holdings of dollars at a time when prospects for the greenback were cloudy. The whole of Gowa's analysis rested on the assumption that US monetary power was in decline. Yet at no time did she offer a definition of the concept, let alone any analysis of its underlying characteristics or sources. Though regrettable, the omission was by no means exceptional. In the years since, many other discussions have gone the same route. The practice is common.

A second cluster takes monetary power more seriously but concentrates mainly on its limits. What might inhibit the exercise of monetary power or cause its erosion over time? Most often the subject is the United States, the post–World War II global hegemon, whose monetary dominance has long been expected, sooner or later, to fade. More than three decades ago, Robert Keohane was already writing about what the world might look like *After Hegemony*.[2] Central attention has been placed on the role of America's persistently rising level of international indebtedness. From Helen Milner to Jonathan Kirshner,[3] scholars have systematically explored the implications of foreign debt for America's position in world politics. But all the emphasis is on how influence may be constrained rather than on where the capacity for leverage comes from.

Third are discussions that bypass questions about monetary power's roots to focus instead on the diverse pathways by which influence might be expected to operate. Though the language of conventional power analysis is rarely invoked formally, such contributions are in fact all about the several faces of power. Some scholars, such as Kirshner,[4] place greatest emphasis on the direct instrumental use of monetary capabilities—the first face of power. The focus is implicit in the title of Kirshner's pathbreaking book *Currency and Coercion*. It is also implicit in his choice of terms like enforcement or expulsion, which certainly seem to suggest self-conscious influence attempts. The bulk of *Currency and Coercion* is about what Kirshner calls the "practice" of monetary power: the deliberate use of leverage to achieve state objectives.

Others are more interested in what might be regarded as structural power—the second face. One example is Beth Simmons, in a pioneering analysis of international capital-market regulations.[5] Regulatory harmonization, she argued, is heavily influenced by the "financial power" (undefined) of the United States. Whatever it does, America "has the potential to change significantly the context for financial markets and hence it affects regulators in the rest of the world,"[6] who then must decide whether to emulate or resist US actions. The logic seems based de facto on a Stackelberg leadership model, with the United States cast as first mover unilaterally establishing a payoff structure for others. Other examples include Eric Helleiner,[7] who aims to demonstrate the relevance of Strange's conception of structural power in monetary relations; and Carla Norrlof,[8] who has repeatedly sought to highlight the unique "structural advantages" that the United States enjoys in monetary affairs. Closely related is Kirshner's notion of entrapment, which operates through a reordering of incentive structures.[9]

And yet others, inspired by constructivism, appeal to a logic of appropriateness—the third face of power. Best known here is Kathleen

McNamara, who in a seminal study highlighted the power of ideas in the historical decision to create a common currency in Europe.[10] The aim of European governments, she contended, was to lock in monetary stability and neoliberal policies. The inspiration was Germany, whose economic success set a standard for its regional partners to emulate—in effect, a demonstration of soft power.

Whatever the pathway chosen, however, the focus remains on the *effects* of power—whether or how behavior is influenced—rather than on its *causes*. One is reminded of what Dahl called the "lump" concept of power. Capabilities are simply assumed, a raw potential. The only question is how those capabilities manage to manifest themselves—whether, to recall Colin Hay's terms, by decision-making, agenda-setting, or preference-shaping.

Finally, there is a fourth cluster—a few brave souls who have actually tried to move beyond the limits or uses of power to systematically explore the concept's underlying meaning and roots. Perhaps most prominent here is Eric Helleiner, who is rightly critical of scholarship that is "more interested in how international monetary power is expressed and what it can accomplish than in its sources."[11] In a notable contribution, Helleiner (2006) emphasizes what he calls the "micro-level" sources of monetary power. These include a dominant state's ability to influence regulatory trends and crisis management in financial markets as well as a capacity to influence perceptions of identity and self-interest. "Attention to how a dominant state can shape these elements," he argues, "provides important insights into the nature of . . . monetary power."[12]

There is no denying the relevance of the factors Helleiner highlights. But there is also a problem. Can these elements really be regarded as *sources* of power? In reality, each is best understood as a manifestation of a state's *capabilities* in monetary affairs rather than as one of monetary power's ultimate roots. Ironically, it turns out that like most others, Helleiner too seems more interested in what power can accomplish than where it comes from. As we saw in the previous chapter, any analysis of power should distinguish clearly between the roots of power and its possible modes of expression. Influence over financial regulation or crisis management may be understood as expressions of the first or second faces of power; an ability to shape preferences is of course what we mean by the third face. As such, they all illustrate the instrumental use of capabilities, not the foundational sources of power. That is the reason why, in this chapter, I emphasize the macro-level of analysis and the central importance of the distribution of adjustment costs. There is where the real roots of monetary power can be found.

Admittedly, my focus on adjustment costs is hardly novel. Other scholars courageous enough to explore the sources of monetary power have also placed the distribution of the burden of adjustment at the heart of their analysis. Inter alia, these have included David Andrews, Michael Webb, Randall Henning, Matthias Kaelberer, and, most recently, Mattias Vermeiren.[13] But most treatments over the years, including previous attempts of my own,[14] have tended to be regrettably ambiguous about what is actually meant by adjustment costs, leaving analysis incomplete. If we are to achieve full comprehension of the sources of monetary power, we need a systematic understanding of what, precisely, the notion of burden is supposed to mean in the context of payments adjustment. In a paper published in 2006,[15] I made a start toward a fuller exegesis of the notion of adjustment costs and the role they play in the genesis of monetary power. This chapter builds on the insights of that earlier paper.

The Burden of Adjustment

Thus we begin with the distribution of the burden of adjustment to external imbalance. Central to the analysis of monetary power, I argue, is a state's capacity to avoid adjustment costs, either by delaying the adjustment process or by deflecting the burden of adjustment to others.

The Balance of Payments

Adjustment is a natural part of the monetary relations among states. Over any given period, a country experiences both monetary inflows and outflows—on the one side, revenues from the sale of exports of goods (merchandise trade) and services ("invisibles") or from various forms of inward capital movement; on the other side, expenditures on imports of goods and services or various forms of outward capital movement. The summary of inflows and outflows is called the *balance of payments*—a record of all monetary transactions between the residents of a country and the rest of the world. Every nation, by definition, has a balance of payments.

The difficulty is that the balance of payments does not always balance. Revenues may either exceed or fall short of expenditures. The economy may run either a surplus or a deficit. That is what we mean by external imbalance (disequilibrium). The question then is: What can the country do about it? Basically, there are two choices: *financing* or *adjustment*. Either the imbalance must be paid for, or it must be eliminated.

Consider a deficit. Financing means finding the wherewithal with which to pay for the excess of foreign spending over revenues. No problem, the uninitiated might think. Most countries have their own currency, created and managed by a central bank. Why not simply print up more money to pay for the economy's external obligations? The answer should be obvious: most local money is unacceptable to foreigners. Few outsiders have much use for obscure currencies like the Eritrean nakfa or the Laotian kip. Deficits, if they are to be financed at all, must be paid for with currencies that, in turn, are likely to be accepted elsewhere. These are the international currencies—the national moneys that play international roles. To finance a deficit, an economy must come up with a sufficient amount of *international* money to pay its overseas bills.

Where does the international money come from? Basically, bills can be paid in one of two ways: by dissaving or by borrowing. *Dissaving* means running down accumulated foreign assets (claims)—for example, by liquidating investments abroad or by drawing on the currency reserves of the country's central bank. *Borrowing* means piling up foreign debts (liabilities) by arranging loans of some kind from one source or another. Either way, whether via dissaving or borrowing, the country's balance of international indebtedness—its net worth—worsens. And therein lies the rub, because the deterioration of net worth cannot go on forever. Sooner or later, external assets and borrowing limits will be exhausted—which means that sooner or later the deficit will have to be eliminated. Foreign revenues will have to be increased or foreign spending will have to be decreased. That is what is meant by adjustment.

In principle, adjustment can be achieved by using any of three classes of policy instrument. These are what may be called the three *D*'s—devaluation, deflation, and direct controls. *Devaluation* (or depreciation) means lowering the exchange rate of the national currency, reducing the price of exports and import-competing production relative to foreign goods and services and thus encouraging an improvement of the trade balance. *Deflation* (also known as internal devaluation or austerity) means acting to reduce the overall level of spending in the economy, thus lowering imports. That may be achieved through either monetary policy (the central bank's control of money supply and interest rates) or fiscal policy (the government's own spending and revenues). Restraints on price increases may also improve the economy's cost competitiveness. And *direct controls* mean making use of available policy instruments to limit import volumes (tariffs and nontariff barriers) or outward flows of capital (capital controls and exchange restrictions).

For surplus economies, the options are the same but with opposite sign. External imbalances can be allowed to result in a buildup of international assets or can be used to pay off foreign debts, improving the nation's balance of international indebtedness; or the disequilibrium can be eliminated by way of exchange-rate revaluation (appreciation), domestic expansion, or easing of trade and capital controls. Revaluation will raise the relative price of home goods and services, reducing a trade surplus. Domestic expansion will stimulate purchases of imports and, through price inflation, may lower the economy's cost competitiveness. And easing direct controls will permit more spending on foreign output or investments.

In practice, however, adjustment choices are tricky, since none is without some cost to the economy at home. As will become clear, this is true whether an economy is in deficit or in surplus. When it comes to eliminating external disequilibrium, there is no free lunch. Adjustment may be costly in either economic or political terms. Each option involves a burden of some kind. Every state, therefore, has an incentive to avoid the costs of adjustment as much as it possibly can. Put differently, every nation has an incentive to maximize its international monetary power.

Autonomy and Influence

In this context, it is clear that the distinction between the two dimensions of power, autonomy and influence, is critical. Avoidance of adjustment costs need not involve any direct attempt to pressure or coerce others. Policy choices may be purposeful, but they do not necessarily involve an "influence attempt." The goal is simply to preserve policy space. Avoidance of adjustment costs is all about autonomy: a desire to maintain as much operational independence as possible. The idea is to maximize "power to," not "power over."

Autonomy, of course, is prized by governments in every aspect of international relations. Its salience, however, is most evident in economic relations, which by definition create a condition of interdependence with other states that is both active and ongoing. Economic relations involve transactional linkages and networks, creating webs of mutual dependency. And in no area of economic relations is the salience of autonomy more evident than in the realm of monetary affairs, where states are inescapably tied through the balance of payments. The risk of unsustainable payments disequilibrium represents a constant threat to policy independence. Excessive imbalances automatically generate mutual pressures to adjust, to help move the balance of payments back toward equilibrium. But no government likes being forced to compromise key domestic policy goals for the sake of restoring external balance. All, if given a choice, would prefer to see others make the necessary sacrifices. In monetary affairs, therefore, the foundation of state power is *the capacity to avoid the burden of adjustment required by payments imbalance.*

The core importance of autonomy in this regard has not always been fully appreciated in the scholarly literature. Indeed, most discussions of monetary power prefer to stress the external dimension—the capacity to control the behavior of others in one way or another—rather than the internal dimension. But we cannot ignore the functionally derivative nature of the external dimension. Only if a state is actually able to avoid the burden of adjustment domestically is it apt to be in a position, in turn, to exert influence elsewhere. Hence if we are interested in getting to the very core of power in monetary affairs, we must go first to the internal dimension. Above all, what matters for the exercise of power abroad is practical freedom of policy action at home.

Not that we can ignore the external dimension entirely. Since monetary relations are inherently reciprocal, a potential for influence, in a real sense, is created automatically whenever policy independence is achieved. By definition, a capacity to avoid adjustment costs implies that if payments equilibrium is to be restored, others must adjust instead. At least part of the burden will be diverted elsewhere. Hence a measure of influence is necessarily generated as an inescapable corollary of the process. That too matters for analytical purposes. But it is also important to keep in mind the distinction between the two *modes* of influence, active and passive. The influence that derives incidentally from a capacity to avoid adjustment costs is passive, not actively targeted; impacts tend to be diffuse rather than directed. A corollary of the adjustment process, such influence is exercised without premeditation and is best understood simply as the alter-ego of autonomy.

In a sense, passive influence in the adjustment process is relatively uncontroversial, broadly accepted as an unavoidable, if regrettable, consequence of interdependence—a veritable fact of life. Active influence attempts, by contrast, are apt to become far more politicized, since they are both elective and purposeful. The active mode seeks to *compel* others to bear the burden of adjustment, taking us well beyond the notion of influence as simply an incidental by-product of autonomy. The active mode, in effect, aims to translate passive influence into practical control through the instrumental use of capabilities. That is very big difference, indeed, and will figure prominently in following chapters.

The Two Hands of Monetary Power

The core message is clear. While payments disequilibria are necessarily shared—one nation's deficit is someone else's surplus—the costs of adjustment need not be shared at all. Governments thus have every incentive, ceteris paribus, to maximize their capacity to avoid adjustment costs—their autonomy—relative to others.

Toward that end, I find it useful to make use of a distinction that I first outlined in a much earlier attempt to explore the concept of adjustment costs.[16] Specifically, I distinguish between two distinctly different kinds of adjustment cost—one *continuing*, the other *transitional*. Corresponding to each of the two kinds of adjustment cost is a very different sort of monetary power. In the spirit of the anatomical bent of the faces-of-power literature, I choose to call these the two "hands" of power. The distinction between the two hands emphasizes that monetary power is fundamentally dual in nature. On the one side, states have the *power to delay*; on the other, they have the *power to deflect*. A two-fisted government prefers both.

The continuing cost of adjustment may be defined as the cost of the new payments equilibrium *prevailing after all change has occurred*. The power to delay is the capacity to avoid the continuing cost of adjustment by *postponing* the process of adjustment.

The transitional cost of adjustment, by contrast, may be defined as *the cost of the change itself*. Where the process of adjustment cannot be put off, the power to deflect represents the capacity to avoid the transitional cost of adjustment by *diverting* as much as possible of that cost to others.

THE CONTINUING COST OF ADJUSTMENT

To understand the power to delay, we must begin with the concept of adjustment. By definition, adjustment imposes on deficit countries a real economic loss that will persist indefinitely once the process is complete. This is the continuing cost of adjustment. Nothing suits the interests of deficit countries more than a capacity to postpone adjustment for as long as possible.

Payments Adjustment

The standard measure of *balance* in the balance of payments is the current account, which comprises all transactions relating to a country's current national income and expenditures—imports and exports of goods (merchandise trade) and services ("invisibles") plus unilateral transfers. Given the conventions of double-entry bookkeeping, any imbalance on current account is, in principle, exactly matched by a corresponding inflow or outflow of funds on capital account (the balance of all financial transactions, including official reserve transactions). A current surplus implies a net increase of international claims. A current deficit implies a net increase of liabilities.

Adjustment, correspondingly, is the process by which imbalances in the current account—surpluses or deficits—are reduced or eliminated. Import and/or export volumes "adjust" to restore payments equilibrium. Countries with deficits experiences a decline of imports relative to exports; countries with surpluses, the reverse.

Not all imbalances need to be eliminated, of course. Standard economic theory teaches that many current-account imbalances are simply the result of what may be regarded as a kind of rational intertemporal trade—deficit countries borrowing resources from the rest of the world for productive investment at home; surplus countries investing savings abroad today to support greater consumption tomorrow. Such imbalances, in principle, are sustainable indefinitely and require no adjustment at all. In practice, however, many imbalances go well beyond what can be readily sustained, for all kinds of reasons—for example, because borrowed funds are not invested productively or owing to financial-market limitations. In such instances, which are all too frequent in the real world, adjustments of trade volumes are indeed required.

Adjustments of trade volumes, however, are impossible without a corresponding reallocation of productive resources, and in a market setting resource reallocations will not occur without the stimulus of a change of relative prices or income. The required price and income changes may be promoted directly by the government via the three *D*'s, or they may be allowed to emerge more spontaneously on their own through the pressure of market forces. Formally, adjustment may be defined as "a marginal reallocation of productive resources and exchanges of goods and services under the influence of changes in relative prices, incomes, and exchange rates."[17] This is the classical concept of "real" adjustment, the basic tool of open-economy macroeconomics.

Adjustment is necessarily a *mutual* process, reflecting the reciprocal nature of monetary relations. Just as one economy cannot be in deficit without others being in surplus, so resources cannot be reallocated in one without equivalent and offsetting reallocations elsewhere. Should a deficit country move resources into export production that were previously employed in producing for the home market, surplus countries will also find themselves obliged to shift resources about as they begin to receive additional imports. Likewise, should a deficit country increase output in import-competing industries, surplus countries will find themselves selling less and thus with additional resources for use in nontraded production or for export elsewhere. In either case, the reallocation of resources is *complementary*. The process of adjustment is *shared*.

Redistributing the Pie

However, while the *process* of adjustment is necessarily shared, the same need not be true of the *burden* of adjustment. In fact, once equilibrium is restored, the deficit country will unavoidably suffer a real economic loss, which will persist indefinitely. This is the continuing cost of adjustment, which is *always* borne *wholly* by deficit countries.

To comprehend why, assume a simple two-country model of payments imbalance. For the deficit country, adjustment requires a reduction of imports relative to exports, which is possible only if its real national "absorption"—the sum total of spending by all domestic residents on goods and services—is reduced relative to that of the surplus country. At the new payments equilibrium, therefore, the deficit country must be worse off than the surplus country, in the sense that it will now receive a smaller proportion of the combined output of the two economies. That is what I mean by the continuing cost of adjustment. I label it a continuing cost because it is open-ended—the ongoing sacrifice imposed by the new equilibrium prevailing after all change has occurred.

In absolute terms, the magnitude of the continuing cost may vary considerably, depending on the particulars of the approach to adjustment. The required change in the current account can be accomplished via very different combination of changes in real national income and absorption in deficit countries—for example, a reduction of absorption relative to a more or less stable national income; an absolute loss of national income as well as absorption (via unemployment or an unfavorable movement of the terms of trade); an increase of national income, all of which, however, is absorbed abroad; or even an absolute increase of absorption as well as national income. Whatever the approach taken, however, the bottom line remains the same. At the new equilibrium, deficit countries will receive a smaller share of combined world output—a thinner slice of the pie. That is a sacrifice no matter how you cut it.

Deficit countries, therefore, have every incentive to put off the process of adjustment for as long as possible. Delay pays. So long as there is no change in the status quo, there will be no redistribution of the pie—hence no new burden. The scale of a state's power to delay is indicated by its capacity, in relative terms, to effectively postpone the payments adjustment process.

THE TRANSITIONAL COST OF ADJUSTMENT

But that is only one hand of monetary power. The continuing cost of adjustment involves an ongoing sacrifice imposed by the new equilibrium prevailing after all change has occurred; that is, after the adjustment process is concluded. But the process itself also imposes a sacrifice—the cost that must be incurred to make the necessary change. Each adjustment implies transition, a once-and-for-all phenomenon, and each transition has its own cost, separate and quite distinct from the presumed burden of the new equilibrium obtaining after the transition is complete. That is what I call the transitional cost of adjustment—in effect, the price of getting from Here to There. Governments have every incentive to avoid that cost, too. No country wants to make more sacrifices than absolutely necessary.

The Adjustment Process

To illustrate the nature of the transitional cost of adjustment, consider a worker who, having lost a job and being unable to find a comparable one, finally accepts a lower-paying position. This process of adjustment imposes two costs on the unfortunate individual. The more obvious one is the real sacrifice implied by the new position—namely, the difference between the new wage and the previous wage. This is an open-ended phenomenon, a loss of income that will go on so long as the worker remains in the new position—the continuing cost of adjustment. But, in addition, the worker must have suffered some loss of income during the period of enforced idleness. There may have been some real cost incurred in searching for a new job, investing in new skills, or moving to a new location. This is a once-and-for-all phenomenon, a singular loss of income associated with the process of change itself. That is what I mean by the transitional cost of adjustment.

The question is: Who pays? In the illustration, the burden falls on the worker. But this need not be so. The government, for instance, might provide unemployment compensation, job training, or other forms of adjustment assistance, thus shifting at least some of the cost to taxpayers. Alternatively, part of the burden might be borne by the worker's former employer in the form of a generous severance package, or even by private charitable organizations dedicated to aiding the involuntarily unemployed. In fact, the distribution of the transitional cost of adjustment is, a priori, indeterminate. Unlike the continuing cost of adjustment, which is never shared, the transitional cost is, in effect, up for grabs.

Recall that the process of adjustment necessarily involves a realignment of relative prices, incomes, or exchange rates sufficient to generate the required reallocation of resources at the margin. The greater the changes of prices, incomes, or exchange rates required, the greater is the transitional cost of adjustment. Most often, equilibrium is restored either by policies of domestic deflation or currency devaluation—what economists call *real depreciation*—in deficit countries, or by domestic expansion or currency revaluation—*real appreciation*—in surplus countries. Implications for the distribution of the burden of adjustment differ greatly depending on which route is taken. Both economic and political elements of cost are involved.

Fixed versus Flexible Exchange Rates

The circumstances under which the transition takes place matter. Consider first a world in which nominal exchange-rate changes are ostensibly ruled out—in today's terminology, a world of "hard" pegs. In that case, distributional implications are reasonably straightforward. With formal devaluations or revaluations largely ruled out, payments equilibrium will most likely require some combination of deflation in deficit economies and expansion in surplus economies. That is, adjustment will be accomplished through either a market-driven fall of prices and incomes in the deficit economies reinforced by restrictive monetary and fiscal policies or a market-driven rise of prices and incomes in the surplus economies reinforced by more expansionary monetary and fiscal policies. In the former case, it is plainly the deficit economies that bear the burden of adjustment. Economically, deflationary conditions will almost certainly result in higher unemployment, slower growth, and perhaps even recession before a new external equilibrium can be established. Politically, austerity is bound to erode a government's popularity with voters. Conversely, in the latter case, it is the surplus economies that pay the price. Accelerated inflation reduces purchasing power and can distort investment incentives. It also tends to be politically unpopular.

Alternatively, consider a world of exchange-rate flexibility, where nominal exchange-rate changes are possible—in today's terminology, a world of "soft" pegs or some manner of floating. In that case, distributional implications are more complex, since governments are no longer limited to domestic deflation or expansion alone. Policy makers can "pick their poison." External adjustment can be allowed to impact prices and incomes in the domestic economy either directly, with the nominal exchange rate fixed; or indirectly, via the effect of exchange-rate movements; or by way of some combination of the two. In such a world, two separate aspects of the process are influential in determining the costs involved—one involving any movements of exchange rates that do occur; the other involving the degree of domestic price and income changes that ultimately are required, whether nominal exchange rates move or not.

First, suppose some exchange-rate movements do occur as part of the adjustment process. Who bears the onus of responsibility? A realignment of rates may be the result of deliberate policy decisions (formal devaluation/revaluation) or may be essentially market driven (depreciation/appreciation). Either way, governments may be held accountable for triggering or tolerating changes in a currency's nominal value.

Does this matter? In a hypothetical two-country world, where currency values are the inverse of one another, it should make no difference who is seen as responsible for the change. Exchange-rate movements would be symmetrical, a decline of one country's money necessarily equivalent to a rise of the other's. But in the real world of more than 150 state currencies, by contrast, the distinction can matter a great deal. The evolution of a given money's value in relation to any other single currency, its bilateral exchange rate, may be substantially different from the evolution of its value against the population of currencies in general—what is called the *effective* exchange rate. A change in one money's effective exchange rate, even if sizable, may have little impact on individual bilateral rates if spread broadly enough. Conversely, even a small change in an effective exchange rate may have a very large impact elsewhere if concentrated on just one or two bilateral rates. In short, exchange-rate movements may be anything but symmetrical. As a practical matter, therefore, some governments may be exposed to much more criticism than others, even if they are not the first mover.

Essentially, this is a political issue. Exchange-rate changes are difficult to ignore. An exchange rate is like the eye of a needle through which prices of all domestic goods and services are linked and compared with the prices of foreign output. Since this role makes the exchange rate a critical variable in determining the pattern of resource allocation as well as the level and distribution of income, governments have every reason to avoid the onus of responsibility insofar as possible. Nominal exchange-rate changes can generate considerable backlash among voters, for symbolic as well as material reasons. Devaluation or depreciation is typically interpreted as a defeat for a government's policies, damaging its reputation and credibility. Conversely, revaluation or appreciation may be resented for its potentially painful impacts on balance sheets and the earning capacity of key sectors of the economy. As a practical matter, few governments wish to be blamed for a sizable change in the value of the national currency in either direction.

Second, consider the effect on the home economy, whether exchange rates move or not. Either way, as Stefanie Walter has recently reminded us, there are likely to be significant price and income changes that will impact adversely on the purchasing power or personal balance sheets of key domestic constituencies.[18] All adjustment strategies, she points out, "are usually painful."[19] Some voters will be hurt more by movements of the exchange rate; others, more by internal deflation. But all are apt to hold the government accountable. It is all too easy to blame policy makers for any domestic austerity or inflation that results from the process of restoring external equilibrium. In Walter's words: "Voters who are hurt by the government's policies are less likely to reelect the policymakers who have inflicted this pain on them."[20]

This matters because we know that domestic impacts, too—not just exchange-rate movements—may be anything but symmetrical between states. In practice, prices and incomes may change much more in some economies than in others, depending on circumstances. Adjustment in one country could generate relatively little macroeconomic change at home but considerable price and income pressures abroad, effectively diverting much of the pain of adjustment to outsiders; or, conversely, most of the impact could be bottled up domestically, with little discomfort elsewhere. As a practical matter, few governments wish to be blamed for a sizable impact on the domestic economy, either.

Summary

Overall, then, the distribution of the transitional cost of adjustment will depend on both aspects of the process: first, who bears the onus of responsibility for any exchange-rate changes that occur; and second—whether exchange rates change or not—who is forced to experience the biggest direct impact on domestic prices and income. In monetary affairs, these are the price of getting from Here to There—also sacrifices, no matter how you cut it. No wonder that governments would want to avoid the transitional cost of adjustment too, deflecting as much as possible to others. The scale of a state's power to deflect is indicated by its capacity, in relative terms, to effectively divert the transitional cost of adjustment to others.

THE POWER TO DEFLECT

What, then, are the sources of monetary power? What are its limits? States obviously differ greatly in their capacity to avoid the burden of adjustment. It is equally obvious that there are limits to the autonomy of even the most powerful states. How can all this be explained?

Given the dual nature of monetary power, it should not be surprising that separate factors might account for the strength of each of the two hands. Begin with the transitional cost of adjustment. Most critical for the power to deflect, I suggest, are fundamental structural variables that determine how much real sacrifice will be required once the process of adjustment gets under way. The easier it is for an economy to resist imposed changes of prices, incomes, or exchange rates, the greater will be its ability to deflect the pressures of adjustment onto others. Most critical for the power to delay, by contrast, are financial variables—above all, a country's international liquidity position, which encompasses both foreign reserves and access to external credit. The more liquidity there is at a country's disposal, relative to other states, the longer it can postpone adjustment of its balance of payments. It should also not be surprising that there might be distinctly different limits to each of the two hands of monetary power.

Structural Variables

The power to deflect derives from fundamental structural variables that distinguish one national economy from another. Two features in particular stand out. These are the degree of openness and the degree of adaptability of each individual economy.

Some observers might wish to add a third feature: whether an economy happens to be in surplus or deficit. But that would be a mistake.

Initial payments positions obviously are relevant to the distribution of the continuing cost of adjustment and therefore to the power to delay. But when it comes to the transitional cost of adjustment, the distribution of the burden—as indicated—is effectively up for grabs. At issue, to repeat, are two questions. First, who bears the onus of responsibility for any exchange-rate changes that may occur? Second, whether exchange rates change or not, who is forced to experience the greatest direct changes of domestic prices and income? These are the two critical aspects of the adjustment process that bear on the distribution of the transitional cost. Each may fall on either surplus or deficit countries.

In my earlier attempt to explore some of these issues, I suggested the notion of "adjustment vulnerability," defined as the proportion of the transitional cost of adjustment borne by each economy.[21] In essence, adjustment vulnerability might be understood as an inverse measure of what I here call the power to deflect. But I would not use the term adjustment vulnerability today because it unfortunately obscures a now more familiar distinction, first introduced by Keohane and Nye decades ago,[22] which helps us to understand why the two structural features of openness and adaptability, defined in relational terms, are of greatest salience in determining the power to deflect.

As indicated in the previous chapter, Keohane and Nye placed great emphasis on asymmetries of interdependence as a source of power. In doing so, they broke ground in distinguishing between two critical dimensions of such asymmetries: *sensitivity* and *vulnerability*. Sensitivity interdependence, as Keohane and Nye put it, involves the *susceptibility* of an economy to impacts from the outside—the degree to which conditions in one country are liable to be affected, positively or negatively, by events occurring elsewhere. Vulnerability, by contrast, involves the possible *reversibility* of impacts from the outside—the degree to which (in other words, the cost at which) a country is capable of overriding or accommodating to the effects of events occurring elsewhere. The distinction is relevant here because it highlights the fact that every adjustment process can be decomposed into two separate elements—stimulus and response. The stimulus is the initial impact of disequilibrium on an economy; response refers to the ease with which the initial impact can be reversed. The sensitivity-vulnerability dichotomy neatly captures these two elements for analytical purposes.

Openness and Adaptability

The power to deflect is a function of both elements of the adjustment process, stimulus *and* response. Openness matters for the power to deflect because it is the key determinant of an economy's sensitivity, relative to others, to payments disequilibrium (stimulus). Adaptability matters because it is the key determinant of an economy's relative vulnerability to disequilibrium (response).

Of these two structural variables, openness is clearly the easier to identify empirically. A standard measure of openness is the ratio of foreign trade to gross domestic product (GDP). The logic of its salience here is equally clear. The more open an economy, the greater is the range of sectors whose earnings and balance sheets will be directly impacted by adjustment, once the process begins. This will be true whether exchange rates remain pegged or are allowed to move. Either way, openness makes it difficult for an economy to avert at least some significant impact on prices and income at home.

Additionally, if exchange rates move, governments in open economies are likely to come in for more criticism than would policymakers in more closed economies. Openness, ceteris paribus, also broadens the range of domestic constituencies that will take an active interest in the value of the country's currency. In a relatively closed economy, even fairly substantial exchange-rate movements may leave the largest part of the population unaffected and therefore indifferent, effectively insulating government from criticism. In a more open economy, by contrast, where more interest groups will be directly affected, even small movements may lead to widespread opprobrium for policy makers, even if the government had nothing to do with starting the process in the first place. A high degree of openness makes it difficult to suppress widespread domestic repercussions when exchange rates change. The authorities will have a hard time trying to deflect blame for any inflation or austerity that may result.

Adaptability is more difficult to measure. Admittedly an amorphous concept, it encompasses a myriad of qualities at the microeconomic level, such as factor mobility, informational availabilities, and managerial resilience. Still, the logic of its salience, too, is clear. For any given degree of openness, the adaptability of an economy determines how readily diverse sectors can reverse a disequilibrium without large or prolonged price or income changes. At issue is allocative flexibility. The more easily productive resources can be switched from one activity to another, overriding or accommodating to outside pressures, the less likely it is that domestic repercussions will involve serious pain; hence the less likely it is, as well, that the process of adjustment will generate widespread resentment or protest. Conversely, the greater are the rigidities characteristic of an economy's labor or product markets, the more serious will be resulting market dislocations and therefore the potential for political fallout. Adaptability may be difficult to define, yet we know it when we see it and we know that it is important.

Implications

Two implications follow. First, it seems clear that the distribution of the transitional cost of adjustment is likely to favor larger and more diversified economies. Large size, as measured by GDP, generally means a relatively lower degree of openness. Greater diversification in production means that the economy offers more opportunities for alternative employment when adaptations are required. Smaller and less developed economies, conversely, are likely to be the least favored in the adjustment process. Some four decades ago, in the midst of the massive dislocations generated by the first global oil shock, I wrote about what appeared to be a "cascading" of the burden of adjustment among oil-importing countries, with the poorest and least developed economies being forced to bear the greatest burden of all.[23] "Power economics," I then called it. Today, with the wisdom of hindsight, I would label it, more precisely, the power to deflect.

The second implication is that the distribution of the transitional cost of adjustment can be expected to be comparatively stable over time, rather than volatile. Structural variables like openness or adaptability tend to change relatively slowly, to the extent that they change at all. The power to deflect, accordingly, is also likely to change slowly, if at all.

From Passive to Active Mode

Finally, we return to the measure of influence that is inherent in the power to deflect. While the essence of the power to deflect is a capacity to avoid the transitional cost of adjustment (autonomy), the practical effect, as noted, is to divert the burden elsewhere, compelling others to bear it instead—a form of influence. In and of itself the influence that is generated in this manner, which I have described as the alter-ego of autonomy, is passive and diffuse, essentially a product of market forces. But a more active mode is also possible, as many sources emphasize. The active mode, stressing the direct use of positive or negative sanctions in government-to-government relations, seeks to translate passive influence into practical control through the instrumental use of power. What is the connection between the two modes?

The connection, clearly, lies in the politics of interstate relations. The active mode is optional. It is also purposeful, seeking to enforce compliance by way of pressure or coercion. In other words, it is policy-contingent. This means that it is not enough simply for a state to enjoy the structural characteristics essential to the power to deflect. For deliberate use of the power to deflect, relative openness and adaptability are necessary conditions, but hardly sufficient.

This brings us back to the potential power problem. We can think of a number of larger and more diversified economies that seem capable of diverting the transitional cost of adjustment to others, including especially the advanced industrial countries. But not many of these are known to engage in direct arm-twisting to get their way on monetary issues. Beyond a *capacity* for influence, a government must also have the *motivation* to put its power to deflect to active use—an agreed policy agenda. Motivation will reflect a host of considerations peculiar to an individual country, involving foreign-policy strategy and domestic institutions as well as underlying constituency politics and political culture. Are the potential costs of an influence attempt too high? Does the government have the requisite political capacity? Are the available instruments up to the task? There is no certainty at all that the capabilities created by the power to deflect will be actively exploited.

THE POWER TO DELAY

The power to delay, by contrast, derives not from structural variables but, rather, more from financial variables that determine each economy's international liquidity position. At issue are both the size of the central bank's foreign reserves and the country's access to external credit. For a privileged few nations, access to external credit is amplified by international use of the national currency.

International Liquidity

A country's international liquidity comprises all available sources of internationally acceptable money. Before the postwar revival of global capital markets, the term was generally assumed to be synonymous with central bank reserves. But once financial globalization began to take hold, understanding was expanded to include access to external credit as well, whether extended to the government or to the nation's private sector. Today, international liquidity is generally defined to encompass the full array of international means of payment owned by or available to a state's residents and public authorities.

The ultimate purpose of international liquidity is financing: to cover deficits in the balance of payments, via either a net reduction of external claims or a net increase of borrowing. The availability of financing to an economy, relative to others, can have a significant impact on the *timing* of adjustment and hence on the *distribution* of adjustment costs among deficit countries. More liquidity means more capacity to stave off any unwelcome reallocation of resources. Every deficit country has an obvious incentive to postpone the continuing cost of adjustment for as long as possible. The longer one deficit country can manage to put off adjustment, the greater will be the pressure on other deficit countries to bear the burden instead.

Of course, surplus countries too may have an incentive to delay the adjustment process—for example, if they believe that once the process begins, it is they who will be compelled to bear the bulk of the transitional cost of adjustment. Moreover, should that be their preference, surplus countries also have a greater ability to delay adjustment, since it is almost always easier to absorb surpluses than to finance deficits. The motivation of surplus countries, however, is unlikely to be as *intense* as that of deficit countries, which have *both* costs to worry about. Moreover, even surplus states must anticipate the possibility that, sooner or later, they will suffer deficits, too. Hence all states have a rational interest in acquiring and maintaining a healthy international liquidity position, on which the power to delay depends.

What, then, are the limits of this hand of monetary power? That requires a closer look at each of the two main components of international liquidity: owned reserves and borrowing capacity. The conditions affecting each are similar but not identical.

Owned Reserves

Superficially, it might seem that a government would want to hoard as many reserves as possible as a form of self-insurance. Insulation from payments pressures would be maximized by the largest possible stockpile of usable liquid assets. But that idea neglects the cost involved in acquiring reserves, which must be balanced against the benefit of greater autonomy. Insurance is not free.

Reserves can be accumulated either as a result of current-account surpluses or by borrowing. Both strategies mean a reduction of real national absorption, either directly as a result of reduced imports relative to exports; or indirectly, as a result of increased interest payments. Neither, therefore, is likely to be pursued without limit, since the cost of acquiring reserves could turn out to be greater than the loss of absorption that might be required by adjustment. Economic theory has long argued that rational policymakers can be expected to seek an *optimal* level of reserves rather than a maximum.

Optimality, however—like beauty—lies in the eye of the beholder. Different policy makers can make very different calculations, depending on their subjective evaluations of the costs and benefits involved. And these evaluations, in turn, will very much depend on politics, international as well as domestic. A government that feels beholden to constituencies who would be especially hurt by a reduction of deficits, such as large-scale importers, would be likely to discount the cost of hoarding additional reserves. By contrast, a government that feels it can count on foreign allies to bail it out in the event of a payments emergency would be less inclined to invest in new reserves. A priori, therefore, no generalization is possible about where the limits are likely to be found in this context. All we know for sure is that the appetite for owned reserves will be considerably short of infinite. Hence the power to delay by this means will be short of infinite, too.

Borrowing Capacity

In most respects, much the same can be said also about external borrowing. Here too it might appear that a government would want to make as much use as possible of borrowing capacity to finance deficits. The more liquidity that can be raised externally, whether by the government itself or by the private sector, the longer adjustment can be postponed. But that too neglects the costs involved. These costs include not just the direct debt-service payments that would be required by foreign loans. Even more critically, they include possible policy compromises that could become necessary if the country finds itself overextended to foreign creditors.

External credit can be raised from a variety of sources, of course. But whatever the source, the liquidity provided can turn out to be too much of a good thing should the level of borrowing appear to rise beyond the economy's capacity to service debt. For poorer and less developed countries, the main source of external credit is the public sector—governments of the more advanced industrial economies or multilateral agencies like the International Monetary Fund. Overextension to public-sector creditors usually means that the borrower ends up negotiating a stabilization program, either bilaterally with creditor governments, multilaterally through the mechanisms of the so-called Paris Club, or with the IMF, with all the attendant conditionality. For middle-income emerging markets or more advanced economies, the main source of external credit is the global capital market. Overextension to private creditors usually means, eventually, a loss of perceived creditworthiness, which can lead to a sudden halt in new lending or a sharp rise of borrowing costs just when credit might be most needed. Worse, excessive borrowing risks provoking panicky withdrawals and crisis, as capital importers around the world have sadly learned, from East Asia in 1997–1998 to some of the members of the euro zone in more recent years. Reputation in financial markets, as we know, is a fragile flower, difficult to cultivate but easy to uproot. Painful policy adjustments may be required to restore a country's access to private investment.

Whatever the source of credit, therefore, autonomy may eventually have to be sacrificed for the sake of restoring external balance—a direct loss of power. Hence with borrowing too, just as with owned reserves, rational policy makers can be expected to seek an *optimum* rather than a maximum. And here too calculations of optimality will very much depend on politics.

But there is also a big difference. The calculations demanded here are inherently more complex than they are with owned reserves, since they necessarily involve tricky questions of probability and risk. With reserves, evaluations of prospective costs are relatively straightforward. Little risk is associated with hoarding reserves, and the real losses from deficit reduction or interest payments can be estimated with a reasonable degree of certainty. With external credit, by contrast, nothing is certain. Borrowing capacity is by definition subjective in nature, often fluctuating widely—and even wildly—in response to the fickleness of creditor governments or changing sentiment in the marketplace. Because of this uncertainty, generalizations about limits are even more difficult than they are with the reserve component of liquidity.

In effect, limits are not set by borrowers at all. Rather they are set by creditors, both public and private. It is they who gain the power that overextended debtors lose. The challenge for borrowers is hard enough when dealing with creditor governments, whose decisions may be ruled as much by politics as economics. Calculations are even more difficult when it comes to market actors, who are constantly judging what they perceive as the quality of policy performance in individual economies. Financial markets are like a perpetual opinion poll. If a country is currently able to avoid deficit reduction owing to ready access to credit, it is because the markets have given it their Good Housekeeping Seal of Approval. Conversely, if a country suddenly finds itself no longer able to put off adjustment owing to a cessation of lending, it is the markets that are enforcing a limit to its power to delay. The more states rely on borrowing capacity rather than owned reserves for their international liquidity, the greater is the role of creditors, public and private, in determining who ultimately will be forced to undergo real adjustment.

Again, two implications follow. First, it seems clear that the distribution of the continuing cost of adjustment among deficit countries will be heavily influenced, if not largely determined, by creditor perceptions of debt-service capacity, which tend to favor the relatively wealthy. Ceteris paribus, the power to delay should be greatest in the advanced industrial economies—the nations that enjoy the highest standing as international borrowers. The power to delay will be least in poorer and less developed economies that have limited access, at best, to foreign finance. Second, it also seems clear that the distribution of the continuing cost among deficit countries, unlike the transitional cost of adjustment, is apt to be highly volatile. That is because of the persistent threat of rapid swings of sentiment about the "soundness" of policy in one economy or another. The perpetual opinion poll often changes its mind—and when it does, the ability to postpone adjustment through borrowing is changed as well. Taken together, these two observations suggest that while wealthier economies may be the most favored in this context, there is no fixed pattern involved. What creditors giveth by way of a power to delay, they may also taketh away.

The Special Role of International Currencies

Finally, we come to the special role of international currencies. For the privileged few countries whose national money is used for international purposes, borrowing capacity is effectively enhanced by the willingness of outsiders to accept and hold the currency as a store of value. These may be market actors or central banks. Expanded foreign holdings are the equivalent of a loan from abroad—an increase of claims on the country of issue. Outsiders in effect take the currency as a form of IOU. But unlike other kinds of credit, the loan is neither negotiated nor even perceived as a debt. It is viewed simply as providing an attractive asset that foreigners can use for a variety of cross-border purposes. The heartier the appetite of outsiders for a given currency, the greater is the issuing country's ability to finance imbalances with its own money—a right to run "deficits without tears," as the French economist Jacques Rueff famously described it.[24] As a result, the state's power to delay is amplified. A need for international liquidity in the conventional sense is obviated when national liquidity is all that is required.

Most notable in this respect, of course, is the United States, which has long benefited from an unparalleled capacity to postpone adjustment of its balance of payments. For well over a third of a century, stretching back to the 1970s, America's current account has been in persistent deficit—a record unlike that of any other nation. The last year the current balance was in surplus was in the recession year of 1991. The United

States clearly enjoys more power to delay than anyone else. First and foremost, that is due to the unique status of America's greenback as the world's preeminent international currency—indeed, the world's only truly *global* currency. Near-universal popularity translates directly into a sustained demand for the dollar or dollar-denominated claims, which in turn enables the United States to go on financing deficits year after year seemingly without constraint. We will have more to say about America's unique advantages in chapter 7.

MEASUREMENT?

That leaves one last question: Can monetary power be measured? For purposes of empirical analysis, it would obviously be helpful if precise numbers could be derived for each of the two hands of power. In principle, it might seem possible to quantify either hand by focusing on the underlying structural or financial variables that determine a state's capacity to avoid adjustment costs. In practice, however, accurate measurement has proved elusive, if not illusory.

Early discussions of monetary power eschewed measurement altogether, concentrating instead on the various roles that a monetarily powerful nation might be expected to play. The idea was to identify specific functions that could be considered as tangible manifestations of power. And what might those functions be? Most familiar is the work of Charles Kindleberger, who wrote a great deal about the roles of a monetary "hegemon." In his justly celebrated book, *The World in Depression*, Kindleberger suggested that a monetary leader would be expected to play three distinct roles: (1) maintain a relatively open market for distress goods; (2) providing contracyclical, or at least stable, long-term lending; and (3) acting as a lender of last resort at times of crisis.[25] Later he added two additional functions: (4) policing a relatively stable system of exchange rates and (5) ensuring some degree of coordination of macroeconomic policies.[26] All five of these roles clearly imply a measure of power. But they can hardly be easily estimated.

Implicitly, an indirect quantitative approach has been suggested by more recent work looking at prospects for competition at the peak of the Currency Pyramid, following creation of the euro and then the rise of China's yuan. Was either currency likely to challenge or perhaps even surpass the dollar as top currency? Econometric exercises have prolifer-ated, seeking to isolate key variables that might be expected to determine the market shares of major currencies over time. For Menzie Chinn and Jeffrey Frankel, focusing on the outlook for the euro, the main factors were thought to be economic size, inflation, exchange-rate variability, and the size of the home financial center.[27] Similarly, for Arvind Subrama-nian, focusing on the RMB, the main variables were said to be GDP, share of global trade transactions, and current account surplus.[28] Though not explicitly intended to measure monetary power as such, studies like these clearly offer a menu of candidates for a composite index comparable to the CINC or other similar constructs that have been developed to mea-sure state power more broadly.

In the tradition of composites like the CINC, Carla Norrlof has calcu-lated an indicator of "monetary capability" based on four key attributes: GDP, volume of trade (exports and imports), capital markets (including openness), and net defense expenditures.[29] Similarly, Leslie Armijo and colleagues have put together a Contemporary Capabilities Index (CCI) incorporating national shares of global output, population, two prox-ies for technology (telephone subscriptions and industrial value added), military spending, and foreign exchange reserves, with variations for four different estimates of national financial capabilities.[30] Efforts like these deserve respect for their ambition. But they also suffer from the same deficiencies as the CINC and its various counterparts, as noted back in chapter 2. Quantitative measures based on the elements-of-power ap-proach to power can be misleading for two reasons—first, because the selection of components is inherently arbitrary; and second, because such indicators omit consideration of strategic or political context. They tell us little about how capabilities may or may not translate into influence. Numbers help, but in the end there is no substitute for careful analysis of the social characteristics of power.

CONCLUSION

To summarize, we may say that monetary power is best understand as being dual in nature, deployable with two hands—the power to delay, aimed at avoiding the continuing cost of adjustment; and the power to deflect, aimed at avoiding the transitional cost of adjustment. The power to deflect has its source in fundamental structural variables—most importantly, the relative degree of openness and adaptability of the national economy—and is limited by the economy's underlying material attributes. The power to delay, by contrast, is largely a function of a country's international liquidity position relative to others, comprising both owned reserves and borrowing capacity, and is limited only by the government's appetite for reserves and by the willingness of foreign actors to lend. By providing an additional channel of access to external credit, currency internationalization amplifies a country's power to delay.

Accordingly, it should be no surprise that states vary considerably in their monetary power, implying a systematic element of hierarchy in monetary relations. In fact, monetary relations have always tended to be distinctly hierarchical, as suggested by the image of the Currency Pyramid. Ultimately, for all states, the issue is adjustment costs. Rank in the Currency Pyramid depends in large degree on the relative capacity to avoid the burden of payments adjustment, making others pay instead. The position of any given country in the Pyramid directly reflects its access to both hands of monetary power.

At the peak of the Pyramid are nations, like the United States, whose currencies are to a greater or lesser extent used for various international purposes. Only such countries may enjoy the special privilege of financing deficits with their own currencies. But that is only the beginning of the story, not the end. While currency internationalization clearly offers advantages for an issuing country, it is not without possible costs or risks as well. The relationship between currency and power is more complex than generally supposed, as we shall now see.

4

From Currency to Power

The sinews of war are infinite money.
—*Marcus Tullius Cicero (106 BC–43 BC)*

Few knowledgeable observers doubt that there must be some kind of causal connection between currency and power—between the international use of a money and the power of the country that issues it. But little systematic analysis exists to tell us what specifically that connection might be. Indeed, it is not always obvious which way the arrow of causation runs. A reasonable premise is that the arrow points simultaneously in both directions in a relationship of mutual endogeneity.

To some extent, clearly, state power plays the role of independent variable, driving currency choice. A money will not come to be used across borders if its issuer does not already enjoy some measure of economic and political standing in the world. Put differently, a currency will not come to be "great" unless its issuer is already "great" as well. Consideration of that side of the relationship, however, will be postponed until chapter 5. In this chapter, we will look first at the causal relationship running the other way.

Here the emphasis will be on the role of power as a dependent variable, driven by the force of currency competition. At issue is what we may call "currency power"—the specific causal pathways that run from cross-border use of a money to the geopolitical capabilities of its home government. For analytical purposes, the issuing state's initial endowment of power will be assumed to be given. The question to be addressed is: What will happen to that endowment of power once the national money comes to be used for international purposes? In short, in power terms, what value is added by currency internationalization?

In formal theory, we actually know very little about currency power. We do know that an international money can play multiple roles. We also know that different moneys may play quite different combinations of roles. What we do not know is how each of these roles separately may affect a government's overall capabilities. Hence we are unable to directly compare the broad currency power of any one issuing country with others. Without an understanding of the distinctive impact of each of a money's separate roles, it is impossible to generalize about how internationalization may—or may not—add to a state's overall power in relation to others.

Therefore, to set the question of currency power within a firm theoretical framework, this chapter disaggregates the concept of currency internationalization into its several distinct functions and seeks to explore the power implications of each function separately. Analysis will rely primarily on deductive reasoning. Attention will be focused on four critical questions: What is the effect on state power of each specific role, considered on its own? Are there interdependencies among the various roles? What are their relative or cumulative impacts? And, finally, what is the role of time in this context?

Two broad findings stand out. First, all three of the traditional faces of power seem to be at work, though in varying degrees. Some roles, more than others, offer a direct capacity for influence; some operate more in the nature of structural power; and some may promote soft power. For each role, the mix can be quite different. In the end, however, only three roles appear to really add value in geopolitical terms. These are a money's roles in financial markets, in trade, and in central-bank reserves. The roles in financial markets and reserves enhance the issuer's monetary autonomy, making it easier to delay adjustment costs, and also reinforces centrality in the global financial network. Both effects in turn create a capacity for influence, though whether that capacity can be effectively actualized will depend on ancillary conditions and limits that may vary considerably over time. A currency's role in trade is important, above all, because of its impact on central-bank reserve preferences. The more a currency dominates in each of these three roles, the greater overall is the value that is likely to be added to the issuer's relative power in the world.

Second, it seems that in some instances an international money might actually be disadvantageous rather than beneficial—a *double-edged sword* that may add to a state's capabilities, but can also cut the other way. Particularly important is the role of time, which can significantly alter the value added by internationalization as foreign liabilities accumulate. A distinct life cycle would appear to characterize the overall relationship between currency and power.

FRAMING THE ISSUE

The concept of state power is not simple, as we know from chapter 2. In the context of international monetary relations, most power analysis tends to focus on overt exercises of influence—the authoritative role that a government might play in, say, crisis management or financial regulation or the supply of payments financing. What can states do, and what are the limits to their leverage? But that tells us little about the underlying nature of currency power. To truly understand the power implications of an international money, we must go behind all such influence attempts to see where, ultimately, the issuer's putative capabilities come from. In other words, we need to look to the *sources* of power.

Whether we are talking of power as autonomy or as influence, the key to analysis of currency power lies in the specific context in which states operate. The internationalization of a money is largely a market phenomenon, reflecting the preferences of diverse actors in global trade and finance. But since currencies tend to be issued by states (or, as in Europe, by a group of states), the power that comes from internationalization is generally manifested in state-to-state relations. Most salient, therefore, is the structure of transactional relationships among states, as emphasized in the social-power approach that has dominated power analysis since the mid-twentieth century.[1] What matters is who depends on whom and for what. How asymmetrical are prevailing relationships among states and how centrally located is a country in the global network of interactions? Relational asymmetries manifestly lie at the root of currency internationalization and therefore may be said to be the source as well of a state's influence, whether passive or actualized.

In turn, currency power may be seen to operate either directly or indirectly. On the one hand the money itself may provide an effective instrument of statecraft, available for direct use as a tool to shape behavior or enforce compliance. This is the usual focus of power analysis in monetary relations. But it is also possible that the role of the currency may be more indirect, reinforcing statecraft by enhancing the utility of *other* pathways to influence. This aspect is more often ignored. For analysis to be complete, the concept of currency power must be understood to encompass both types of impact, indirect as well as direct, on overall state capabilities.

Framing the central issue for this chapter, then, is relatively straightforward. The connections run from (1) mutual dependence to (2) a capacity to avoid the burden of adjustment to (3) passive or actualized influence. The agenda for analysis can be outlined in the form of a series of four interrelated sets of questions. The first three questions have to do with the meaning and sources of currency power. Only the last question has to do with uses and limits.

1. What is the effect of an international currency on the issuing state's position within the global monetary network? In particular, is dependence reduced or centrality of position enhanced?
2. What is the effect of an international currency on the state's monetary autonomy?
3. What is the effect of an international currency on the state's capacity for influence?
4. What is the likelihood that influence will be actualized, either directly or indirectly?

CONVENTIONAL WISDOM

Conventional wisdom generally holds that currency internationalization must add to the power of the state that issues it. As Susan Strange put it years ago: "It is highly probable that any state economically strong enough to possess [an international money] will also exert substantial power and influence. The rich usually do."[2]

Remarkably, however, this convenient presumption has never been put to a serious, systematic test. A broad causal relationship is casually assumed, linking currency to power, and much has been written about how the resulting capabilities might be used as an instrument of statecraft.[3]

But no one has previously tried to spell out the connections in detail, to see just how or why any of the diverse cross-border uses of a national money might actually affect the autonomy or influence of its issuer. In the words of Hubert Zimmermann, "It is simply assumed that a national currency that takes on an international role enhances the power of the issuing country. . . . However, substantiating in what sense the possession of a global currency actually bestows power on the issuing country is not so easy."[4]

Part of the difficulty is that international currencies play a variety of roles, and not all of those roles need have the same impact on state power. Some roles might turn out to be disadvantageous rather than beneficial; on occasion, the effect of a role might even change significantly over time. To test the conventional wisdom, therefore, we must take a closer look to see what specific characteristics of international money make the most difference, and how.

The logic of the conventional wisdom is impeccable. Given the "rich tapestry" of hierarchy among the world's diverse moneys, it hardly seems implausible to assume that there must be a connection between currency and power. The very notion of hierarchy, after all, is inherently political, suggesting varying degrees of reciprocal influence—differential impacts on the ability of governments to achieve goals at home or abroad. So why not just connect the dots? The stronger the currency, presumably, the stronger the country.

In the extant literature, however, we find only the vaguest clues as to how the dots might actually be connected. Most observers tend to limit themselves simply to repeating the usual litany of benefits and costs of an international money, as summarized in chapter 1. Remarkably little effort has gone into analyzing the specifics of causation. Currency internationalization, typically, is treated as a more or less holistic phenomenon, with little regard for the distinctively separate roles that any given international money might play. The possibility that these separate roles might have differential impacts on the capabilities of issuing states has never been formally addressed.

Thus, impeccable as the logic of the conventional wisdom may be, it still leaves critical gaps in our understanding. We have a standard taxonomy to describe an international; currency's several roles. But we know little about how each of these roles individually may (or may not) connect to state power. To improve understanding, we need to systematically disaggregate the concept of currency internationalization in order to isolate the impact of each individual function. The challenge is to look carefully at each function separately and ask: What is the effect on state power of each specific role, considered on its own? Are there interdependencies among the various roles? What are their relative or cumulative impacts? And what is the role of time in this context? Only then can we begin to get a real handle on the specifics of causation in currency power.

THE PRIVATE LEVEL

In international markets, selected national currencies—whether top, patrician, or elite—may play any of three roles: in foreign-exchange trading, trade invoicing and settlement, or financial markets. Examining each role on its own, it becomes evident that their respective implications for state power differ noticeably. All three roles may generate economic dividends, but only the role in financial markets, where currencies serve as an investment medium, can prove advantageous in political terms as well. The big dividing line is between the medium-of-exchange and unit-of-account functions of money, on the one hand, and the store-of-value function on the other.

Foreign-exchange Trading

Nothing better illustrates the network-like quality of international monetary relations than the foreign-exchange market—that vast agglomeration of banks and other financial institutions around the world where currencies are actively traded for one another. Given the more than 150 distinct state-issued moneys presently in existence, it is evident that the total of bilateral relationships numbers in the thousands, constituting a gigantic web of interactions. The metric for all of these relationships is of course the rate of exchange between each pair of currencies.

Not all relationships are of equal importance, however. In most cases, the direct connections between pairs of currencies are thin at best, meaning that the expense of direct purchases is likely to be high, if not prohibitive. Most wholesale trades therefore tend to go through a more widely used intermediary, a "vehicle" currency, in order to minimize transactions costs. The idea is to take advantage of scale economies, otherwise known as network externalities. One peripheral currency is used to buy the vehicle currency; the vehicle currency is then used to buy another peripheral currency. Data on the currency composition of global foreign-exchange transactions are provided in a triennial survey by the Bank for International Settlements (BIS), a kind of central bank for central banks located in Basel, Switzerland. According to the bank's most recent survey, conducted in 2013, the US dollar is by far the most dominant vehicle currency, appearing on one side or the other of some 87 percent of all market transactions.[5] (Percentages add up to 200 percent because every transaction involves two currencies.) Trailing far behind are the two patrician currencies, the euro (33 percent) and the yen (23 percent), and a small handful of elite currencies.

Vehicle currencies clearly enjoy a position of centrality in the global currency network, since so many exchanges pass through them. For issuing states, that almost certainly translates into economic benefit. Transactions costs are likely to be reduced for local enterprises; banks and other financial institutions may gain some "denomination rents"[6] from the volume of business done in their home currency. Political benefits, on the other hand, seem slight, since the role appears to have little impact on monetary autonomy. Widespread use as an intermediary for currency trading involves no long-lasting holdings. Hence it has little impact on the issuing country's ability to delay or deflect adjustment costs. No constraint on state action is removed or alleviated. Nor is there likely to be much value added in terms of global prestige or reputation. The vehicle role is a purely technical one and can be easily replaced.

Trade Invoicing and Settlement

Much the same can also be said of a currency's role in trade invoicing and settlement. Whenever goods or services are bought and sold internationally, the parties to the transaction must agree on the monetary unit to be used to denominate contracts and effectuate payments. And here too scale economies dictate a dominant role for a small handful of currencies at the center of the global monetary network. Available data suggest that roughly half of all world exports today are invoiced and settled in US dollars. Partly this is because of America's large market size and still predominant place as an importer and exporter, all providing a large transactional network that enhances scale economies. And partly it is because of the greenback's central role in the markets for virtually all reference-priced and organized exchange-traded commodities—including, most notably, the global market for oil, the world's most widely traded product. The dollar's dominance in commodity trading dates back to the first decades after World War II, when the United States and its major mining and petroleum companies ruled global markets on both the export and import sides.

Next in importance today is the euro, which accounts for perhaps 15 to 20 percent of world exports, mainly in and around the European region and roughly equivalent to the euro zone's share of global trade. Most other moneys play a marginal role at best.

The benefits of the trade role too appear to be largely economic rather than political. On the economic side, local enterprises need worry less about the issue of exchange risk; financial institutions may enjoy a competitive edge in providing commercial credit or other trade-related services in their own home currency. These are definite advantages. But on the political side gains again seem slight, and for much the same reason. The market's choice of a national currency for invoicing and settlement, on its own, adds nothing directly to the issuing government's ability to delay or deflect adjustment costs. Again, no constraint is removed or alleviated. Bills must still be paid on time, whatever the currency used.

Financial Markets

Effects are quite different, however, in financial markets, where currencies play a role as an investment medium. One of the principal functions of financial markets is to facilitate the management of investor risk by creating opportunities for portfolio diversification. At the international level this means widening the range of currency choice. To spread risk, global portfolio managers typically invest across a variety of currencies, including all the familiar moneys near the peak of the Currency Pyramid. Most popular here too is the US dollar, though by a slightly declining margin in relative terms. Representative are the figures for the outstanding stock of international bonds (defined as issues in a currency other than that of the borrower's home country). At the end of 2012 the greenback's share of the global bond market stood just above 52 percent. The euro's share was a little more than one-quarter, and at least a half-dozen other moneys, including the yen and a number of elite currencies, accounted for the remainder.

Like the vehicle and trade roles, the investment role clearly yields economic benefits. Most significant is the seigniorage gain that automatically results from the willingness of outsiders to acquire a currency that is not their own. Additional benefits may also accrue to local banks or other financial institutions that generate or manage the claims owned by foreigners. But unlike the vehicle and trade roles, the investment role also yields distinct political benefits since it does involve long-lasting holdings. State capabilities are augmented in two ways. First, autonomy is enhanced, since it becomes possible to finance external deficits, at least in part, with the nation's own currency. Traditional balance-of-payments constraints on policy are relaxed, and adjustment costs can more easily be delayed or deflected. And second, the potential for influence is increased, since centrality in the global financial network is reinforced. The more the currency is used for investment purposes, the greater will be the number and strength of links that must go through that particular node. Dependence is amplified.

Can the potential for influence be actualized? Indirectly, a relaxed payments constraint makes it easier to use more traditional instruments of statecraft—whether diplomatic, economic, or even military—to pursue foreign-policy goals. Side-payments can be offered or costly sanctions imposed with less concern for where the money is coming from. Military protection can be promised or force threatened without worrying about the risk of a payments crisis. The key is the enhanced borrowing capacity afforded by an international currency. "The sinews of war are infinite money," Cicero said. The borrowing power afforded by an international currency is not infinite, but it is generous.

Rosella Cappella, for example, notes how for Britain in the nineteenth century, the attractiveness of sterling assets made it relatively easy for the British government to finance its involvement in conflicts abroad by selling bonds to foreigners.[7] London had a clear wartime advantage vis-à-vis adversaries—its own "exorbitant privilege." Likewise, in the more recent era it is evident that sustained foreign demand for dollar-denominated claims has played a major role in supporting US military spending around the world.[8] Being able to run "deficits without tears" means that Washington can borrow its way out of almost any budget squeeze. International security specialist Paul Viotti calls the greenback the monetary component of America's hard power:

> The dollar's privileged position has facilitated the conduct of American foreign and national security policy since the end of World War II. . . . Given the global position of the dollar . . . American policy-makers deploy U.S. armed forces at will. When U.S. policy-makers want to conduct military operations or finance other projects abroad, they spend those readily accepted dollars.[9]

As in the classic board game *Monopoly*, it is like having a handy Get Out of Jail Free card.

Directly, the currency itself may become an effective instrument of leverage owing to the investment role's impact on autonomy and centrality. As a corollary of the enhanced power to delay or deflect adjustment, the issuing country is now in a position to use the payments process per se as an instrument of leverage. And as a corollary of greater network dependence, access to the currency itself can be manipulated to advantage. Consider two examples. First is the case of Panama, which back in 1988 found itself in a grim political dispute with the United States. Determined to force General Manuel Noriega, the country's leader at the time, from power, Washington froze Panamanian assets in US banks and prohibited all payments or other dollar transfers to Panama. The impact was devastating. Most local banks were forced to close their doors, and the economy was squeezed by a severe liquidity shortage, significantly weakening Panamanian resistance to American pressure. Coercion via private financial markets worked.[10]

Second is the more recent case of Iran, hit with financial sanctions by the United States as part of Washington's campaign to curb the Islamic Republic's ambitious nuclear program. Particularly since 2011, the United States has imposed an aggressive currency blockade on Iran, effectively denying it access to greenbacks through the international banking system. Any financial institution anywhere doing business in dollars with Iran is subject to heavy penalties. Hence Iran has been hampered in its ability to repatriate funds held abroad to finance payments deficits. As one source puts it, Washington "forced foreign banks to choose between access to the US financial system or doing business with Iran. . . . The major direct consequence of banking sanctions was that Iran was locked out of leading payment and credit networks."[11] Here too the impact has been devastating, slowing growth dramatically and weakening Iran's resistance. Many observers are convinced that it was largely due to these sanctions that Tehran finally agreed in 2013 to sit down to formal negotiations on the future of its nuclear efforts.

Caveats, however, are in order. The investment role does not automatically make a country a superpower. There are limits. Fundamentally, the possibility for actualizing leverage depends on two ancillary conditions— first, the availability of alternatives to the issuer's currency; and second, the magnitude of existing foreign holdings of the currency. The former variable is important because it determines the issuer's ability to control the *supply* of investment opportunities. How much monopolistic power does the issuing authority enjoy as a source of investment-grade assets? How absolute is its control at the center of the financial network? The latter is important because it helps shape market sentiment regarding the attractiveness of those investment opportunities, thus affecting *demand*. We cannot forget the pivotal role that creditors play in determining borrowing limits. In acquiring claims in a currency, outsiders are automatically extending credit to the issuing country. From their point of view, as previously indicated, the issuer's liabilities are no more than a kind of IOU, always subject to the market's perpetual opinion poll. Confidence in a currency may vary considerably, strengthening or weakening the issuer's capacity for leverage. The larger the total amount of claims at risk, the shakier foreign demand is apt to become—hence the smaller is the possibility of a successful activation.

To illustrate, consider two contrasting scenarios. At one extreme would be a situation like that enjoyed by the United States immediately after World War II, when market actors had few alternatives to the greenback and dollar holdings were low. America had a near-absolute monopoly on quality outlets for savings, and few feared for the dollar's future value. As a result, Washington was in a position to make access to its financial markets an explicit instrument of foreign policy, welcoming friends or barring adversaries. At the other extreme would be a situation like the present, when alternatives to the greenback are more plentiful and the accumulated overhang of foreign dollar liabilities has grown enormously.

The United States may remain at the center of the international financial network, but not to the same degree it once did. As we shall see in chapter 7, many observers therefore worry that further attempts by Washington to exploit its potential for leverage could prompt a shift away from the greenback—perhaps even an abrupt flight. That would certainly be more disadvantageous from America's point of view.

On balance, therefore, the power implications of the investment role are ambiguous. Autonomy is initially increased, but currency influence may or may not be facilitated, depending as it does on ancillary conditions that can vary considerably over time. Gains in the shorter term might well eventually be reversed in the longer term, as liquid liabilities accumulate. There is no denying that the investment role of a currency is potentially valuable. But there is also no denying that it could be quite dangerous as well—in effect, a double-edged sword that could cut either way.

The Official Level

At the official level, involving relations between governments, national currencies may also play any of three roles, as an exchange-rate anchor, an intervention currency, or a reserve asset. Here too each role, considered separately, has its own implications for state power. Likewise, here too the biggest difference is between the medium-of-exchange and unit-of-account functions, on the one hand, and the store-of-value function on the other.

Exchange-rate Anchor

Since the breakdown of the Bretton Woods pegged-rate system in the early 1970s, governments have been free to choose whatever exchange-rate regime they desire, from various versions of a "hard" or "soft" peg to managed flexibility or an independent ("clean") float. States that prefer to retain some form of peg have a wide range of units of account to choose from. In practice, only a few currencies figure prominently as exchange-rate anchors, either for single-currency pegs or as a prominent part of basket pegs.

Most dominant, once again, are the dollar and euro. About sixty states presently align their exchange-rate policy, wholly or in part, with

America's greenback, and use the dollar as their principal medium of currency intervention. These nations range in size from tiny islands in the Pacific to China. Their anchoring to the greenback would certainly seem to be evidence of a kind of Stackelberg leadership model at work—a form of structural ("go-it-alone") power. The United States acts unilaterally, as it typically does, taking advantage of its "exorbitant privilege." Others then decide whether or by how much to follow in Washington's wake. In parallel fashion, close to forty countries are tied in some degree to the euro.

As with trade invoicing at the private level, the anchor role at the official level appears to produce gains that are largely economic rather than political. The relative stability of a peg is likely to reduce the cost of doing business with aligned countries, as compared with economies with more variable or freely floating rates. Power implications, by contrast, appear to be as ambiguous as with the investment role. On the one hand, an anchor role certainly enhances the centrality of a currency, putting it at the core of a formal or informal monetary bloc. That may help promote the issuing state's soft power, by adding to the country's prestige and reputation. But hard power, on the other hand, benefits little, since on its own the pegging function—understood simply as a currency *numéraire*—does nothing to augment monetary autonomy.

Indeed, the net impact on the issuing state's power position could even turn out to be negative—an illustration of how structural power, emerging without conscious intent, may actually operate to the leader's disadvantage rather than to its benefit. The problem here is that pegging by followers can turn out to constrain the issuing government's ability to resort to exchange-rate shifts as part of the adjustment process.[12] The nominal value of the anchor currency is determined not by the home government but by the intervention practices of others; and foreign preferences cannot always be expected to coincide with the interests of the issuer. Faced with external deficits, the United States might wish to engineer a depreciation of the greenback, to gain a competitive edge in foreign trade. But depreciation is impossible unless it is ratified by the interventions of America's trading partners, who might prefer otherwise. Other countries retain the freedom to manage their own exchange rates. The price of the dollar simply adjusts as a residual. The United States thus actually loses a degree of policy autonomy—in effect becoming, in the words of historian Harold James, "a hostage of the international monetary system."[13] America's power to delay or deflect adjustment costs is not aided but eroded. Here too an international role can turn out to be a double-edged sword.

Intervention Currency

Except for an absolutely clean float—relatively rare in practice—all exchange-rate regimes involve some degree of government intervention in the exchange market, whether modest or substantial. But what foreign currency should be bought or sold in order to manage an exchange rate? Here too, as in foreign-exchange trading, scale economies matter. Efficiency criteria dictate choosing a currency that is as widely traded as possible, to ensure that the effects of intervention will be quickly and smoothly generalized. That means relying on one of the most popular international moneys such as the dollar, euro, or yen. Use for intervention purposes generally tends to mirror a money's prominence as a vehicle currency.

Effects of the intervention role, for the issuing state, appear to parallel those of the anchor role. On the one hand, there is likely to be some economic benefit, insofar as widespread use of the currency provides advantages to home financial institutions. On the other hand, power implications are ambiguous. There is nothing in the intervention role, considered on its own, that augments monetary autonomy. There is, however, a risk of loss of influence over the exchange rate in the adjustment process to the extent that bilateral rates are controlled by the intervention practices of others. Once again, we find a double-edged sword.

Reserve Currency

Finally, we come to the role of reserve currency—the function that most readily comes to mind when we think about international money. For central banks, reserve assets serve as a store of value that can be used directly for intervention purposes or else can be more or less quickly converted to a usable intervention medium. For historical reasons gold is still included in the reserve stockpiles of many countries, despite the fact that it is no longer directly employable as a means of exchange. So too is the IMF's own reserve asset, the SDR, which like gold must be exchanged for a more usable instrument when the need for financing arises. But the great bulk of reserves is held in the form of liquid assets denominated in one of the small handful of moneys at the peak of the Currency Pyramid. Once again the US dollar predominates, accounting near end-2014 for some 62 percent of global reserves according to the IMF. This was down from 71.5 percent in 1999 but well up from a low of around 45 percent in 1990. And once again the euro is second, with a share of 22.6 percent in late 2014, up from 18 percent in 1999 but down from a high of 27 percent as recently as 2011.

Effects of the reserve-currency role most closely resemble those of the investment role. On the one hand there are clear economic benefits, including a gain of seigniorage for the economy as a whole as well as heightened profit opportunities for local financial institutions—at least for those in a position to assist foreign central banks in the management of their reserves. On the other hand power implications are ambiguous and highly dependent on ancillary conditions that can vary over time.

Here too autonomy is increased initially and centrality in the global financial network is reinforced. The more foreign central banks are willing to add to their reserve holdings, in effect extending credit to the country of origin, the easier it is for the issuer to delay or deflect adjustment costs. Likewise, dependence on the center country is amplified by the tightening of financial links. A capacity to exercise leverage emerges. But once more, whether that potential can be actualized is another matter entirely. Here too there are limits. Much depends on the same ancillary economic considerations that make the investment role so contingent: the availability of alternatives and the magnitude of existing holdings. Because here we are speaking of official state institutions, and not just private market actors, much also depends on geopolitical considerations, including especially the nature of the issuing state's diplomatic and security relations with reserve holders. Possibilities vary enormously, from a condition of potentially great strength early on to later, as liabilities accumulate, a position of decided weakness—yet again, the double-edged sword.

Interdependencies

Overall, a distinctive pattern emerges. All six roles generate economic benefits of some magnitude. Political effects, however, tend to be more differentiated. Only the two store-of-value roles—the investment role at the private level and the reserve role at the official level—seem able to add directly to the issuing state's capabilities, creating a potential for effective leverage (though in time this advantage may be eroded or even reversed by an accumulation of foreign debt). In this respect, there is a clear dividing line between the store-of-value function and the other two functions of international money (medium of exchange and unit of account).

That does not mean, however, that the two store-of-value roles are the only ones that add geopolitical value. Analysis cannot stop with a consideration of each role on its own. The possibility of interdependencies among the various roles must also be considered. For example, we know that the intervention role of an international money is closely tied to its importance as a vehicle currency. As indicated, scale economies matter in exchange-rate management. Likewise, it is evident that a close link exists between the invoicing role of a currency in international trade (a unit-of-account function) and its settlement role (a medium-of-exchange function). It is no accident that typically these are spoken of, as I have done here, in tandem: the trade role. Most parties to international trade find it convenient to use the same currency for both purposes.

The real question, however, concerns the two store-of-value roles and the dividing line between them and the other two functions of international money. Is either the investment role or the reserve role in any way dependent on a currency's use as a medium of exchange or unit of account at either the private or official level?

At the private level, the answer is clear: No. For most portfolio managers, seeking diversification to manage risk, use of any given currency as an investment medium is most closely tied to the critical qualities of exchange convenience and capital certainty—a high degree of transactional liquidity and reasonable predictability of asset value. The key to both, to repeat, is a set of broad and well-developed financial markets for claims denominated in the issuing country's currency, sufficiently open to ensure full access by investors of all kinds. Neither exchange convenience nor capital certainty appear to depend in any way on how much a money may or may not be used as a vehicle in currency markets or for trade invoicing and settlement. In currency markets the vehicle is not held as a store of value at all. In trade a species of investment instrument is created in the form of commercial paper, but the claims involved are very short term and effectively self-liquidating.

At the official level, the answer is trickier. In principle central banks are no less free than market investors to diversify the currency composition of their holdings, so long as the assets they hold can be quickly converted when needed into a medium useful for intervention purposes. To that extent the qualities they seek are the same as those valued by private actors: exchange convenience and capital certainty. In practice, however, reserve preferences in most countries tend to be distinctly skewed, favoring one currency in particular. In Latin America, the Middle East, and much of Asia, the US dollar typically predominates, while around Europe and in parts of Africa the euro is more popular. Why is that?

Superficially, it might appear to have something to do with the anchor and intervention roles. If a country's money is formally or informally aligned with one anchor currency in particular, it would seem to make sense to intervene in that currency as well; and that in turn would logically encourage concentrated holdings of the currency, to facilitate easy entry or exit in the exchange market. In effect, reserve preferences could be said to reflect the map of exchange-rate linkages. As one recent study puts it, "Currency geography is portfolio destiny."[14] But that fails to explain why we also see the same kind of skewed reserve preferences in states with floating currencies, which may not actively manage their exchange rate on a regular basis. Nor, for states that do intervene frequently, does it account for the choice of anchor to start with. Such decisions are not made arbitrarily.

Looking deeper, it seems evident that the really crucial link lies elsewhere—in the trade role. Politics aside, reserve preferences are most likely to reflect the pattern of currency choice in a country's foreign commercial relationships. The popularity of the dollar in Latin America, the Middle East, and Asia is a direct reflection of either or both of two considerations: the importance of the United States as a market or supplier, and/or the importance of reference-priced and organized exchange-traded commodities in each country's exports. Since the greenback is the main monetary unit used for invoicing and settlement in both bilateral trade with the United States and global commodity trade, it is hardly surprising to find it dominant in the reserves of these nations as well. Conversely, the euro naturally dominates in the European region, where trade relations are focused more toward members of the EU.

Plainly, therefore, the investment and reserve roles are not the only ones that add value. In terms of direct implications for state power, the dividing line between the two store-of-value roles, on the one hand, and money's other two functions (medium of exchange and unit of account), on the other hand, remains essential. But indirectly, the role of a currency in trade can be seen to play a vital part, too, insofar as it helps to shape central-bank reserve preferences. Overall, three of an international money's six possible roles—specifically, the trade, investment, and reserve-currency roles—are critically involved, not just the two store-of-value roles.

RELATIVE AND CUMULATIVE IMPACTS

What are the relative or cumulative impacts of these three roles? Ultimately, it seems not unreasonable to conclude that a currency's reserve role has the greatest effect on state power, owing to the enhanced capacity that emerges for direct leverage on governments. By comparison, the investment and trade roles would appear to be of secondary importance. Their relevance derives mainly from the part they play in making a reserve role possible.

There are two reasons for discounting the relative impact of the investment role considered on its own. First, as compared with the reserve-currency role, it is clearly more difficult to actualize any potential capacity for influence. We know that both store-of-value roles enhance autonomy, by relaxing traditional external constraints on domestic macroeconomic policy. A capacity for leverage is the automatic corollary of any increase in the power to delay or deflect adjustment costs. But when the enhanced autonomy results from decentralized investment decisions in the open marketplace rather than from centralized government choices, impacts are bound to be more dispersed and diffuse, making it harder to target specific actors with self-conscious intent. When a currency is held just by private investors, pressures can be brought to bear on other states only indirectly. When the same currency is held by public agencies, pressures on foreign governments can be applied directly, to much better effect.

Second, the investment role also offers a lower degree of control over supply, again as compared with the reserve-currency role. That is evident from the differing degrees of diversification in private markets and official reserves. At the private level, as many as eight to ten currencies figure prominently in global finance. It is not like the immediate aftermath of World War II when just one country, the United States, could enjoy anything like a monopoly over available alternatives. Given the much higher level of currency competition today, few issuing states are in a position even to try to exercise deliberate leverage through the role of their money as an investment medium. Though assets denominated in the monetary units of countries like Australia, Canada, and Switzerland are all actively traded in global markets, no one would claim that this translates into any kind of real power for their issuing governments. At the official level, by contrast, where just two currencies dominate, something closer to a duopoly prevails. More room, accordingly, is offered for actualizing influence.

On the other hand, it is clear that an investment role is essential if a currency is ever to rise to the status of a reserve currency. While a given money can play an investment role even if never used as a reserve currency, the reverse is unlikely ever to happen in a market-based currency system. Monetary history suggests that the investment role comes first and then is followed by a reserve role *in addition*. Certainly that was the pattern followed by the pound sterling in the nineteenth century, which first found an international role as a consequence of London's preeminence as a financial center, and only later began to be held by central banks as well. Likewise, it was true of the US dollar, which first rode the rise of New York as a rival to London for foreign lending well before it surpassed sterling as a reserve asset. It is necessary to think in terms of cumulative effects. A state whose currency is used as a store of value in private markets alone gains only the marginal influence created by that role. But a state whose currency is used as a store of value by central banks as well gains the cumulative impact of both roles.

The link is the trade role, which plays a critical part in determining which among several investment currencies will emerge as a favored reserve asset as well. The issuer of an international money that is used only as investment medium can aspire to just some modest increment of power at best. But add widespread use for trade invoicing and settlement leading to a reserve role, and soon the issuer becomes much more centrally placed in the global monetary network, enhancing its influence considerably. Combined dominance in all three—financial markets, trade, and reserves—produces the "exorbitant privilege" enjoyed by a true top currency.

TIME

Finally, it is critical to recall the importance of the element of time, as noted back in chapter 1. The analysis in this chapter strongly suggests that the power implications of an international money may change quite dramatically over time.

Deficits?

First, a caveat. The single most important consequence of time would appear to be a gradual accumulation of foreign liabilities, reflecting the dynamics of both the investment and reserve roles. For a surprisingly large number of observers, that means that over time the issuing state has no choice but to run a persistent current-account deficit, accepting the burden of an ever-increasing amount of net debt. In fact, as I have suggested elsewhere, that is a serious mistake.[15]

Superficially, the idea would seem plausible. It is all a matter, we are told, of elementary balance-of-payments accounting. If there is to be any substantial accumulation of claims denominated in the home money—a net capital inflow—a current-account deficit is needed to provide the requisite supply. In the words of one recent commentary, a "reserve currency nation must be a net debtor, running a current account deficit, and other countries must run current account surpluses so that they can invest in these securities."[16] Echoes another analysis, even more bluntly, "the country issuing a reserve currency must be able to generate a trade deficit."[17] The assertion comes up especially often in commentaries on prospects for the euro or yuan. Regarding Europe's joint money, one source writes, "an increase in the demand for euros would . . . require that the eurozone run a substantial external deficit in order to satisfy the external demand for euros."[18] Regarding China's RMB, another observer insists that "China needs to be a large net importer of goods . . . in order to allow its partner nations to accumulate renminbi assets in significant size."[19]

In truth, the idea is simply wrong. There is no necessary connection at all between a country's current-account position and enhanced use of its money. As a practical matter, internationalization can occur even when the current account is in balance or surplus, through a process of intermediation on capital account—in effect, by borrowing short and lending long. Liquidity can be provided to foreigners in the form of short-term or easily marketable liabilities; working their way through the domestic financial system, the proceeds of this borrowing can then be used to lend or invest abroad at longer term. That is precisely how sterling became top currency in the late nineteenth century. It is also how the dollar came to replace the pound at the peak of the Currency Pyramid by the middle of the twentieth century. And more recently it was the pattern for currencies like the DM, yen, and euro as well, as we shall see in the next chapter. In every case, internationalization started alongside surpluses, not deficits, in the current account.

Of course, for both Britain and the United States it is also true that eventually those surpluses did turn into deficits. Net creditors became net debtors. But there is nothing in either the British or US experience to suggest that such an outcome is either required or somehow inevitable. Britain's current balance did not turn negative until the exigencies of World War I. America's current deficits did not emerge until the oil shocks of the 1970s. In theory, the issuer of an international currency could sustain the position of its money indefinitely through intermediation on capital account alone. That logic was articulated decades ago in a celebrated monograph by Emile Despres, Charles Kindleberger, and Walter Salant,[20] and has since been reiterated inter alia by Barry Eichengreen.[21] Yet many commentators continue to ignore it, seeming to be blissfully unaware of the error they are committing.

Life Cycles

Even with the caveat, however, it seems undeniable that fortunes can change over time. Along the lines suggested by Gallarotti's notion of a power curse,[22] growing vulnerabilities and feedbacks may well be ignored until it is too late. Indeed, it does not seem far-fetched to speak of something approximating a distinct life cycle for international currencies— first a rise and then a fall of popularity. Were there no terminal stage in the cycle, we might all still be using the Athenian drachma or Byzantine solidus. It was not so long ago that we saw the demise of sterling, after decades of preeminence as a top currency. Today many are persuaded that we may be witness to the beginning of the end of the dollar's dominance as well, though opinion on that prospect continues to be divided (as we shall see in chapter 7).

Taking time into account, it seems evident that the value added by internationalization is most likely to accrue at the earliest stages of cross-border use, when a money is most popular. Seigniorage gains and policy flexibility will be at their height, and both hard and soft power will be enhanced. Later, however, gains may well be eroded by a growing overhang of liquid liabilities that could intensify external constraints on the nation's autonomy. The power curse starts to kick in, and the sword becomes double-edged. The two edges appear to cut in sequence, offering considerable advantage in the early days of a currency's internationalization but, over time, possibly also becoming quite burdensome. Summarizes one recent survey, "the benefits of issuing an international currency are likely to decline over time, while its costs are likely to increase."[23]

Britain's pound offers an obvious example. After long dominance as a top currency a century or more ago, sterling suffered through an extended and painful decline;[24] and that decline in turn eventually erased any advantage that London might once have enjoyed in projecting power abroad. Cappella has amply documented the pound's role in Britain's sad transformation from swaggering imperialist to chastened mendicant.[25] During the Crimean War (1853–1856) and even during the first years of World War I, sterling's widespread acceptability enabled the British to successfully finance expensive foreign interventions, providing a distinct edge over its adversaries. London could borrow all it needed to pay for its war efforts. But with sterling's gradual eclipse over the interwar years, that edge eventually disappeared, forcing Britain during World War II to rely on credits from its American ally to sustain its military role. By 1956, when Britain (along with France and Israel) tried to seize control of the Suez Canal from Egypt, it was humiliatingly clear that any residual advantage had by now evolved into distinct disadvantage owing to the pressure of an excess of external debts. London was effectively stopped in its tracks by the possibility of a run on the pound threatened by the Eisenhower administration in Washington.[26]

Along similar lines, many observers today worry about the risk that a decline in the US dollar's long-standing global "hegemony" will adversely affect America's ability to project military power internationally. Washington could lose its Get Out of Jail Free card. Representative is Jonathan Kirshner, who asserts that "Dollar diminution would significantly affect international power politics, in particular by presenting new and under-appreciated restraints upon American political and military predominance."[27] Christopher Layne is even more emphatic. "The dollar's reserve currency role is central to America's geopolitical preeminence," he contends, "and if it loses that status US hegemony will be literally unaffordable."[28]

The issue, as Eric Helleiner notes,[29] is well expressed in Susan Strange's distinction between a top currency and a negotiated currency. A top currency appeals to foreigners because of the issuing country's innate economic and political qualities. No persuasion is needed to encourage adoption. But once decline sets in, continued use may have to be actively promoted to prevent defections. Terms and conditions may have to be *negotiated*, either via explicit diplomatic bargaining or through implicit understandings—in effect, dropping the money from the top of the Currency Pyramid to the next lower rank of patrician currency. The consequences of such a demotion can be considerable. Not only are many of the benefits of internationalization apt to be lost. Worse, additional resources may have to be invested—in the form of, say, aid packages, market access, or enhanced military protection—in order to keep outsiders "on side." The costs of a negotiated currency, as Strange feared, could be considerable.

Time in this context, however, is apt to be quite lengthy, measured not in years but rather in decades, given the well-known inertias that tend to prevail in international currency choice. Lags are inevitable owing to the high cost of switching. Consider how long it took the greenback, despite its many attractions, to displace Britain's pound at the peak of the Currency Pyramid after World War I. According to research by Barry Eichengreen and Marc Flandreau, the dollar first surpassed sterling in trade transactions and official reserves as early as the 1920s.[30] But that was already decades after the emergence of the United States as the world's greatest industrial and trading nation; and as Eichengreen and Flandreau show, the dollar did not fully consolidate its dominance until after World War II. As Paul Krugman has commented: "The impressive fact here is surely the inertia; sterling remained the first-ranked currency for half a century after Britain had ceased to be the first-ranked economic power."[31]

As a practical matter, the downside of internationalization is likely to assert itself only in the very long term. In the shorter term, policy makers understandably may be inclined to discount the potential risks involved, focusing on the benefits instead.

CONCLUSION

What, then, may we conclude about the impact of currency internationalization on state power? How are the dots connected? Four generalizations are possible.

To begin, it is clear that disaggregation of the concept of internationalization into its several distinct functions matters a great deal. The conventional practice of treating internationalization as a holistic phenomenon obscures more than it reveals. Different roles have distinctly different effects on a state's overall capabilities and tend to work through different faces of power. Most critical are the two store-of-value functions—a currency's use in financial markets or central-bank reserves—both of which, initially at least, offer the prospect of greater autonomy for the issuing country, adding to its power to delay adjustment costs, as well as greater network centrality. A capacity to exercise leverage is generated by the store-of-value functions, though whether that capacity can be actualized will depend on other ancillary conditions.

Second, it follows that different issuers may find themselves with very different outcomes, depending on what combination of roles is played by their respective currencies. A national money whose use is limited primarily to the foreign-exchange market or to trade invoicing will add very little to a state's power endowment. Much more value is added if a money is used extensively for investment or reserve purposes.

But recall, third, the critical indirect impact of a currency's role in trade. Power is not enhanced directly, since the trade role does little to add to a government's ability to delay or deflect adjustment costs. But material capabilities can be augmented indirectly through the impact of the role on the reserve preferences of central banks. The more widely a currency is used for trade invoicing and settlement, the more likely it is to be adopted as a reserve asset as well.

Finally, it is vital to acknowledge the possible downsides of currency internationalization. The conventional wisdom, that internationalization must add to a state's power, may be right much of the time—but by no means always. The sword is potentially double-edged. Limits emerge for a pair of reasons. First, some international roles put the issuing country in the position of Stackelberg leader, effectively hostage to the decisions of followers. This is most evident in the anchor role, where the issuer's power to manage its exchange rate is largely transferred to others. The anchor role may be seen as a form of structural power, but it does not necessarily operate to the benefit of the leader. And second, there is the element of time, which clearly can work to the disadvantage of an issuing country as external liabilities accumulate. Currency power is not a one-way escalator, always going up. It may also go down.

5

From Power to Currency

Money: power at its most liquid.
—*Mason Cooley (1927–2002)*

The message of chapter 4 is clear. The relationship between currency and power is more complex than the conventional wisdom would have us believe. An international money manifestly does have an impact on its issuer's geopolitical capabilities, as most observers suppose—but in a variety of ways that defy facile generalization. Implications for state power may vary considerably, depending on the mix of roles that a currency happens to play. Effects can turn out to be negative as well as positive and may change considerably over time.

Yet that tells only half the tale: how currency internationalization affects state power.

Chapter 4 assumed a causal arrow that ran from money to capabilities, with state power as the dependent variable. We also need to consider matters the other way around. We need to address as well the impact of state power on currency internationalization—the specific causal pathways that run from geopolitical capabilities to a money's cross-border use. That is the purpose of this chapter.

Here the causal arrow is reversed, treating state power not as a dependent variable but as an independent variable. Once again, for analytical purposes, a country's initial endowment of power will be assumed to be given. But in this chapter we will ask not how currency internationalization may affect a state's broader capabilities, but rather how a state's broad capabilities may affect competitive currency choice. The aphorist Mason Cooley suggests that money is simply a liquid distillation of power. Our aim is to go behind the witty saying to explore, in more mundane fashion, how the process of distillation actually works. Attention is directed toward three questions in particular: What role does state power play in the internationalization of a currency? Can an international money be "manufactured" by deliberate government strategy? And what is the effect of geopolitical decline on cross-border use of a currency?

More than chapter 4, this chapter relies heavily on inductive reasoning, drawing substantially from the historical record of currency internationalization in the modern era. My focus will be on the period since the end of World War II, when the US dollar reigned supreme. In the decades since 1945, several other currencies have emerged to gain acceptance for at least some cross-border purposes. Most notable among them were West Germany's old Deutsche mark, Japan's yen, and the euro (the EU's successor to the DM and other European "legacy" currencies). Each of the three in its time seemed destined to soar to the peak of the Currency Pyramid—perhaps even to supplant the greenback as top currency—only to fall short of expectations. Limits intervened to slow down and ultimately to stall the process of internationalization. Though the sample is small, much can be learned from the stories of these currencies—first, about what elements of state power may drive the internationalization of a money; and second, about what, ultimately, may set a limit to the process.

Three broad findings stand out. First, four elements of state power appear to play the most critical role in driving currency internationalization. They are economic size, financial development, foreign-policy ties, and military reach. Each of these capabilities may enhance the competitive appeal of a currency. In general, this observation would appear to confirm the general expectations of specialists as outlined in chapter 1. Missing from the extant literature, however, is any attempt to disaggregate the analysis to take account of a money's separate roles. The evidence reviewed in this chapter suggests that the impacts of each of the four power resources are likely to turn out to be quite uneven across the range of a currency's functions. The finding is important because we know that different states have different mixes of capabilities. Hence it should not be surprising to see so much variation in the combination of roles played by different currencies.

Second, while it may be tempting for a country to try to make use of its power resources to promote its money, there are clearly limits to a government's ability to "manufacture" an international currency. Inertia, costs of implementation, domestic politics, and fungibility problems may all conspire to limit a money's rise. The Currency Pyramid turns out to be much like a greased pole, harder to climb than it looks.

And third, harking back to the end of chapter 4, it is evident that the currency escalator can go down as well as up. Combining observations from both chapters, we may conclude that the life cycle of an international currency can be characterized as a succession of two broadly self-reinforcing processes—first a "virtuous circle" in which power resources promote internationalization and internationalization simultaneously promotes state power; and then a "vicious circle" in which the reverse is true, geopolitical decline sapping the appeal of a currency which in turn further erodes economic and political capabilities. How long either circle persists will very much depend on the attractiveness of available alternatives.

The Deutsche Mark

At the end of World War II, the global monetary picture was clear. There was just one international currency of any consequence—the dollar. Within the so-called sterling area, Britain's pound was still in use for some cross-border purposes but had already begun its long twilight decline to fringe status. Ironically, when the first new challenger emerged in the 1960s and 1970s, it was a money that had not even existed in 1945—the Deutsche mark. The DM was created in 1948 as part of a major economic reform in the Western zones of occupied Germany, presaging the inauguration a year later of the new Federal Republic of Germany (otherwise known as West Germany). By the 1980s the DM was firmly established as the second most important currency in the world, before being absorbed into the newborn euro in 1999. Both economic and political considerations played pivotal roles in the story.

History

The Federal Republic's beginnings were not auspicious. Following the devastation of war, the country lay in ruin, its cities and industries largely destroyed. But then began the *wirtschaftswunder*—West Germany's economic miracle—which generated rapid growth and persistent export surpluses. By the end of the 1950s the Federal Republic could already be described as the leading economy on the European continent and the region's preeminent monetary power. By the 1960s the DM's internationalization was well under way. By the 1970s evidence of the currency's growing prominence was manifest. Though never more than a distant second to the US dollar, it was leagues ahead of all other currencies apart from Japan's yen.

At the private level, the DM quickly emerged as one of the world's most widely used currencies for both foreign-exchange trading and trade invoicing and settlement. Early estimates for turnover in the interbank market in New York put the DM share of trades against the dollar in the range of 31 to 34 percent over the decade of the 1980s.[1] The triennial BIS surveys suggest that globally, in 1989, the DM was involved on one side or the other of 27 percent of all currency trades—far below the dollar's share of 90 percent but well above that of any other money aside from the yen, whose share as a vehicle currency was comparable. In 1998, just prior to the birth of the euro, the DM's share of global currency transactions was up a bit to 30 percent.[2] Similarly, by as early as 1980 the DM's share in the denomination of global trade was estimated at 13.6 percent, rising to 15.3 percent by 1992, some 40 percent greater than West Germany's share of total world exports.[3] Only the dollar, with a share of global trade close to 50 percent, accounted for a larger proportion of invoicing.

The DM also gained some popularity in financial markets. Most indicative is a composite index of the currency composition of international assets constructed at the BIS for the years 1980–1995.[4] This "international assets" aggregate combined holdings of bonds, notes, and cross-border banking claims for purposes of ready comparison. Over the period covered by the index, the DM attained a market share in the range of 14 to 15 percent. Again, this was second only to the greenback, though well below the dollar's share of half or more.

At the official level, West Germany's currency was quickly adopted by a number of European neighbors as a de facto anchor for the exchange rates of their own currencies. Stability vis-à-vis the DM became a high priority, for reasons to be explained later. Correspondingly, West Germany's money also became the preferred intervention medium for neighboring central banks, mostly replacing the dollar. According to one informed source, the DM share of exchange-market interventions within Europe rose from some 25 to 30 percent in 1979 to as much as three-quarters by the end of the 1980s.[5] And that development in turn encouraged accumulations of DM in reserves, also in preference to the greenback. Estimates culled from various issues of the IMF annual report suggest that the West German currency came to account for anywhere from 12 to 16 percent of global reserves during the 1980s and 1990s.

Rise

What explains the successful rise of the DM? The roots of its internationalization lay in economics but were reinforced by politics. Two economic factors in particular stood out. One was West Germany's growing importance in world trade, which mainly affected the DM's role as a medium of exchange and unit of account for private market actors. The other derived from West Germany's disproportionate influence on general macroeconomic conditions, particularly within Europe, which mostly affected the currency's use at the official level. Both factors were amplified at the political level by the process of regional integration begun with the Coal and Steel Community in 1950 and Rome Treaty of 1955—what has since been known as the "European project."

Together, these economic and political considerations promoted a broad, albeit uneven scope to the DM's internationalization. All six roles of an international currency were played to a greater or lesser extent. In terms of domain, however, the DM was quite localized, prevailing mainly in the Federal Republic's natural hinterland around Europe. Elsewhere the currency was less competitive. The DM's geographic range was regional, not global like the dollar's.

Trade. As indicated back in chapter 1, a broad transactional network, reflecting a large and open economy, is generally considered essential to the internationalization of a currency. That proposition certainly seems to be confirmed by the West German case. There is little doubt that the increased use of the DM for trade invoicing and settlement was directly linked to the Federal Republic's growing importance in commerce, both as exporter and importer. By the 1990s West Germany had become the world's second-largest trading nation, with a share of global trade (exports plus imports) of around 10 percent—well behind the United States but ahead of Japan. On the selling side, West Germany ranked as second

biggest exporter, with a pronounced comparative advantage in differentiated manufactured goods like machinery, transport equipment, and the
like. These are the sort of products that, among advanced economies,
typically are priced in the seller's own currency. (The major exception to
this norm was Japan, as we shall see later.) Conversely, on the buying side
the large size of the Federal Republic's domestic market gave the country's importers leverage to insist on denominating trade in DM, to avoid
exchange risk. On both sides, therefore, use of the DM was stimulated.

The effect, however, was distinctly regional in scale, limited primarily to the Federal Republic's immediate neighbors. In the broader global
economy, West Germany was by no means a giant among nations—only
about one-fifth the size of the US market and equal to no more than
60 percent of Japanese GDP. Its place in the world was substantial but
hardly overwhelming. Within Europe, however, the Federal Republic was
dominant—about 30 percent bigger than France and 40 percent bigger
than Britain. In its own hinterland, West Germany's large market was
bound to exercise a strong gravitational pull.

In turn, the regional bias was reinforced by the European project of
integration. By the 1980s nearly the entire continent west of the Iron Cur-
tain was drawn together by a network of trade agreements, reducing or
eliminating barriers to commerce in the region. Some countries were full
members of the so-called Common Market, known today as the European Union (EU). Others were effectively included under other accords.
Europe's increasingly close commercial ties naturally added to the weight
of the regional leader's currency. With barriers falling, intra-European
trade could logically be expected to grow faster than trade with countries
elsewhere; and no economy was more important within the region than
the Federal Republic. As nearby countries grew increasingly dependent
on West Germany, both as market and source of supply, it was only natural that they would be prepared to do more business in DM.

Macroeconomics. A record of low inflation is also considered essential
to internationalization. That proposition too seems to be confirmed by
the West German case. Germans have a well-known aversion to inflation,
dating back to the hyperinflation that swept their country after World
War I. A pronounced "stability culture" has long prevailed, fully reflected in the hard-line policies of the Federal Republic's central bank, the
Bundesbank. Throughout the post–World War II period, West Germany

consistently ranked among the least inflationary of all economies. And that preference in turn was bound to have a disproportionate influence on general macroeconomic conditions across Western Europe, given the Federal Republic's central position in regional import and export markets. Neighboring states were driven to keep their own prices in line in order to avoid a loss of competitiveness relative to Germany. The imperative was to stop real exchange rates (nominal exchange rates adjusted for inflation differentials) from rising.

This meant that many European governments felt under pressure to match the DM's high interest rates as best they could. It may have been a bit of a caricature to suggest, as some observers did, that the Bundesbank now in effect was making monetary policy for all of Europe—a simplification that came to be known as the *German dominance hypothesis*. Econometric evidence suggests a more nuanced picture, where interest rates often moved in tandem but were less than perfectly correlated.[6] But there is little question that a distinct asymmetry prevailed that looked very much like a Stackelberg leadership model. The Bundesbank was the acknowledged leader. Other central banks then decided whether (or by how much) to follow West German policy in response.

The same imperative also explains why stability vis-à-vis the DM became a high priority. Neighbors felt compelled to anchor their nominal exchange rates to the DM as a kind of check to their own inflationary propensities. As one informed commentary put it: "The gradual hardening of exchange rate commitments . . . became the mechanism by which previously high-inflation members chose to discipline their own monetary policies, and it was to the Bundesbank and its anti-inflationary credibility that these countries turned for monetary policy leadership."[7] By the end of the 1980s the Bundesbank was boasting that the DM "performs the function of a key currency, acting as a 'stability anchor' for the other pertinent currencies."[8]

It was only natural, therefore, that most interventions in Europe would be carried out in the West German currency and that a larger share of reserves would now be maintained in DM. And here too the impact was reinforced by the European project, which from the late 1960s onward featured repeated attempts to promote some form of regional monetary integration. First, in 1972, came the so-called snake, a mutual intervention system aiming to link the currencies of West Germany and its Common Market partners together in a joint float. And then, when that experiment proved unsustainable, agreement was reached in 1978 to launch a new European Monetary System (EMS), designed in effect to create an improved "supersnake" for Europe. At the heart of the EMS was the Exchange Rate Mechanism (ERM), where in principle all interventions to sustain the joint float would be symmetrical within a matrix of bilateral cross-rates. In practice, however, the ERM soon evolved into something more like a spoke-and-wheel construct with West Germany's money at the center—a de facto DM zone. Studies show that by the 1980s almost all of Europe's currencies were shadowing the DM to a greater or lesser extent.[9]

Limits

Yet for all its achievements, West Germany's currency never came close to true global status. Even before its absorption into the euro, the DM had clearly reached its limit—a distant second to America's greenback. Four factors, both economic and political, explain why.

First was sheer inertia, reflecting the dollar's undoubted incumbency advantages in most parts of the world. Outside Europe, the DM offered no significant gains relative to the greenback. Only within the European neighborhood was West Germany's gravitational pull sufficient to make the DM truly competitive. Elsewhere, the dollar retained its traditional edge.

Second was the inaccessibility and relative backwardness of West Germany's financial markets, as compared with the global market for the dollar. Although convertibility of the DM for current-account transactions was introduced as early as 1958 (along with most other European currencies), a panoply of capital controls persisted until as late as the mid-1980s, restricting foreign participation; the financial system could hardly be described as open. Moreover, institutional development was hindered by a variety of complex regulations and taxes. West German bond and equity markets were notably thinner than corresponding markets in New York or London, offering a limited menu of financial instruments. Accordingly, trading in DM-denominated claims was narrow and expenses were high, hampering transactional liquidity. It was hardly surprising, therefore, that use of the Federal Republic's currency as an investment medium, though not insignificant, would lag considerably behind its other international roles.

Third was a notable reluctance on the part of the West German government to do much to promote internationalization of the DM. Indeed, until the early 1980s the Bundesbank actively sought to restrict cross-border use—for example, by exercising firm command over the issue of DM obligations in the external bond market.[10] At issue was control of monetary policy, so critical to German anti-inflationary stability culture. Public authorities feared that in time an undue constraint might be imposed on policy at home by an excessive accumulation of liabilities abroad—an apprehension that was widely shared by financial interests and other key constituencies across West German society.[11] Over the longer term, it was thought, shifting currency preferences could generate much exchange-rate volatility and uncertainty, threatening both price stability and export revenues. At no point did the government take a proactive stance on internationalization. If the DM was to emerge as a rival to the dollar, it would have to do it on its own.

Finally, there was the security dimension. The Federal Republic may have been a stable democracy with full respect for property rights and a hard-earned reputation for effective policy management. But it was also a divided nation on the front line of the Cold War, hardly what might be considered a safe haven for investors. As Susan Strange wrote at the time:

> It is just possible to imagine a future scenario in which West Germany is overrun by an exuberant Red Army while Fortress America remains inviolate across the Atlantic, but it is impossible to imagine the converse: a West German state surviving while the United States is overrun or the North American continent laid waste by nuclear attack. As long as this basic political asymmetry persists, there is no chance whatever of the Deutsche mark being the pivot of the international monetary system.[12]

For understandable historical reasons, the West German government was reluctant to rebuild a strong military machine capable of projecting power abroad, relying instead on the protection of the United States. Foreign governments, therefore, had no reason to look to West Germany for leadership on security issues. If they were to be attracted to use the DM, it would have to be for economic, not political reasons. And as we know, the DM's economic appeal was limited largely to the European region, setting a natural limit to the currency's scope and domain.

THE YEN

In many ways, the story of the Japanese yen was similar. At the end of World War II, Japan too lay in ruin, its economy shattered and its currency virtually worthless. And then Japan too enjoyed an economic miracle, sustaining growth rates from the late 1950s onward that were the envy of the world. By the late 1960s Japan's GDP had come to be the second largest anywhere, bigger even than West Germany's. By the late 1970s, the international standing of the yen was well established. Yet Japan's currency too ultimately reached its limit; indeed, more recently, it has in most respects gone into seemingly irreversible decline. Here too both economic and political considerations played pivotal roles.

History

The rise of the yen was impressive but uneven in both scope and domain. At both the private and official levels, the currency came to be used much more as a store of value than as a medium of exchange or unit of account. Geographically its reach, like that of the DM, remained primarily regional, for the most part limited to the nations of East Asia. Overall, the yen never managed to climb above third place among international currencies, behind not just the dollar but the DM as well.

The yen's internationalization was most notable in financial markets, where persistent appreciation made the currency an especially attractive store of value. According to the composite index constructed at the BIS, the yen's share of claims in international asset markets accelerated swiftly from little more than 3 percent in 1980 to some 12.4 percent by 1995.[13] Growth was especially rapid in the offshore bond market, where the proportion of new issues denominated in yen more than tripled between 1980 and 1995, from under 5 percent to above 17 percent.[14] By the 1990s the yen's share of the bond market matched that of the DM, though both remained well short of the dollar. The Japanese currency was especially popular in the East Asian region, where the yen supplanted the dollar as the predominant vehicle for foreign borrowing. Included, most notably, were larger neighbors like Indonesia, Korea, Malaysia, Philippines, and Thailand. Within Japan, nonresident holdings of both bank deposits and securities expanded steadily through the 1980s and into the 1990s.

Likewise, for central banks the yen became an attractive complement to the dollar or DM for purposes of portfolio diversification. IMF estimates suggest that during the 1980s and early 1990s the yen's share of global reserves more than doubled, from just over 3 percent to close to 8 percent. That was only half the portion accounted for by the DM but well ahead of any other currency. Once again the yen was favored most by East Asian nations, where the currency's share of reserves topped 17 percent by 1990.[15]

For other uses, the yen's performance was respectable but by no means overpowering. In foreign-exchange markets, the yen share of currency trades accelerated over the course of the 1980s to a peak of 27 percent in 1989 but never did surpass the proportion accounted for by the DM.[16] Here too the appeal was mainly regional. Japan's currency was most favored as a vehicle in East Asia, in financial centers like Hong Kong and Singapore, where the proportion of business done in yen was considerably higher than anywhere else. Likewise, in the invoicing of global trade, available evidence suggests that there was some expansion of use, but from a very low base and again concentrated mainly in East Asia. The yen's share in the denomination of trade more than doubled during the 1980s but in 1992 still accounted for less than 5 percent of the world total. That represented little more than half of Japan's share of global exports.[17]

Finally, there was the yen's potential as a possible anchor for the exchange rates of other currencies. Over the course of the 1980s and into the 1990s there was much debate about whether—or to what extent—Japan and its neighbors might be coalescing into some kind of yen bloc, comparable to the emerging DM zone in Europe. In fact, most governments in East Asia preferred to maintain a managed float. Usually the float was in line with a currency basket of some kind, though the components of their baskets were rarely disclosed. Econometric analysis suggests that increasingly some of Japan's neighbors—including, in particular, South Korea, Singapore, and Thailand—did begin to shadow the yen more closely, putting greater weight on the yen relative to the US dollar.[18] But in no economy other than Korea did the yen actually surpass the greenback as an anchor, and no country ever pegged to the yen formally.

If there was a yen bloc, it was a feeble one. In the words of one contemporary analysis: "From a policy perspective, it appears that the yen has not yet been perceived as a key regional currency to the extent that the deutsche mark is incorporated as an anchor currency in the European Monetary System."[19] Declared another source more bluntly: "The yen zone is [limited] to Japan."[20] Correspondingly, there was also very little increase in use of Japan's currency for intervention purposes.

Rise

As with the DM the roots of the yen's internationalization lay mainly in economics, though in the yen's case—in contrast to the DM—there was little reinforcement from politics. Unlike Europe, post–World War II Asia never sought any sort of formal integration; there was no local equivalent of the European project. Nor did the Japanese government at the time actively promote foreign use of its currency. Widespread adoption of the yen occurred in the absence of—not because of—affirmative political support. Economic motivations dominated.

To begin, there was Japan's enviable inflation record, confirming again the importance of monetary stability in the process of internationalization. Over the course of the 1980s Japan recorded the lowest price increases of any advanced economy. Annual inflation averaged about 2.6 percent, lower even than Germany's 2.9 percent.[21] At the same time, decades of trade surpluses had made Japan the world's greatest creditor nation, even as the United States was becoming a net debtor. Together with the sustained strength of the yen's exchange rate and a seemingly stable political system, these considerations were bound to make the currency an attractive store of value for investors and central banks alike. A strong demand for yen-denominated claims was assured.

In turn, a series of regulatory reforms supported increased access to a growing yen supply as well. During the first decades after World War II, Japan's financial system was the most tightly managed of any industrial nation, inhibiting wider use of the yen. Domestic markets for equities and securities were relatively underdeveloped, and financial institutions were rigidly segmented. Beginning in the mid-1970s, however, a gradual process of deregulation began, prompted in particular by a slowing of Japan's economic growth. Interest rates were soon freed, encouraging investor appetite for a rapidly rising volume of public debt, and new markets were created or expanded for government liabilities, certificates of deposits, and other financial instruments. The traditional segmentation of institutions was relaxed and supervisory practices were strengthened, gradually increasing both exchange convenience and capital certainty.

Most importantly, capital controls were largely eliminated, opening the domestic system to greater foreign participation. Earlier, strict limitations on the movement of funds had restricted both inward and outward investments, even though convertibility of the yen for current-account transactions was restored as early as 1964. But that too eventually began to change. In 1980, nonresident access was eased by a new Foreign Exchange and Trade Control Law, which established the principle that cross-border capital flows should now be free unless specifically restricted. And then in 1984 Tokyo committed to a panoply of further liberalization measures outlined in an agreement negotiated with the United States. The so-called Yen/Dollar Agreement grew out of discussions of the Working Group on Yen/Dollar Exchange Rate Issues—the Yen/Dollar Committee—that had been created jointly by the US Treasury and Japanese Ministry of Finance in 1983. Subsequent years saw a flurry of measures widening of the scope of allowable foreign activity in domestic banking and capital markets.[22] Overall, the process of liberalization was by no means complete, as contemporary accounts emphasized.[23] But cumulatively the government's initiatives did suffice to increase Japan's integration into world financial markets and to promote use of the yen for investment and reserve purposes.

Finally, there was the massive size of Japan's economy and foreign trade, exerting a strong gravitational pull on markets elsewhere. Without the promise of a broad transactional network, the yen would never have become the third most popular vehicle in foreign-exchange trading, nor would East Asian governments have given it so much weight in the management of their exchange rates. In the 1980s Japan was seen as a new giant on the world stage, destined perhaps even to surpass the United States as a global economic power. The appeal of the yen for international use naturally followed. For many, it was only a matter of time before the currency would take its rightful place alongside the dollar and the DM at the peak of the Currency Pyramid.[24]

Limits

Yet it failed to happen. Here too, as in the case of the DM, a limit was eventually reached. Effectively, internationalization of the yen peaked somewhere near the mid-1990s. Ever since, the currency's standing has withered quietly like a dying plant. In banking markets, the yen share of cross-border claims has declined from 14 percent in the early 1990s to under 4 percent by 2010. Similarly, in bond markets the share has fallen from above 17 percent to under 3 percent. In currency markets the drop has been from 27 percent to 19 percent; and in central bank reserves, from near 8 percent to under 4 percent. No one today speaks of Japan's currency as a future number one (or even number two). What happened? In this instance, five factors may be cited.

First, once again, was the force of inertia. By the time the yen came on the scene in the 1980s, there were already two well-established rivals— the dollar globally and the DM on its own turf in Europe. The incumbency advantages of these two currencies were hard to overcome. Outside East Asia, the yen offered no significant gains relative to either one.

Second was the crash of the Japanese market after the bursting of its so-called bubble economy in 1989. In ensuing years the country was plagued by stagnation, frequent recessions, and persistent price deflation, even as neighboring China charged ahead with double-digit growth rates. Over time the gravitational pull of the Japanese economy simply became less and less forceful.

Third was the unique pattern of invoicing in Japanese trade, which discouraged foreign adoption of the yen as a medium of exchange. Unlike most other advanced economies, Japan did relatively little of its overseas business in its own currency. Whereas in the United States virtually all exports were denominated in dollars, and in Germany 80 percent, in Japan the corresponding figure at the time was only some 30 to 35 percent. Most exports were denominated in dollars, reflecting the Japanese economy's high degree of dependence on the US market. In effect, Japan's autonomy in currency choice was constrained. A practice of "pricing to market" was a rational strategy to maintain market share in the United States. Only sales to developing countries, where Japan enjoyed relatively more commercial leverage, tended to be denominated in yen. Over time, there was some increase in yen invoicing, mainly due to the growing salience of East Asia as an export market.[25] But as noted, even at its peak the currency's share in global trade remained remarkably small.

Fourth was the role of public policy in Japan, which for years was notably unhelpful. Like the Germans, the authorities in Tokyo were long resistant to internationalization of their currency, which they too feared might in time impose an undue constraint on domestic monetary management. Some in the government did take a more positive tone. Most notable was the Council on Foreign Exchange and Other Transactions, an advisory body to the Ministry of Finance, which in 1985 called for further financial liberalization to enhance the yen's international appeal. For the most part, however, the regulatory reforms of the 1980s were adopted reluctantly, partly to stimulate domestic growth, as indicated, but also as a grudging concession to the United States. Through the Yen/Dollar Committee, Washington pressured Tokyo to liberalize its financial structure in hopes of raising demand for the yen. The idea was to engineer an appreciation of the yen that would improve the competitiveness of US goods vis-à-vis Japan. Yen internationalization was seen by most Japanese not as a goal to be sought but rather as a price to be paid to retain the good will of the Americans.

In fact, appreciation did occur, particularly after the well-publicized Plaza Accord of 1985—but with consequences that were not anticipated at the time. In order to soften adverse effects of the appreciation, Japan's central bank pushed interest rates to historically low levels. The result was a marked increase of speculation in equity and real estate markets, feeding the bubble that finally burst in 1989. Many in Japan have blamed the United States, at least in part, for the prolonged deflation that followed, harking back to the pressures Washington exerted through the Yen/Dollar Agreement and Plaza Accord.[26]

Interestingly, as Tokyo struggled to come to grips with the country's post-bubble downturn, opinion on internationalization shifted. Over the course of the 1990s an international role for the yen now became a declared policy objective, in hopes that it would help promote economic recovery at home.[27] Most dramatic was a multiyear financial liberalization program announced in 1996, dubbed the Big Bang in imitation of the swift deregulation of Britain's capital markets a decade earlier. Under the Big Bang all remaining capital controls were to be eliminated and a variety of other ambitious measures were scheduled, including tax reductions and increases in the range of available financial products. Especially after the Asian financial crisis of 1997–1998, a concerted effort was made to promote broader use of the yen for a variety of purposes, guided by the recommendations of a newly established Study Group on the Promotion of Yen Internationalization. But by this time it was too late. As economic stagnation dragged on, the government's campaign failed to reverse the decline of interest in the yen. Defeat was admitted in 2003 when the strategy was officially abandoned. In the words of one Japanese observer, "it was clear that any further attempt to internationalize the yen . . . would be futile."[28]

Finally, here too there was a security dimension. Like West Germany, post–World War II Japan could be considered a stable democracy with full respect for property rights and effective policy management. Investors were probably attracted for those reasons. But as powerful as it was in economic terms, Japan lacked political means to influence the currency preferences of foreign governments. On the one hand, it was in no position to offer leadership on security issues. Limited by its Occupation constitution to a modest self-defense force, Tokyo was incapable of projecting military power beyond the country's home islands. Indeed, Japan was itself obliged to seek protection under the security umbrella of the United States. On the other hand, there were no nations in the region prepared to follow Japan's lead. Memories were still fresh of Tokyo's wartime atrocities and prewar attempts to build an imperial Greater East-Asia Co-Prosperity Sphere. Here too, as in the case of the DM, it appeared that if others were to be attracted to use the yen, it would have to be for economic, not political reasons.

THE EURO

The last currency to be considered is the euro, Europe's joint money. In 1999 the European Union began its grand experiment—the new Economic and Monetary Union (EMU), with the euro as its centerpiece. Although still a story in progress, the contours of the tale are by now clear, bearing a strong resemblance to the experience of the yen (albeit on a more compressed time scale). After a fast early start following the currency's birth, euro internationalization appears to have quickly reached a limit. In more recent years, it may even have gone into reverse.

History and Rise

A fast early start was not unexpected, given the euro's credentials. From the moment of its birth, Europe's new money clearly enjoyed many of the qualities necessary for competitive success on the world stage. These included a large economic base in the membership of the euro zone, initially numbering some eleven countries—including some of the world's richest economies—and now up to nineteen. They also included deep and resilient financial markets, political stability, and an enviably low rate of inflation, all backed by a joint monetary authority, the European Central Bank, that was fully committed to preserving confidence in the currency's future value. For many observers, the global future of the euro seemed secure; for some, it seemed that Europe's money might even overtake the dollar as the world's preeminent currency.[29] Hence it was no surprise that in the euro's early days, international use seemed to expand exponentially.

Very soon, however, momentum slowed. The currency's fast start appears to have peaked sometime around 2003–2004; thereafter, use for cross-border purposes leveled off at rates well below those enjoyed by the dollar. In effect, the euro did little more than hold its own as compared with the past aggregate market shares of EMU's "legacy" currencies. Given the fact that the old Deutsche mark had already attained a number-two ranking in global monetary relations, second to the greenback, anything less would have been a real shock. But beyond that, a limit does appear to have exerted itself. Straight-line extrapolation of the euro's early acceleration far into the future does not seem to have been warranted.

Limits were evident in terms of both scope and domain. On the one side growth of euro usage was broad but, like the DM before it, sharply uneven across functional categories. The early expansion of international use was especially dramatic in the issuance of debt securities, reflecting the promised integration of Europe's financial markets. There was also some modest increase in the euro's share of trade invoicing and central-bank reserves. But in other categories, such as foreign-exchange trading or banking, there was little penetration. The ECB's polite way of putting this was that use of the euro turned out to be "heterogeneous across market segments."[30]

On the other side, the euro's domain turned out to be starkly bifurcated, just as it had been for the DM. For the most part, internationalization of the euro has been confined to economies with close geographical and/or institutional links to the EU and euro zone. These include the EU's newest members, all destined eventually to join the monetary union, as well other candidate states (for example, Bosnia or Montenegro) and nonmember neighbors like Norway and Switzerland. They also include several nations around the Mediterranean littoral as well as a number in sub-Saharan Africa. Where trade and financial ties are deep, the euro obviously enjoys a special advantage. But elsewhere, in stark contrast, scale of use drops off abruptly. The evidence, concludes the ECB, clearly confirms "the strong regional character of the euro's international role."[31]

Worse, in more recent years, some of the euro's achievements have even been reversed as global crisis has lingered along with Europe's debt and banking problems. Given the adverse circumstances, says the ECB, the currency has remained notably "resilient."[32] But that is at best a backhanded compliment, referring mainly to the relative stability of the euro's exchange rate. In terms of actual use, key indicators seem to have started trending downward. The global share of international bonds issued in euros, for example, which had peaked above one-third in 2004, began to slide in 2009 and by the end of 2012, as indicated in chapter 4, was down to little more than one-quarter. Similarly, the euro's share of global reserves, which had exceeded 27 percent as recently as 2009, fell to below 23 percent by 2014. "Resilience," plainly, is in the eye of the beholder. The best we can say, truthfully, is that it could have been worse.

Limits

The reasons for the euro's early rise are clear. Despite the skepticism of some, including myself,[33] the currency's credentials appeared obvious. Yet it failed to live up to potential. Why? Four factors may be briefly mentioned here. Later, in chapter 8, I will have more to say about the unrealized power of the euro.

First is the familiar force of inertia, which in this instance acted like a double-edged sword. Within the European region itself, where the Deutsche mark had already predominated, adoption of the euro as the DM's successor was only to be expected. In the eyes of many, the euro was simply the DM writ large. Inevitably, the new currency would inherit the natural hinterland of the old. But beyond the immediate neighborhood the force of inertia worked the other way, to favor America's greenback with all its incumbency advantages. In this respect, the euro was able to make no more headway than the DM or the yen before it.

Second has been the absence of any proactive policy by European authorities to promote a major role for the euro. Like the West German and Japanese governments before it, EMU has been at best ambivalent about internationalization. From the beginning policy has remained studiously neutral, in principle neither discouraging nor encouraging wider use by foreigners. According to an authoritative early statement by the ECB, repeated many times since, internationalization "is not a policy objective [and] will be neither fostered nor hindered by the Eurosystem. . . . The Eurosystem therefore adopts a neutral stance."[34] Development of the euro as an international currency—if it was to happen at all—was to be a market-driven process, simply one of many possible by-products of monetary union. Policy makers would take no action to directly enhance the currency's appeal.

Third, once again, is the security dimension. How could the EMU—a gaggle of states with limited military capabilities and divergent foreign-policy interests—possibly substitute for the global influence of the United States? How could others look to Europe for protection? As economist Adam Posen comments: "The European Union, let alone the euro area itself, is unable or unwilling to offer these systemic or security benefits beyond a very limited area."[35] Few governments saw any political interest in switching their currency allegiance to a weaker patron.

Finally—and most important of all—is the issue of the euro's internal governance. For all their other limitations, this was never a question for the DM or yen. No one doubted that West Germany and Japan were capable of effective policy management. But the euro, as the joint money of a club of sovereign states, is obviously different—a currency, in effect, without a country. A fundamental mismatch exists between the domain of EMU and the jurisdictions of its member governments, making decision-making problematic at best. Europe's money is the product of an interstate treaty rather than the expression of a single sovereign power. For outsiders, therefore, the currency can be considered only as good as the political agreement underlying it; and as recent experience in Europe has vividly demonstrated, the requisite accord is often tenuous at best. Foreigners cannot be blamed for not wishing to put too many eggs into that fragile basket.

SOURCES AND LIMITS

What do we learn from these stories? Several lessons stand out.

Sources

To begin it is obvious that state power, broadly defined, does indeed matter. Admittedly, it helped that in each case the currency was supported by the key microfoundations of political stability and accountable government. That was true of both West Germany and Japan, each reborn after World War II as functioning pluralistic democracies. Gone was the unpredictability of earlier autocratic governments; now, in each, agents could reasonably assume that contractual obligations would be fairly enforced. And of course it is true of the euro zone as well. But while effective governance was a necessary part of each story, it was hardly sufficient. In none of the three cases could the currency have attained the standing that it did without at least some disproportion of capabilities favoring the money's issuer. As Mundell suggested, it is "great" powers that have "great" currencies, not the likes of Luxembourg or Liechtenstein.

Power, however, may have many roots. What are the *sources* of power in this particular context? Overall, four elements stand out as particularly salient. These are economic size, financial development, foreign-policy ties, and military reach. All can be regarded as expressions of geopolitical capacity. The historical record suggests that all can also have a significant influence on the competitive appeal of a currency. Over the period since World War II some of these elements have demonstrated their importance by their presence, acting to drive adoption of a currency for cross-border purposes; others have demonstrated their importance by their absence, which acted to limit the process of internationalization.

First is the factor of *economic size*—the magnitude of the issuer's GDP and importance in world trade. In all three cases the gravitational pull of the issuer's economy played a decisive role in driving the process of internationalization, just as it did in earlier times when Britain and then the United States first emerged as rich and influential trading nations. Size clearly does enhance capabilities. It is no accident that among the many statistical indicators that have been developed in the IR literature to measure the elusive concept of state power (chapter 2), nearly all include some measure of GDP and/or share of world trade. And the same is true as well of the indicators of monetary or financial capability described in chapter 3.[36] Nor is it happenstance that virtually every study of future prospects for currencies like the euro or yuan also emphasize economic size.[37]

But it is not just size alone that matters. That would imply a rather crude elements-of-power approach to the subject. Even more salient is the *structure* of relations that derives from the issuer's economic weight, opening opportunities for influence—a social power perspective. It is significant that West Germany, Japan, and EMU all enjoyed a central position in their respective regional economies. In each instance a network of asymmetrical relationships emerged that tended, at least for a time, to lock in the relative dependence of neighboring nations. Increased use of the central node's currency naturally followed. At work was a form of structural power that constrained and shaped the decisions of others. Trading partners had a strong incentive to follow the center's lead.

Second is the factor of *financial development*—the sophistication and openness of the issuer's banking and capital markets. In Japan's case, the role of finance was distinctly positive, particularly once the country's process of deregulation began in the mid-1970s. A deepened financial sector clearly promoted the yen's competitiveness. Outsiders were attracted to take advantage of the currency's liquidity and prospects for appreciation. And, initially at least, much the same could be said for EMU, which could also boast of a well-developed financial sector. Back when the euro was born, no one doubted the monetary union's ability to assure a high degree of exchange convenience and capital certainty. In the earlier West German case, by contrast, the role of finance proved to be more negative—a limit on, not a driver of internationalization. The importance of financial development was demonstrated by its absence. For a long time, the inaccessibility and relative backwardness of the Federal Republic's capital market acted as a drag on the otherwise impressive rise of the DM.

Third are *foreign-policy ties*, present or absent. In the West German case and in EMU, the closeness of relations with regional neighbors clearly helped to drive internationalization. As indicated, the European integration project naturally added to the weight of the leader's currency.

The multiplication of institutional links could be said to have amplified structural incentives to follow the Federal Republic's lead—an apt example of "go-it-alone" power, where monetary management at the center decisively, even if unintentionally, influenced the choice sets available to other. In the Japanese case, par contra, regional relations were anything but close. Internationalization, therefore, was not helped but hindered. Any hope for an Asian yen bloc was effectively precluded by lingering resentments and animosities toward Japan. During its brief effort in the 1990s to promote yen internationalization in the neighborhood, Tokyo ran into a solid wall of resistance. The contrast with European experience could not have been greater.

Last, but by no means least, is the factor of *military reach*: the security dimension. In none of the three cases was the issuer of a potential international currency capable of offering the kind of security assurances that had long been provided by the United States. In the opinion of many, America's military superiority, sustained ever since World War II, is a key reason why the dollar has remained at the peak of the Currency Pyramid.[38] In the words of political scientist Bessma Momani: "While there are viable currency alternatives to the US dollar, there are no alternatives to the US military security umbrella."[39] The United States could offer both protection for governments abroad and a safe haven for investors within its borders. The greenback's rivals found it difficult to offer either advantage.

This list of factors should come as no surprise. In general, it conforms closely to the expectations of most specialists as outlined back in chapter 1. The four attributes are clearly the most decisive in determining the competitiveness of a currency. But once again, as in chapter 4, we find that in the extant literature there is a tendency to casually assume a broad causal relationship without going into much detail. Here too, the dots remain largely unconnected. What matters is how much more we can do to connect the dots—what we can say about the specific causal pathways that run from power resources to currency internationalization. Identifying the qualities needed for competitive success is just the beginning of the tale, not the end.

Limits

Together, the four factors make a formidable package. We know that, in practice, none of the three currency issuers we have discussed—West Germany, Japan, or EMU—managed to complete the package. Though all three economies in their time exercised a strong gravitational pull in trade relations, particularly in their own regional neighborhood, in other respects each lacked one or two essential ingredients.

Suppose, however, that one of them (or some future challenger, such as China) had actually been able to put the whole package together. Would that suffice to elevate a money to the top tier of the Currency Pyramid? A combination of economic size, financial development, foreign-policy ties, and military reach would seem an ideal recipe for enhancing a currency's appeal. Would internationalization inevitably follow?

The answer, sadly, is indeterminate. As emphasized in chapter 2, power is not absolute but relative. The limits of power are elastic and depend very much on the structure of competition prevailing at the time. A DM or yen or euro (or RMB?) would have a much easier task gaining acceptance if it were the only player in the game; in other words, if it enjoyed an effective monopoly. The more a currency must contend with others, the lower will be the "weight" of its power. The complete package may increase the probability of successful internationalization, but it does not guarantee it.

Moreover, new players must contend not only with other entrants like themselves but also with incumbents, since cross-border currency use is so path dependent. Incumbency advantages raise the bar even higher, as noted in chapter 1. To be competitive, a challenger must not just match but must visibly surpass the qualities of existing international currencies. The force of inertia was evident in all three cases, vividly demonstrating the limits to even the most promising aspiration to power.

Currency Roles

More importantly, we need to look closely at the several separate roles that an international money can play. Any one of the four sources of power highlighted by the historical record may promote cross-border use of a currency. But across the full range of a money's possible functions, impacts may be quite uneven. This is where the details begin to matter. Just as each role of a currency may have quite different effects on a government's overall geopolitical capabilities, each element of power may have quite different effects on a money's overall internationalization.

Economic size, for example, will obviously encourage use of a currency for trade invoicing and settlement. That was amply evident in the cases of both the DM and the euro (though, significantly, not in the case of the yen, owing to Japan's heavy reliance for so long on a "pricing to market" strategy for exports to the United States). And the trade role, in turn, might be expected to have some positive influence on central-bank preferences as well, as suggested in the previous chapter. But on its own, the factor of size will offer little support for use of a currency as an investment medium in financial markets; and that in turn will limit development of a reserve-currency role, since historically an extensive investment role has seemed necessary before a money began to be added to reserve portfolios (chapter 4). Put differently, the gravitational pull of GDP and trade will promote the medium-of-exchange function of a currency, but at best may have only some indirect impact on the store-of-value functions that are the real key to currency power.

Conversely, financial development will obviously do more to encourage the store-of-value functions of a currency rather than its medium-of-exchange functions. A trade role relies little on a deep and resilient financial sector. At most, some amount of export financing may be required; no long-lasting currency holdings are involved. But for the investment and reserve roles, a sophisticated and open capital market is essential, to provide the exchange convenience and capital certainty that investors and central banks crave. Without financial development, prospects for a significant amount of currency power are limited.

Foreign-policy ties, for their part, can be expected to have their greatest impact on the roles of a money at the official level, as an exchange-rate anchor, intervention medium, and reserve currency. For example, both Quan Li and Adam Posen find strong evidence that formal alliances have a distinct impact on a country's choice of anchor currency.[40] Preferences of market actors at the private level, on the other hand, are less likely to be affected. Military reach, by contrast, could have a major impact at both levels, though the effect may be either positive or negative depending on circumstances. If the issuer is seen as a guardian of stability, as many view the United States, investors may be attracted by the prospect of a safe haven for their assets and governments may be attracted by formal or informal security assurances. The opposite will be true if the issuer is seen as a destabilizer or aggressor. In Posen's words, "military misadventures will erode the willingness of other countries to rely on [a currency], and thus create a negative feedback loop between economic and security capacities."[41]

Collectively, these more fine-grained observations help to explain why we see such wide variation in the combination of roles played by different currencies. Ceteris paribus, states that are economically large but lag behind in terms of financial development can expect their currencies to develop a substantial role in trade but little else. Conversely, even relatively minor economic powers that happen to have well developed financial markets may hope to see their currencies claim some investment role and possibly a reserve role as well. Middle-ranking nations such as Australia and South Africa, with well-established ties to smaller neighbors, may find their currencies used more at the official level than at the private level. Countries able to offer credible security assurances are more likely than others to see their currencies adopted for use by both investors and governments.

INFLUENCE ATTEMPTS

All of this assumes, however, that the Darwinian struggle for market share is entirely demand driven, reflecting no more than the autonomous preferences of currency users. But what about the issuing governments, the decision makers on the supply side of the market? Here too, the details matter. Can suppliers make use of their power resources to alter demand for their money? Put differently, can an international currency be "manufactured" by deliberate "influence attempts"—what one source describes as "managed internationalization"?[42] The aim of managed internationalization would be to raise a previously uncompetitive money to the rank of elite currency or perhaps even patrician currency in the global Currency Pyramid.

History provides little guidance. A common impression is that most international currencies have been manufactured. Jonathan Kirshner, for example, casually asserts that "great powers have routinely sought to expand the international use of their currencies."[43] But little evidence exists to substantiate the claim. Of the several moneys that have managed to scale the heights of the Currency Pyramid in the modern era—including the pound sterling and dollar as well as the DM, yen, and euro—none came into widespread use as the result of official effort.[44] On the contrary, all their issuers were initially quite reluctant to promote internationalization. If a currency attained broader standing, it was largely because of inherent qualities, economic or political, that came to make the money attractive to traders, investors, and other interested agents. Internationalization was driven by the spontaneous evolution of preferences on the demand side of the market, not by deliberate influence attempts on the supply side. There is no successful prior model of managed internationalization.

But that need not always be so. As a practical matter, it is easy to imagine that some governments at some moment might be tempted to adopt more proactive policies to push demand in favor of their currency. For them, the experiences of the DM, yen, and euro might seem a cautionary tale. That none of the three moneys managed to achieve its full promise as international money cannot be blamed entirely on the ambivalence of their issuing authorities; as indicated, other factors were also involved. But the lack of official backing surely did not help. It is clear that affirmative government action may not be *sufficient* to attain top currency standing. But decision makers should not be blamed if they were to conclude from those experiences that greater backing by public policy might be *necessary*.

More proactive policies would mean attempting to activate capabilities to alter the behavior of outsiders: a matter of statecraft. The goal could be pursued either by manipulating incentives (the first and second faces of power) or by seeking to alter underlying preferences (the third face of power). The question is: Can such influence attempts succeed? The answer is not self-evident.

Certainly there is no lack of means. Broadly speaking, two classes of strategy are possible—corresponding to what I have elsewhere described as either "informal" or "formal" aspirations to currency leadership.[45] Eric Helleiner proposes a roughly similar distinction between what he calls "indirect" or "direct" channels of political influence.[46] For both of us, the basic idea is that states do have options if they wish to manage internationalization.

Informal leadership (or indirect political influence) refers to a policy strategy designed to enhance the market appeal of a money—to improve the currency brand, as it were. The aim would be to alter demand by manipulating the economic attributes that determine currency choice: in effect, to exploit the issuer's structural power (the second face of power) to mold incentives and payoffs.[47] Targets could include foreign governments as well as market actors. Ostensibly "sound" monetary and fiscal policies—meaning high interest rates and low budget deficits—might be implemented to build confidence in the currency's future value. Financial development might be emphasized to offer lower transactions costs or greater liquidity. Or network externalities might be promoted by lowering import barriers and opening new trade markets. In Helleiner's words: "Politics can help determine international currency standing through these indirect channels of influencing confidence, liquidity, and transactional networks in ways that influence the economic choices of both market and state actors."[48]

Formal leadership (or direct political influence), by contrast, refers to a strategy designed to alter demand directly, by manipulating currency choice itself—in this regard, more an exercise of the traditional first face of power. Targets here would be mainly other governments. Currencies might be directly imposed on client states in a manner similar to what Susan Strange meant by a master currency. Recalling again Kirshner's language,[49] countries could be threatened with *enforcement* or *expulsion* if they do not align themselves monetarily—a threat of sanctions, say, or a withdrawal of past commercial or financial privileges. In effect, elite or patrician currency status could be imposed on others. Alternatively, attractive inducements of an economic or political nature might be offered to reshape policy preferences in a manner analogous to Strange's notion of a negotiated currency. Elite or patrician status could be the result of inducement. Again in Helleiner's words: "In the second category . . . politics matters more directly by prompting states . . . to support a currency's international position for reasons unrelated to their inherent economic attractiveness."[50]

So if such abundant options are available, why do we not see more attempts at managed internationalization? Why is monetary force not activated more? Evidently, in this context we definitely have something of a potential power problem. Several explanations are possible.

First, as suggested back in chapter 2, is the issue of costs. Measures to promote use of a currency are rarely costless. Quite the contrary, the advantages of internationalization may be more than offset by disadvantages. Tight monetary and fiscal policies, for instance, might achieve low inflation but only at a high price in terms of unemployment and lost growth. Similarly, as noted in the previous chapter, the expense of measures intended to sustain use of a negotiated currency—generous aid packages and the like—could turn out to be considerable. Rational policy makers may well calculate that the game is not worth the candle.

Likewise, as attractive as the possibility of internationalization might seem, policy makers could be stymied by resistance from key domestic interest groups. Some constituencies, we know from chapter 4, can be expected to benefit from internationalization—for example, banks that will gain some denomination rents or traders who would like to worry less about exchange risk. But other more domestically oriented interests may well resent the expenses that could be involved in prolonging conservative macroeconomic policies at home or paying to sustain a negotiated currency abroad. Internal political struggle could hamstring efforts to pursue an ambitious agenda for the nation's currency in external relations.

Last, there is the fungibility problem—the possible lack of fit between the broad goal of internationalization and the practical instruments available to achieve it. Since the impacts of relevant elements of power on currency use tend to be uneven, power resources that are available to promote one or two monetary roles could turn out to be quite ineffectual at encouraging others. A large trading nation, for example, might be able to exploit the gravitational pull of its economy to boost interest in its currency for invoicing purposes, but that will do little to encourage an investment role in the absence of adequate financial development. Conversely, opening a country's capital market may encourage adoption of its currency as a store of value but may be of little value in encouraging a trade role. And lavish security guarantees may be effective in attracting use by foreign governments but could leave private market actors indifferent. A particularly poignant illustration of the fungibility problem was provided by Japan's belated and abortive drive to internationalize the yen in the 1990s. Tokyo's ambitious financial liberalization program—its Big Bang—was intended to encourage the coalescence of a yen bloc in East Asia. But the effort failed owing to lingering distrust of the Japanese in their own neighborhood. The attractions of the Japanese capital market could not compensate for conflicted foreign-policy ties. To be successful, influence attempts must be carefully designed to match instrument and objective.

GEOPOLITICAL DECLINE

Finally, we come to the question of geopolitical decline. The three cases reviewed in this chapter all involved powers on the rise—states (West Germany and Japan) or a group of states (EMU) whose broad capabilities were clearly growing. As their endowment of power mounted, outside demand for their currency expanded. But what about the reverse—a monetary power in decline? What then happens to the currency?

Given enough time, demand for the currency of a declining power is most likely to evaporate. International use will dwindle, and the money will slide down the Currency Pyramid to the rank of plebeian currency or even lower. To revive a term I first used decades ago, the money will become *domesticated*, reverting to a purely domestic role, and may even disappear altogether.[51] Eric Helleiner speaks of "de-internationalization" or "downsizing";[52] Kirshner's preferred term is currency "contraction."[53] Domestication (de-internationalization or contraction) has eventually been the story of every "great" currency over the ages, from the silver drachma of ancient Athens to the Spanish-Mexican silver peso, which in the eighteenth and nineteenth centuries was a virtually universal money throughout the Western Hemisphere before being supplanted by the US dollar.[54] No international money has ever outlasted the "great" power that issued it.

The reason is evident. Once the foundations of a currency's popularity begin to erode, outsiders have an incentive to look elsewhere for a more appealing alternative. Slow economic growth or a falling share of world trade will diminish the money's usefulness in trade invoicing and settlement. Stalled financial development, perhaps compounded by the weight of an accumulation of foreign liabilities, will encourage investors to look for safety or liquidity elsewhere. And a fraying of political ties or military capabilities will open opportunities for geopolitical rivals to attract the attention of former clients or allies. At issue, fundamentally, is the question of credibility—a form of soft power. Can the currency still be trusted? Once confidence is undermined, it is difficult to restore.

All this spells considerable loss for the currency's issuer. Not only are the past benefits of internationalization compromised. Worse, as Kirshner has pointed out, additional costs are likely to be associated with managing a money in decline.[55] What is to be done, for example, about the overhang of external claims? Special measures may be required—for example, in the form of higher interest rates or exchange-rate guarantees—to avoid a messy rush for the exits by foreign investors and governments. In effect, a kind of vicious circle may be created. Geopolitical decay diminishes the competitiveness of the currency, which leads to yet more economic and political losses, which in turn erode the currency's appeal even more, and so on. Unlike internationalization, which can emerge with little or no government initiative, domestication is likely to be both challenging and expensive.

What is striking, however, is how long domestication may take. Lags are an integral part of the process. Perhaps most remarkable is the example provided by the Byzantine gold solidus—later also called the nomisma and still later, under Italian influence, the bezant—which was first struck by Constantine the Great in the early fourth century. Not much later the Byzantine Empire began to sink into irreversible decay. Yet for nearly eight hundred years, the bezant remained the premier international currency of its day—in the words of historian Robert Lopez, the "dollar of the Middle Ages."[56] Its circulation, according to one authority, stretched "from Ceylon to the Baltic. . . . Bezants struck with the imperial seal became the accepted medium of exchange throughout the civilized world."[57] Although it was partially supplanted from the seventh century onward by the dinar of the new Islamic empire, not until the collapse of the last shreds of Byzantium in the fifteenth century was the bezant finally and definitively eclipsed.

Less dramatic—but equally representative—was the experience of the pound sterling, as noted in the previous chapter. Britain's decline as a great power began even before the end of the nineteenth century, when its GDP was surpassed first by the new German Empire and then by the United States. Yet it was not until the period between the World Wars when the pound was initially displaced by the dollar as top currency. Or even more recently, we could look to the Japanese yen, which continues to occupy a high rank in the Currency Pyramid despite a quarter century of stagnation since the bursting of the country's "bubble economy." The currency's standing has withered but is by no means yet dead.

Here again the reason is evident. The explanation lies in the highly path-dependent character of international currency use, reflecting the potentially high cost of switching from one money to another. The choice by any given agent to adopt a new currency will depend greatly on what others can be expected to do; and others, similarly, will be watching to see what new market practices emerge. Given the network qualities of money, decision making is inherently interdependent. Absent an adventurous first mover, inertia is only natural. The advantages of incumbency assure that replacement will not come quickly. Much depends on the attractiveness of available alternatives. The bezant lasted for as long as it did in good part because until the Renaissance there were no adequate substitutes outside Muslim realms. Today, by contrast, when there are several currencies at or near the peak of the Currency Pyramid, the corresponding lag might be considerably shorter.

LIFE CYCLES

Combining observations from both this chapter and chapter 4, it seems evident that the relationship between currency and power is indeed mutually endogenous. The working premise suggested back in the introduction seems justified. Currency internationalization does influence state power; state power does influence currency internationalization. The arrow of causation points simultaneously in both directions.

In turn, this appears to confirm the notion of a distinct life cycle for international currencies. The life cycle can be characterized as a succession of two broadly self-reinforcing processes. First comes a "virtuous circle" in which power resources promote a money's internationalization via the several channels described in this chapter; while simultaneously currency internationalization promotes state power along lines suggested in the preceding chapter. The double-edged sword cuts in the issuer's favor. But then, sooner or later, comes a more vicious circle in which the reverse is true. Ultimately, geopolitical decline will sap the appeal of a currency, while simultaneously a weakening currency will erode economic and political capabilities. The double-edged sword cuts the other way.

The critical question, of course, is when the cycle turns. When does the virtuous circle end and the vicious circle begin? In practical terms, the moment comes when outsiders begin to abandon the currency, limiting the borrowing capacity—the ability to run "deficits without tears"—that is the foundation of a money's contribution to state power. The timing of such a tipping point is obviously difficult to predict. But we do know the factors that are most likely to influence outcomes.

On the one hand is Gallarotti's power curse,[58] which may lead an issuer to waste capabilities or underestimate vulnerabilities, thus affecting the demand side of the equation. Most at stake is the vulnerability associated with the accumulation of an excessive overhang of foreign liabilities. We know that the greater the overhang, the more likely it is that investors and central banks will begin to look elsewhere for a more reliable store of value. On the other hand is the availability (or not) of sufficiently attractive alternatives, affecting the supply side of the equation. How strong is the currency's monopolistic power? Investors and central banks may wish to find a safer store of value, but will there be any out there? Even if vulnerable, an incumbent benefits from path dependency. Challengers may find it difficult to offer advantages sufficient to persuade agents to make a potentially costly change.

CONCLUSION

In conclusion, six generalizations seem warranted. First, it is clear that state power does play a critical role. Competition among currencies is not a purely economic affair, devoid of politics. Quite the contrary, geopolitical capabilities matter a great deal. At the international level, states may not enjoy the same capacity for coercion that they do at the domestic level; except in limited circumstances, they cannot normally *compel* adoption of their money by outsiders. But when given a choice, users naturally gravitate toward currencies that can best promise stable value and accessibility over time. Trust is essential. The backing of a powerful state can make all the difference.

Second, it is also clear that more than one element of state power is involved. The four most important factors seem to be economic size, financial development, foreign-policy ties, and military reach. No one power resource is decisive on its own. Most or all of them would appear to be necessary for a currency to rise to the peak of the Currency Pyramid. Prospects for successful internationalization will depend greatly on how many rival players there are in the game, and in particular on the residual advantages enjoyed by existing incumbents. Inertia is only to be expected.

Third, the effects of a state's power resources can be expected to be quite differentiated across the range of a money's possible roles. While some factors, such as economic size, are more apt to promote the medium-of-exchange functions of a currency, others, such as financial development, will have their biggest impact on the store-of-value functions. Political ties will have their greatest influence at the official level; military reach will offer a safe haven for both private investors and central banks.

Since individual states may have quite different mixes of capabilities, it follows that separate currencies can be expected to play very different combinations of roles.

Fourth, it is evident that room exists for deliberate influence attempts—strategic efforts by governments to "manufacture" an international currency, either by manipulating incentives or by altering underlying preferences. Power resources can be used either to enhance the market appeal of a money, nudging demand indirectly, or to shape demand directly via diverse side-payments or sanctions. Managed internationalization may be a real option.

Managed internationalization, however, is unlikely to be easy. That is the fifth generalization. A government may aspire to push its money up through the ranks of the Currency Pyramid. But desire alone is no guarantee of success, no matter how seemingly irresistible the country's power resources may be. There are distinct limits to the process, imposed inter alia by inertia, costs of implementation, domestic politics, and/or fungibility problems. There may be a causal arrow that runs from state power to currency internationalization, but its path is by no means a direct or simple one.

Finally, it is evident that geopolitical decline is an important part of the picture—emphasizing the likelihood that, sooner or later, the virtuous circle of a currency's rise will be succeeded by a vicious circle of decay and decline. International moneys may last a very long time. But they do not live forever.

6

Currency Competition Today

(with Tabitha M. Benney)

> A world of multiple international currencies is coming.
> —*Barry Eichengreen*[1]

With this chapter we turn from theory to praxis. What is the state of play among today's major international currencies? How is power distributed at the peak of the Currency Pyramid, how has the balance of power changed (if at all) over time, and what are the most likely prospects for the future?

Half a century ago matters were simple. There was just one truly full-bodied international currency, the US dollar, and its reach was global. The currency system could fairly be described as unipolar, a virtual monopoly. America's greenback enjoyed genuine "hegemony." But then new rivals gradually emerged to challenge the dollar, including for a time West Germany's Deutsche mark, later Japan's yen, and most recently Europe's euro (replacing the DM). And just over the horizon looms the Chinese yuan, which many see as the international money of the future.

More and more, therefore, we hear loose talk about the diminished power of the greenback. The world, we are told, is moving toward a multicurrency system, with several poles. Barry Eichengreen's prediction is typical.[2] Declares the World Bank, "the most likely scenario for the international monetary system is a multicurrency system centered around the U.S. dollar, the euro, and the renminbi."[3] Echoes Jonathan Kirshner, the advent of a multiple currency order is "highly probable."[4]

Indeed, for some, the future has very nearly arrived. In the words of Fred Bergsten, "the international monetary system is already becoming bipolar, and may soon be tripolar."[5] Or as the European Central Bank puts it, "the international monetary system is already on the verge of becoming tripolar."[6] Another source calls it the "new triumvirate."[7] Two French economists speak of "the long march towards a multipolar monetary regime."[8] A survey of financial elites in leading emerging market economies finds near-unanimous expectation of a multicurrency system in coming years.[9] Multipolarity, it appears, is the new normal. The implication is that the currency system is becoming increasingly competitive.

Polarity, however, is a notoriously crude measure of the level of competition in any kind of system, economic or political. As Edward Mansfield long ago reminded us, using polarity alone implies that any inequalities among the major players are basically unimportant.[10] In effect, poles are assumed to be structurally equivalent—not significantly different from one another in terms of capabilities or influence. That is an improbable notion at best. In reality, the competitiveness of key players is apt to be anything but uniform. If description of a system is to be at all accurate, it should take into account not only the number of poles but also the inequalities among them –an alternative approach encompassed by the concept of *concentration*. If we really want to know how competitive a system is, we need to think in terms of concentration, not just polarity. Concentration can integrate inequalities and polarity in a single measure of competitive structure.

This chapter makes use of the concept of concentration to provide a more accurate picture of the competitive structure at the peak of the currency system today. At issue is the degree of rivalry among the world's major currencies. Is the system really becoming more competitive, as the popular idea of multipolarity implies? Are we already on the verge of something like an oligopoly, with several top currencies (poles) contesting for market share? Or has the erosion of the dollar's hegemony been exaggerated, despite the emergence of challengers?

Analysis indicates that loose talk of an increasingly competitive currency system is at best premature. A future of multipolarity may yet arrive, but there is no evidence that any of this is happening *yet*. Taking account of concentration as well as polarity, it appears that the competitive structure of the system has changed little over a period stretching back nearly a quarter of a century. The dollar's dominance seems undiminished. Assertions to the contrary are simply not consistent with the facts.

Prior Efforts

Monetary scholars are not insensitive to the issue of inequality among international currencies. A basic question, however, is what metric (or metrics) to use for the purpose of comparative analysis. As indicated back in chapter 3, accurate measurement of monetary power is difficult, if not impossible. Statistical indices of capability, based on the traditional elements-of-power approach, are arbitrary at best. Is there a better alternative?

Market Shares

Typically, analysts rely on measures of market share as a proxy for competitiveness. How widely used is each currency for one or another international role? The logic, derived from microeconomic theory, is that market shares are a reasonably objective indicator of demand, an expression of "revealed preference." The assumption is that if a currency dominates in some market segment, it must be because it has succeeded in the Darwinian process of natural selection. The popular good money has driven out the bad.

As a proxy, however, market share has its limitations. Despite the claims of some experts,[11] use cannot be easily equated with power, whether understood as autonomy or influence. We have seen that internationalization may well turn out to be a double-edged sword. Wider use as an anchor, for example, may mean less control over the issuer's exchange rate, rather than more. Likewise, increased central-bank holdings may reflect not strength but weakness if they are the result of purchases required to support a reserve currency under stress. After World War II, more than a decade passed before the US dollar's share of global reserves came to surpass that of the pound sterling. Is there anyone who would argue that Britain's pound, undermined by war and recurrent exchange-rate crises, was actually more powerful than the American greenback at the time? Market shares, on their own, are at best an imperfect indicator of competitiveness and must be handled with care. They certainly tell us little about where basic capabilities come from or how they might be used.

Yet what else is there? As the expression goes: In the land of the blind, the one-eyed man is king. In lieu of anything better, we have little choice but to rely on market shares (usage) as the best indicator of competitiveness we have, no matter how imperfect. We just have to be careful not to put too much blind faith in what the numbers tell us.

Incomplete Analysis

Unfortunately, prior efforts to use market shares to determine relative currency competitiveness, while often quite sophisticated, have been sadly inadequate. Typically, in another manifestation of the Fallacy of Misplaced Concreteness, one single role is selected for comparative analysis and is treated as a proxy for all the diverse functions that an international money may perform, ignoring available data on other roles. Analysis, consequently, tends to be regrettably incomplete.

Most frequently, studies focus on the reserve-currency role, widely regarded as the ultimate confirmation of a money's international acceptability. The share of each currency in the total of world reserves is assumed to stand for its relative ranking among its peers or its prospects for the future. Representative is the work of Menzie Chinn and Jeffrey Frankel, who not long ago made waves by predicting that the euro would surpass the dollar as an international currency by as early as 2015, making the system more competitive.[12] Their forecast, based on formal modeling and rigorous econometric analysis, was technically impeccable. Their projections, however, were limited exclusively to central-bank reserve holdings, ignoring all other uses.

Chinn and Frankel's timing, obviously, was unfortunate. Soon after their work appeared, the euro zone was plunged into a prolonged sovereign debt and banking crisis. As a result, the ascent of Europe's currency has clearly stalled, at least for the moment. Its power remains unrealized, for reasons that are explored in chapter 8. But that has not stopped other analysts from emulating the Chinn-Frankel methodology, particularly to assess prospects for the dollar's newest challenger, the RMB. Most widely publicized has been the work of economist Arvind Subramanian, who confidently predicts a glowing future for the yuan.[13] Using a model similar to that of Chinn and Frankel, he makes an equally audacious forecast, concluding that the rise of the RMB is unstoppable. In his words: "The renminbi could rival or even overtake the dollar as the primary reserve currency as soon as the early years of the next decade."[14] He too focuses exclusively on the reserve-currency role.

In fact, it should be clear that selecting just a single role for comparative analysis is a risky research strategy. The practice is typically defended in terms of linkages among an international currency's diverse functions, which are assumed to be tightly connected. As one source puts it:

> The assumption is that reserve currency holdings are a good proxy for the overall international role of a currency. . . . the international roles of a currency tend to be related and jointly determined by more fundamental factors. There are economies of scope.[15]

But is that persuasive? Interdependencies among a currency's international roles undoubtedly exist, as noted in chapter 4. Economies of scope cannot be denied. But that does not rule out large differences in actual use for various purposes. In practice, the correlation across market segments for any given currency is far from strong. To believe otherwise is to succumb to another logical fallacy: the Fallacy of Composition. That is the notion that one can infer that something is true of the whole from the fact that it is true of some part of the whole. The premise of the strategy is, to say the least, dubious.

Somewhat more persuasive are studies that explicitly acknowledge the relatively low level of correlation across market segments. This is done by selecting several roles for comparative analysis, rather than just one function alone. Market shares are compared across multiple sectors of activity. That is the approach, for instance, traditionally followed by the European Central Bank, which every year publishes a comprehensive report on the international role of the euro. The euro's share of various sectors of activity, from the foreign-exchange market and trade invoicing to international debt markets and central-bank reserves, are calculated and contrasted with other currencies like the dollar. The same approach has been widely used to evaluate prospects for both the euro[16] and the yuan.[17] The advantage of the approach is that it gives a more realistic picture of the global system's inherent complexity, explicitly allowing for varying inequalities among the players.

But that still leaves a problem. The approach fails to integrate inequalities and polarity in a way that would permit generalization about the system's overall competitive structure. In most instances, each role is compartmentalized and addressed more or less on its own. On one occasion the ECB did try to construct a "summary indicator" of the international role of the euro, aggregating available information on reserve holdings and financial-market activity into a single dimension, but conceded defeat by "conceptual, practical and methodological challenges."[18] In practice, few attempts have been made to produce a more comprehensive portrait of the system as a whole.

A rare exception comes from economist Christian Thimann, who has developed a composite measure of what he calls a currency's "global role" based on the size and stage of development of its financial markets and the scope of financial instruments available in the currency.[19] Measurement and rankings are calculated using fifteen size indicators and sixteen structural indicators for each of twenty-two currencies. The research design is ambitious and points in the right direction. Regrettably, however, for all its plethora of statistical variables, it is limited to just one of the six roles of an international currency—namely, the investment (store-of-value) role in financial markets—and thus falls far short of truly comprehensive coverage.

Perhaps closest to what is needed is a composite indicator developed recently by the World Bank as part of a major study of multipolarity in the global economy.[20] The indicator is intended to provide a broad overview of the relative importance of international currencies, encompassing three of the six roles identified back in chapter 1. Based on principal components analysis, the measure is calculated according to shares of foreign-exchange market turnover (vehicle currency role), outstanding international bank claims and bonds (investment currency role), and official reserves (reserve currency role). Unfortunately, the data cover only a short time span, from 1999 to 2009, making it difficult to generalize about longer-term trends. The Bank's results would appear to signal a modest increase of competitiveness among leading currencies, showing an increase of about ten percent in the euro's importance after its birth in 1999 (mostly in its first five years), mirrored by a 6 percent decline for the dollar, a 5 percent decline for the yen, and minor changes elsewhere. But measurement over a longer time horizon, as we shall soon see, suggests that the apparent increase of competitiveness is in fact illusory. Extending the period of analysis, this chapter finds little net change in the general pattern of currency rivalry.

CONCENTRATION

In contrast to prior efforts, a more fruitful approach to estimating the currency system's competitiveness would make use of the concept of *concentration*, borrowed from the discipline of economics. The concept of concentration first gained traction in political science as the original basis for the Correlates of War project.[21] That foundational work used a concentration of power formula to calculate the polarity of a given international system. The purpose was to test whether different distributions of power might systematically influence the likelihood of political-military conflict. Though students of international relations today may quarrel about the usefulness of the COW data set, they continue to make use of the idea of concentration, particularly as a means to gauge the distribution of power among states. Concentration helps IR scholars to distinguish among different types of international political systems at a given period of time. Typically, four types of system are distinguished: unipolar, bipolar, tripolar, or multipolar.

In economics the concept of concentration was first developed for the study of industrial organization—the size of firms in an individual sector and the degree of competition among them. The greater the concentration of a market, the lower is its level of competition. The concept is widely applied in competition law and studies of anti-trust regulation and has also been used to analyze the commodity or geographic composition of international trade.[22] This chapter argues that concentration can also be usefully deployed to help estimate the structure of competition in the currency system.

For purposes of practical analysis, two tools have become standard among economists to measure market competition—concentration ratios (also known as N-firm ratios) and the so-called Herfindahl–Hirschman Index (HHI). Concentration ratios are relatively easy to calculate. First, the leading firms in the industry are identified, with the number N determined by sectoral characteristics. Where some industries (such as large commercial aircraft or automobiles) have very few rival firms, warranting a small N, in other sectors a larger number might be more appropriate. Second, an appropriate measure of market share (for example, percentage of profits or sales) is calculated for each firm. And then, finally, the market shares of all the selected firms (expressed as fractions) are simply added up to give an overall percentage. But concentration ratios are also of limited analytical value, since they provide little insight into the distribution of firm size and also take no account of smaller firms below the selected threshold. All they measure is the aggregate market share of a given number of firms. They are thus a relatively crude indicator of competitive *structure*.

A more complete picture is provided by the HHI, named after the Orris Herfindahl and Albert Hirschman, two economists who came up with the idea independently but more or less simultaneously.[23] The HHI is defined as the sum of the *squares* of the market shares of all the firms in an industry (again expressed as fractions)—not just the biggest firms but all others as well to ensure that the total of percentages adds up to 100 percent. Squaring market shares prior to summation gives added weight to larger firms, thus taking account of the distribution of firm size as well as the number of leading players. Results are proportional to the average of market share, weighted by market share. Formally, the HHI is calculated as follows:

$$\text{HHI}_t = \sum_{i=1}^{Nt} S_{it}^2$$

where HHI is the Herfindahl–Hirschman Index at a given time t, S is the market share of firm i at time t, and N is the number of firms at time t. Increases in the HHI indicate a decrease in competition and can range from $1/N$ (the equivalent of perfect competition) to 1.00 (monopoly). Anything above 0.25 (25 percent) is generally considered by US anti-trust regulators to be an excessively high level of concentration.

To illustrate the contrast between the two approaches, consider two alternative cases of an industry in which the top four firms together (CR4) are assumed to account for 80 percent of sales and twenty other firms account for the remaining 20 percent (one percent each). In one case, each of the four large firms controls 20 percent of the market; in the other, one firm controls 50 percent and the other three control 10 percent each.

Case 1. CR4 = .20+.20+.20+.20   Case 2. CR4 = .50+.10+.10+.10
       = .80 or 80%   = .80 or 80%

Plainly, the degree of competition is greater in the first case. The second comes closer to dominance by one firm, approaching monopoly. But the difference between the cases is obscured if we use a simple concentration ratio, since with that approach the two appear to be identical. In both, the ratio is 80 percent.

Using the HHI, by contrast, we clearly see the difference.

Case 1. $HHI = 4(.20^2) + 20(.01^2)$ Case 2. $HHI = .50^2 + 3(.10^2) + 20(.01^2)$
$$= 4(.04) + 20(.0001) \qquad\qquad = .25 + 3(.01) + 20(.0001)$$
$$= .16 + .002 \qquad\qquad\qquad = .25 + .03 + .002$$
$$= .162 \qquad\qquad\qquad\qquad = .282$$

While the HHI or some variant thereof have frequently been employed by IR scholars to explore the nature of the global political system and the risk of international conflict,[24] it has appeared only rarely in the IPE literature. To my knowledge, the HHI has previously been used just once in a discussion of currency hierarchy—a brief aside by Herman Schwartz in his masterful book *Subprime Nation* suggesting that recent years have seen some erosion in the dominant position of the US dollar.[25] Applying Susan Strange's labels, Schwartz contended that the greenback was slipping from top currency status to becoming more like a negotiated currency. This chapter, by contrast, making fuller use of both concentration ratios and the HHI, comes to a rather different conclusion.

DATA

Our objective is to evaluate the competitive structure of the currency system today. Ideally, in such an analysis, we would wish to include measures of use for all six of the roles of an international currency. In practice, however, that is just not possible. For two of the roles—trade invoicing and settlement at the private level and currency intervention at the official level—adequate statistics are lacking. For trade invoicing and settlement, some survey material is available,[26] but the coverage is far from complete. For currency interventions, most governments prefer to keep their operations confidential.

More is known about the anchor role of international currencies, but measurement for comparative purposes is also problematic. A money functions as an anchor when other currencies are pegged to it in one way or another. But it is not always easy to know when such an exchange-rate relationship exists. The link is obvious when a formal (de jure) peg is announced but more difficult to specify when pegs are informal (de facto) or maintained in relation to a "basket" of currencies. And there is also a problem of estimating the relative importance of diverse exchange-rate links. Simply adding up the number of currency pegs, formal or informal, is clearly inadequate. As previously noted, as many as forty countries currently align their currencies to some extent with the euro (as compared with some sixty countries that align more or less closely with the dollar). But of the euro's forty, four are European mini-states (Andorra, Monaco, San Marino, and the Vatican); and another sixteen include the fourteen members of the CFA franc zone in Africa (Communauté Financière Africaine–African Financial Community), a long-standing monetary union among mostly French former colonies, together with two affiliated economies (Cape Verde and Comoros)—all small and poor countries. How do we compare these anchor relationships with the links to the dollar maintained by much larger economic powers like China, Hong Kong, and Saudi Arabia? Recent studies have tried weighting existing pegs by either income or trade shares, with mixed results.[27]

That leaves us, therefore, with just three of an international money's six functions. Not coincidentally, these are the same three functions that are included in the World Bank's composite indicator—the roles as vehicle currency, investment currency, and reserve currency These are the categories for which adequate data are available. The analysis here will focus on these same three roles but with considerably more detail than in the World Bank study and over a longer time span. The data show that five currencies clearly dominate across all three roles: the dollar, euro, yen, pound sterling, and Swiss franc. These are today's top, patrician, and elite currencies. A few other moneys have begun to achieve some prominence, including most notably the Australian and Canadian dollars, but overall still lag considerably behind in most functions. Notably absent is China's tightly controlled yuan, which has yet to make any significant impact in any of the three market segments.

For the vehicle and investment currency roles, the best source we have is the Bank for International Settlements. Data on the vehicle role have been available since 1989, when the BIS first began its triennial surveys of global foreign-exchange market activity. The latest survey was published in 2013.[28] A summary of market shares for the most widely used vehicle currencies since 1989 is provided in table 6.1. Changes over time are charted in the corresponding figure 6.1. Market shares in the

TABLE 6.1. Vehicle currency role: Currency shares of the global foreign exchange market (percentage of average daily turnover)

	1989	1992	1995	1998	2001	2004	2007	2010	2013
US dollar	90.0%	82.0%	83.3%	87.3%	89.9%	88.0%	85.6%	84.9%	87.0%
Euro	33.0%	55.2%	59.7%	52.5%	37.9%	37.4%	37.0%	39.1%	33.4%
Japanese yen	27.0%	23.4%	24.1%	20.2%	23.5%	20.8%	17.2%	19.0%	23.0%
Pound sterling	15.0%	13.6%	9.4%	11.0%	13.0%	16.5%	14.9%	12.9%	11.8%
Swiss franc	10.0%	8.4%	7.3%	7.1%	6.0%	6.0%	6.8%	6.4%	5.2%
Other currencies	25.0%	17.4%	16.2%	21.9%	29.7%	31.3%	38.5%	37.7%	39.6%

Source: Bank for International Settlements.

Note: Percentages add up to 200 percent.

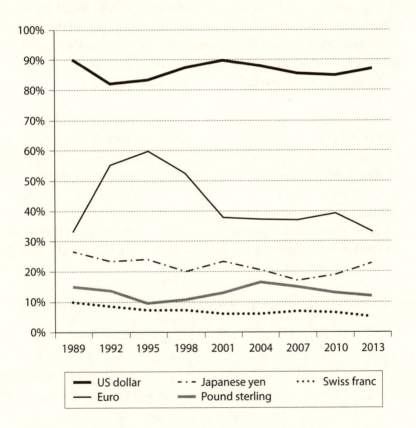

Figure 6.1. Vehicle currency role: Currency shares of the global foreign exchange market (percentage of average daily turnover).

Source: Bank for International Settlements.

foreign-exchange market are measured by the percentage of transactions in which each currency appeared. (Again, since every transaction involves two currencies, percentages add up to two hundred percent.) The survey is always taken at the same time of year, once every three years, on or near April 30. In table 6.1 and figure 6.1, as in all subsequent tables and figures, the shares shown for the euro prior to its birth in 1999 are calculated as the sum of the shares of the Deutsche mark, French franc, and other so-called legacy currencies (including the old European Currency Unit). The apparent sharp drop in the recorded share of the euro after 1998 can be attributed to the formal start of Europe's monetary union, which eliminated trading among the euro's constituent currencies. From 1999 onward, transactions among members of the euro zone became effectively domestic and thus were no longer treated as part of the foreign-exchange market. Unfortunately, there is no easy way to strip out these domestic transactions from the data prior to 1999.

Statistics on international banking and securities, including data on the main currencies used in global financial markets, have long been published by the BIS on a regular basis in the quarterly reports of its Monetary and Economic Department. A summary of market shares of the principal investment currencies is provided in tables 6.2 and 6.3, with changes charted in the corresponding figures 6.2 and 6.3. Table 6.2 and figure 6.2 show trends in the currency composition of the international banking market, comprising all cross-border banking claims. Table 6.3 and figure 6.3 show the currency composition of the international securities market, encompassing money-market instruments as well as notes

TABLE 6.2. Investment currency role: Currency shares of the international banking market (percentage of total cross-border bank claims)

	1989	1992	1995	1998	2001	2004	2007	2010	2013
US dollar	58.4%	52.3%	45.0%	48.5%	48.4%	43.1%	41.9%	42.7%	44.3%
Euro	17.4%	22.8%	27.5%	26.0%	31.8%	39.1%	39.6%	39.4%	36.5%
Japanese yen	13.8%	12.3%	14.1%	10.0%	8.1%	4.9%	3.4%	3.7%	4.5%
Pound sterling	3.5%	3.9%	3.5%	5.0%	5.0%	6.4%	7.7%	5.7%	4.8%
Swiss franc	4.1%	4.3%	3.9%	2.9%	2.3%	1.8%	1.6%	1.5%	1.6%
Other currencies	2.8%	4.5%	5.9%	7.6%	4.5%	4.8%	5.8%	7.0%	8.3%

Source: Bank for International Settlements.

TABLE 6.3. Investment currency role: currency shares in the international securities market (percentage of total issues outstanding)

	1992	1995	1998	2001	2004	2007	2010	2013
US dollar	42.4%	38.5%	48.0%	51.4%	40.4%	36.0%	37.8%	36.6%
Euro	24.7%	26.8%	24.2%	30.0%	43.0%	47.3%	46.0%	44.0%
Japanese yen	13.1%	16.2%	11.7%	6.9%	4.3%	2.7%	2.6%	2.4%
Pound sterling	7.1%	6.8%	8.0%	7.2%	7.5%	8.6%	8.0%	9.5%
Swiss franc	7.3%	6.8%	3.8%	2.0%	1.8%	1.5%	1.4%	1.7%
Other currencies	5.5%	4.9%	4.3%	2.5%	3.0%	4.0%	4.2%	5.8%

Source: Bank for International Settlements.
Note: Securities markets include international bonds, notes, and money market instruments.
No data are available for 1989. The data in the first column are from September 1993.

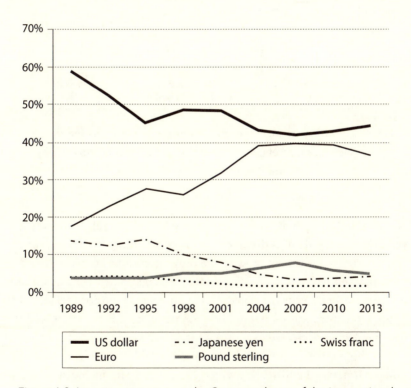

Figure 6.2. Investment currency role: Currency shares of the international banking market (percentage of total cross-border bank claims).

Source: Bank for International Settlements.

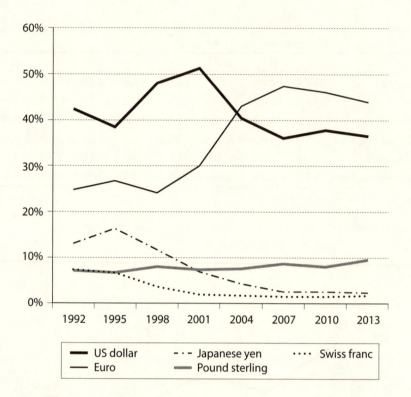

Figure 6.3. Investment currency role: Currency shares in the international securities market (percentage of total issues outstanding).
Source: Bank for International Settlements.

and bonds. The data are presented at three-year intervals to parallel the vehicle-currency data and depict claims outstanding at the end of the first quarter of each year shown. The only exceptions are to be found in table 6.3 and figure 6.3, due to the fact that comprehensive statistics for the international securities market were not available prior to September 1993. No entries are shown in table 6.3 or figure 6.3 for 1989, and the data for 1993 are treated as a proxy for 1992.

For the reserve currency role the best available source is the International Monetary Fund (IMF), which for many years included information in its annual reports on the foreign-exchange holdings of central banks. Since 2005 the IMF's presentation has been formalized in a public database on the Currency Composition of Official Foreign Exchange Reserves (COFER), published quarterly. The COFER data are regrettably

TABLE 6.4. Reserve currency role: Currency shares of foreign exchange reserves
(percentage of total "allocated" reserves)

	1989	1992	1995	1998	2001	2004	2007	2010	2013
US dollar	52.4%	55.1%	56.8%	65.7%	72.3%	67.1%	65.1%	61.7%	62.0%
Euro	34.8%	26.0%	22.9%	14.5%	17.7%	23.4%	25.0%	27.3%	23.6%
Japanese yen	7.4%	7.5%	6.8%	5.3%	5.5%	4.5%	3.1%	3.0%	3.9%
Pound sterling	2.6%	3.0%	3.1%	3.8%	2.8%	2.8%	4.6%	4.3%	3.9%
Swiss franc	1.6%	1.0%	0.8%	0.7%	0.3%	0.2%	0.2%	0.1%	0.2%
Other currencies	1.2%	7.4%	9.6%	10.0%	1.4%	2.0%	2.0%	3.6%	3.2%

Source: International Monetary Fund.

incomplete, since not all countries report the currency distribution of their reserve holdings. Most importantly, several Asian central banks—including, most prominently, China—are absent. Moreover, since the onset of the global financial crisis in 2008, the share of these "unallocated" reserves in global reserve totals has risen sharply, from no more than 25 percent in the 1990s to nearly half in 2013—mainly because of disproportionately big increases in the holdings of China and some of its neighbors. *Faute de mieux*, however, the numbers for so-called allocated reserves are the best we have and must be considered sufficiently representative to be useful for analytical purposes. A summary of market shares for the principal reserve currencies is provided in table 6.4, with changes over time charted in figure 6.4. Shares are calculated as a percentage of allocated reserves. Again, the data are presented at three-year intervals to parallel the vehicle-currency data and depict amounts outstanding at the end of the first quarter of each year shown.

ANALYSIS

What do the data tell us? Much can be learned about both the presumed polarity of the currency system and its overall degree of concentration.

Multipolarity?

To begin, the data suggest that predictions of a new normal of multipolarity are, at best, premature. Even a quick glance confirms that in reality the global system today is dominated in varying degrees by just two

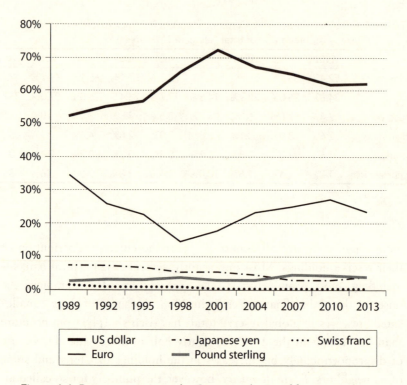

Figure 6.4. Reserve currency role: Currency shares of foreign exchange
reserves (percentage of total foreign exchange reserves).
Source: International Monetary Fund.

currencies: the dollar and the euro. This is a pattern that has persisted
consistently for more than two decades. Routinely, the dollar and euro
together predominate across the board. Though the yen, pound sterling,
and Swiss franc are used widely enough to warrant separate mention, they
are clearly no more than "also-rans" in the international currency race.
For no role is their market share more than a few percentage points—
certainly not great enough to qualify for description as a distinct pole.

And even further back, still, is the yuan, which is nowhere to be seen in
any sector, owing in particular to China's extensive exchange restrictions
and capital controls. In the foreign-exchange market the RMB's share in
2013 amounted to just over 2 percent of total transactions—admittedly
a notable increase from less than one-tenth of one percent as recently as

2004, but still way back in the pack, running neck and neck with the likes of the Mexican peso and New Zealand dollar. In the international bond and banking markets, as we shall see in chapter 9, China's share is even smaller, and any incentive for central banks to hold RMB in their reserves is severely blunted by the money's continuing inconvertibility. Overall, the yuan remains a midget among international currencies, despite all the hype lately about an emerging tripolarity.

Bipolarity?

What about bipolarity? As indicated, the dollar and euro together clearly dominate the data. Does that mean, as some suggest,[29] that the system today can therefore be described as a duopoly? Even that is doubtful, given the evident disparities between the two currencies.

Much depends on how we measure bipolarity. We know that the notion of a pole is somewhat ambiguous. It is not always easy to know when an actor might, or might not, qualify as a polar power. But a variety of indicators have been suggested in the IR literature in hopes of giving the concept of polarity more precision. Perhaps the most useful is a set of definitions outlined by Mansfield,[30] based on previous efforts of Ray and Singer, Modelski, Thompson,[31] and others:

1. In a *unipolar* system, one state controls 50 percent or more of the relative capabilities that matter.
2. In a *near-unipolar* system, one state controls more than 45 percent but less than 50 percent of relative capabilities and no other state possesses as much as 25 percent.
3. In a *bipolar* system, two states control at least 50 percent of relative capabilities and each of the two leading actors possess at least 25 percent.

By these definitions, the euro would not appear to qualify as a pole co-equal with the dollar. The disparities between the two currencies can be clearly seen in table 6.5, which summarizes the shares for the dollar and euro in all four market segments in 2013. For illustrative purposes, a simple average of the four ratios is also shown, though without any pretense that this can be considered as anything other than a very raw indicator of the overall competitive structure of the system. In calculating the overall

TABLE 6.5. Summary of currency shares: US dollar and euro (2013)

	Vehicle	Banking	Securities	Reserve	Average
US dollar	43.5%	44.3%	36.6%	62.0%	48.7%
Euro	16.7%	36.5%	44.0%	23.6%	26.9%

average, the banking and securities segments are assigned a weight of 0.5 each, combining them together into one investment category with a weight equal to that of each of the other two roles (vehicle and reserve). The table does not appear to portray a genuine duopoly. Arguably it would be more accurate to depict the system as falling somewhere between bipolar and near-unipolar—an "asymmetric monetary bipolarity," one source calls it.[32] This may not be the starkly unequal "one-and-a-half currency system" that has been described elsewhere,[33] but it is certainly not a relationship of parity.

Admittedly, the two currencies are comparable and clearly competitive in the international banking and bond sectors, with roughly equal market shares going back nearly a decade. In these two segments, the relationship is indeed effectively bipolar. But that is by no means the case in the foreign exchange market or official reserves, where America's greenback has persistently outstripped the euro by ratios well in excess of 2:1. Since trading among the euro's legacy currencies was eliminated in 1999, use of Europe's money as a vehicle currency has barely budged in relative terms. As a reserve currency, the euro's market share of allocated reserves has actually declined as compared with the aggregate share of its legacy currencies in 1989. In the first years after its birth in 1999, the euro did improve its reserve-currency position somewhat at the expense of the dollar. But this was from an artificial peak for the greenback, reflecting the success of the Clinton administration's "strong dollar" policy in preceding years. The dollar's share of allocated reserves in 2013 was still higher than it had been in the mid-1990s. The euro's share, meanwhile, as noted in the previous chapter, peaked in the mid-2000s and in more recent years has actually declined, falling from above 27 percent in 2009 to below 25 percent by 2013.

Is the euro's role as a reserve currency underestimated because the calculation of shares is based solely on allocated reserves? The biggest reserve holder that is missing from the data is of course China. According to one reputable source, the euro's share of China's reserves might actually have risen to as high as one-third by the end of 2011, while the dollar's share had fallen to just 54 percent.[34] However, even if we add these amounts to the existing figures for total allocated reserves at end-2011, we find that the dollar still accounts for as much as 59 percent of the total, while the euro's share is no higher than 28 percent. The greenback still outstrips the euro by a ratio of more than 2:1.

As a practical matter, the euro appears to have already passed its peak as an international currency. Most informed observers no longer see it as a potential rival to the greenback. In the words of economist John Williamson: "For a time it looked as though the euro might become a serious competitor, but given the recent [difficulties] in the euro area, it no longer threatens the preeminence of the dollar."[35] Not everyone agrees, of course. Kirshner, for example, contends that "Europe is down but not out, and in the longer run, the euro will resume its encroachment on the dollar's international role."[36] The evidence to the contrary, however, seems overwhelming. The euro's relative decline is evident in central-bank reserve holdings, as noted, and also in the international securities market, where the euro share of new issues has dropped sharply. Moreover, it is well known that while the dollar continues to be used virtually everywhere, the euro's domain has remained confined to a limited number of countries with close geographical and/or institutional links to the European Union. Considerations like these highlight why it is essential to think about not only the number of poles in the system but also the inequalities among them.

Concentration Ratios

Moving, therefore, beyond polarity to concentration, we begin with some simple concentration ratios as shown in table 6.6 and figures 6.5 and 6.6. Even admitting their limited analytical value, concentration ratios represent an improvement over crude notions of polarity alone.

To ensure representative coverage, two ratios are shown for each market segment. One is for the dollar and euro alone ($N = 2$), the two dominant international currencies. The second includes as well the three also-rans—the yen, pound sterling, and Swiss franc ($N = 5$)—which at the present time can be considered the only other international currencies

TABLE 6.6. Concentration ratios

Currency role	1989	1992	1995	1998	2001	2004	2007	2010	2013
Vehicle (N = 2)	61.5%	68.6%	71.6%	70.0%	64.0%	62.7%	61.3%	62.1%	60.2%
Vehicle (N = 5)	87.5%	91.3%	92.1%	89.2%	85.3%	84.4%	80.8%	81.3%	80.2%
Banking (N = 2)	75.8%	75.1%	72.5%	74.5%	80.2%	82.2%	81.5%	82.1%	80.8%
Banking (N = 5)	97.2%	95.6%	94.0%	92.4%	95.6%	95.3%	94.2%	93.0%	91.7%
Securities (N = 2)	NA	67.0%	65.3%	72.2%	81.4%	83.4%	83.3%	83.8%	80.6%
Securities (N = 5)	NA	94.5%	95.1%	95.7%	97.5%	97.0%	96.0%	95.8%	94.2%
Reserve (N = 2)	87.2%	81.1%	79.7%	80.2%	90.0%	90.5%	90.1%	89.0%	85.6%
Reserve (N = 5)	98.8%	92.6%	90.4%	90.0%	98.6%	98.0%	98.0%	96.4%	93.6%
Average (CR = 2)	74.8%	75.6%	75.9%	76.8%	77.3%	77.3%	76.7%	77.0%	76.2%
Average (CR = 5)	94.5%	95.1%	95.1%	94.0%	93.6%	93.3%	91.9%	91.8%	91.2%

Note: $N = 2$ is the sum of the market shares of the dollar and euro. $N = 5$ is the sum of the market shares of the dollar, euro, yen, pound sterling, and Swiss franc. For the vehicle currency role, market shares have been reduced uniformly by one-half from the percentages shown in table 6.1.

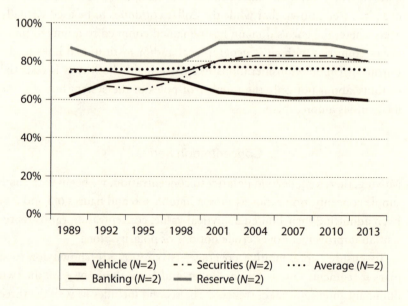

Figure 6.5. Concentration ratios ($N = 2$).

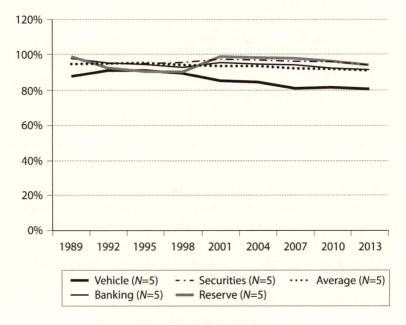

Figure 6.6. Concentration ratios (N = 5).

of consequence. Once more, for illustrative purposes, a simple average of ratios for each year is also shown, again combining the banking and securities segments into a single investment category.

Notably, the ratios show virtually no net change in the level of concentration in the system. Over the years there have been some fluctuations up and down in the individual measures, especially in the securities sector, but for the most part we see a quite stable trend. Whether calculated for N = 2 or N = 5, most of the ratios have barely budged from where they were a quarter of a century ago.

In the foreign exchange market there is some sign of increased competition as a result of declining shares for the yen, pound sterling, and Swiss franc. The relatively modest amount of business lost by the three also-rans appears to have gone primarily to smaller currencies like the Australian and Canadian dollars or the Swedish krona rather than to the greenback or euro. China's RMB has also begun to stake out a role but, with a market share in 2013 of little more than 2 percent, remains a very

TABLE 6.7. Herfindahl–Hirschman indices

	1989	1992	1995	1998	2001	2004	2007	2010	2013
Vehicle HHI	0.272	0.272	0.287	0.286	0.279	0.272	0.269	0.268	0.274
Banking HHI	0.394	0.346	0.305	0.322	0.346	0.348	0.343	0.347	0.341
Securities HHI	NA	0.271	0.258	0.313	0.365	0.357	0.363	0.363	0.341
Reserve HHI	0.402	0.383	0.390	0.467	0.558	0.508	0.490	0.459	0.447
Average HHI	0.356	0.321	0.320	0.357	0.398	0.378	0.371	0.361	0.354

minor player. In the banking and securities sectors, by contrast, concentration has actually risen a bit because of notable increases in foreign use of Europe's money. Once the new currency was born, outside borrowers were attracted by the opportunity to tap into the much broader pool of savings created by the consolidation of European financial markets. Both bank lending and securities issues denominated in euros increased substantially. Overall, however, the average level of competition in the global system, as shown by concentration ratios, seems to indicate little net change from the late 1980s to 2013.

Herfindahl–Hirschman Indices

Even more telling is the picture drawn by calculation of Herfindahl–Hirschman Indices over the same period, as shown in table 6.7 and figure 6.7. Where concentration ratios simply add up the market shares of top players, the HHI gives us a more complete sense of competitive structure by taking explicit account of functional inequalities. Two contrasting observations demonstrate the value added by the HHI.

On the one hand, we again see for the most part a remarkable stability, rather than decline, in the overall level of concentration in the system, despite some fluctuations in individual sectors. Indeed, if we start with 1992 rather than 1989, there actually appears to have been a small net increase of concentration over time. Only in the foreign exchange market is a rise of competition confirmed, and that is only by a quite modest margin. In all other segments, the trend of the HHI is stable or even modestly upward, indicating greater concentration.

On the other hand, we see that concentration and polarity do not always move in tandem. The data, as noted, clearly suggest a high degree

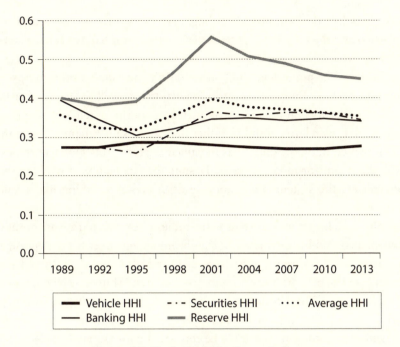

Figure 6.7. Herfindahl–Hirschman indices.

of unipolarity in both the foreign exchange market and official reserves. In both segments, the dollar share is more than twice that of the euro. Yet the levels of concentration as measured by the HHI in the two segments are vastly different—strikingly low in the foreign exchange market but much higher in reserves. Inequalities differ significantly for the two roles. A result like this illustrates why reliance on the notion of polarity alone can be quite misleading.

Conclusion

Keeping in mind the limitations of market share as an indicator of competitiveness, the general conclusion seems unmistakable. Contrary to the popular impression of an emerging multipolarity in the global currency system, there seems little evidence of a higher level of competition. Quite the opposite, in fact. Even today there appears to be just one major pole in the system—namely, the US dollar. The euro lags behind considerably;

also-rans like the yen, pound sterling, and Swiss franc are at best niche players; and the yuan is so far back in the race that it barely even registers as yet.

More to the point, levels of concentration have shown no sign of significant decline. Taking account of inequalities as well as the number of poles, it appears that the most striking feature of the system's competitive structure is its relative stability, rather than any secular change. For more than two decades, the dollar has remained the only truly global currency, still dominant for most purposes. Despite the emergence of rivals to the greenback, the system still cannot be described as anything like a true oligopoly.

This conclusion is consistent with studies of exchange-rate anchoring, which also find little evidence of significant change over time. Representative is an ECB survey dating from 2011, which found that "there have been over the past 30 years no systematic or trend shifts in exchange-rate practices. . . . The US dollar has remained the main anchor currency, with the euro as a distant second."[37] According to a recent World Trade Organization study, it appears to be consistent with available evidence on trade invoicing and settlement as well.[38]

By contrast, the conclusion would seem to conflict with the analysis of the World Bank,[39] whose composite indicator suggests a considerable shift of competitive positions—in particular, a substantial rise for the euro at the expense of the dollar. As noted, however, the Bank's calculation starts only from 1999 when the greenback was at an artificial peak. Going back to a starting point a decade earlier clearly demonstrates the dangers of generalizing about secular trends on the basis of a limited number of years. Over the longer time horizon reviewed in this chapter, the boost of the euro's fortunes in its first half-decade appears to be little more than a kind of regression to the mean. After two and a half decades, the general pattern of currency competition remains little changed.

Of course, even a quarter century covers only a relatively short period in historical terms. Going back even further would undoubtedly show greater variation in competitive structure. Concentration in the currency system was undoubtedly higher in the first decades after World War II and may well have been lower in the last decades before World War I. But data limitations prevent us from extending detailed analysis back any further than the late 1980s.

The important point is the stability of the system *today*. Nothing in this chapter's analysis rules out the possibility of greater change in the future. Were Europe to get a real grip on its prolonged crisis, the euro might yet stage an effective challenge to the dollar; China's RMB might eventually take a place commensurate with the size of the Chinese economy; conceivably, even the currencies of other emerging market economies, such as India or Brazil, could begin to attract international use. The message is simply that none of this has happened *yet*. Loose talk about the shape of the currency system as it presently exists is misleading and a deterrent to serious analysis. Multipolarity is not (yet) the new normal.

7

The Dollar: Power Undiminished

The dollar is finished as international money.
—*Charles Kindleberger*[1]

The reports of my death have been greatly exaggerated.
—*Mark Twain (1835–1910)*

The demise of the dollar has been reported for decades. More than half a century ago, the celebrated economist Robert Triffin was already warning about of "the imminent threat to the once mighty US dollar."[2] After Washington ended the greenback's gold convertibility in 1971, Charles Kindleberger was convinced that the dollar was "finished." And even today advance obituaries continue to appear, anticipating the currency's fall. Dollar pessimists abound.

One prominent example is economist Barry Eichengreen, who writes gloomily about the risk of a "dollar crash." Following the global financial crisis in 2008, he notes, "doubts are pervasive about whether the dollar will retain its international role."[3] Another is political scientist Jonathan Kirshner, who expresses no doubt about the prospect of "dollar diminution."[4] Over the coming years, he confidently declares, "the dollar's international role is likely to come under pressure." Most sensationalist is James Rickards, an investment manager and former government official, who shrilly predicts the imminent demise of the dollar and with it the collapse of the international monetary system. "Threats to the dollar are ubiquitous," Rickards writes.[5] "It is too late to save the dollar."

Yet America's currency continues to prevail. The greenback remains the only truly global money, the one major pole in the system. Not even the gale-force winds of the recent crisis seemed able to topple the dollar from its perch at the peak of the Currency Pyramid. Indeed, if anything the greenback's predominance appears to have been reinforced. Observes Eric Helleiner: "In the wake of the crisis, the dollar quickly faced new challenges. . . . [Yet] the dollar's status as the world's dominant currency emerged remarkably unscathed."[6] Forecasts about the greenback's perils, like reports of Mark Twain's death, appear to be greatly exaggerated. The power of the dollar remains undiminished.

What explains the dollar's endurance? The aim of this chapter is to explain why, despite decades of doubts, the greenback remains the world's top currency—and more importantly, why it is likely remain on top for years to come. Back when she was secretary of state under President Bill Clinton, Madeleine Albright liked to describe the United States as the "indispensable nation." This chapter argues, similarly, that there is cause to believe that the dollar is the *indispensable currency*: the one money that the world cannot do without. In John Williamson's words: "The dollar is unrivaled."[7] The greenback offers unique advantages as an international store of value. No other currency can match its appeal as an investment medium or reserve asset, the two roles that matter the most in geopolitical terms.

We begin with the doubts. Over the years, many adverse factors have been cited by dollar pessimists—including, most prominently, America's persistent payments deficits and mounting external debt. Surely, it could be reasonably argued, it must be just a matter of time until a tipping point will be reached in the greenback's life cycle as an international currency. The virtuous circle supporting the dollar's global standing will give way to a vicious circle of self-reinforcing decline. But so far at least, the tipping point has never managed to arrive. This chapter will explain why. Dollar pessimism, I submit, is by no means unwarranted, but it misses a good part of the story. The greenback also benefits from multiple strengths that sustain its international appeal. First and foremost is the advanced level of financial development in the United States. The appeal of the US capital market is an indisputable source of power for the dollar. In addition, America still offers broad network externalities in trade, a wide range of political ties, and unsurpassed military reach—the complete package needed to gain and hold top currency status. There simply is no credible alternative.

Doubts

Why have so many, for so long, expressed doubts about the dollar? The reasons are myriad but boil down to one basic concern: America's ever-expanding overhang of foreign liabilities. Will the United States be able to honor its financial commitments? Dollar pessimists divide broadly into two groups. On the one side are those who put the onus of responsibility on America's creditors—skittish investors and risk-averse central bankers who, at any moment, might suddenly opt to flee from the dollar, precipitating an irreversible downward spiral. On the other side are those who are inclined more to blame America itself for policies that have allowed the threat to grow so ominous. The United States, it is said, has abused its exorbitant privilege, putting at risk the value and ultimately the usability of its currency.

Gold-exchange Standard

Fears of a run on the dollar first emerged in the 1960s, when the greenback was still formally convertible into gold. In the monetary regime that was so carefully constructed at Bretton Woods in 1944, America's national currency was expected to be the primary component of international liquidity. Formally, the system was a gold-exchange standard. Although gold was to be at the core of the regime, a limited supply of the precious metal would be supplemented by a paper currency, the greenback, on the condition that the currency could be readily exchanged for gold upon demand. To sustain confidence in the dollar, America's so-called gold window would be open to any foreign central bank that wished to exchange its greenbacks for ingots.

For a while, the system worked well. Throughout most of the 1950s, the US balance of payments was in modest overall deficit (as measured at the time). But those deficits were greeted as a welcome relief from a postwar "dollar shortage." Surplus nations could rebuild reserves that had been depleted by the exigencies of the Great Depression and World War II. The imbalances of the period were rightfully termed a "beneficial disequilibrium."[8] By the end of the decade, however, America's deficits were ballooning, and perceptions of a dollar shortage were quickly replaced by worries over a growing "dollar glut."

The earliest warnings came from Triffin in his classic book *Gold and the Dollar Crisis*.[9] Negotiators at Bretton Woods, he argued, had been too complacent about the gold-exchange standard. In fact, as he sagely pointed out, the regime was fatally flawed because it was based on an illusion—an unquestioned faith that its fiduciary element, the dollar, would always be convertible into gold at a fixed price. The system relied on US deficits to avert a world liquidity shortage. But those deficits, by adding to the swelling total of US liabilities, seemed bound in time to undermine confidence in the greenback's continued convertibility. In effect, governments were caught on the horns of a dilemma—what came to be known as the Triffin Dilemma. To forestall a flight from the dollar, US deficits would have to cease. But that would confront policy makers with a liquidity problem. To forestall the liquidity problem, US deficits would have to continue. But that would confront policy makers with a confidence problem. The quandary was real. Governments could not have their cake and eat it, too.

Throughout the 1960s, monetary authorities struggled to cope with the Triffin Dilemma. On the one hand, a variety of ad hoc measures were implemented to help alleviate pressures on the dollar, including a network of reciprocal short-term credit facilities, known as "swaps," between the Federal Reserve and other central banks, as well as restraints on capital outflows from the United States. On the other hand, negotiations were undertaken to establish a substitute source of liquidity growth in order to reduce reliance on dollar deficits in the future. The result was creation of the IMF's Special Drawing Rights, an entirely new type of world reserve asset. In the end, however, all these efforts proved futile. Confronted with accelerating demands on America's rapidly dwindling gold reserves, the Nixon administration in August 1971 dramatically closed the gold window. The gold-exchange standard passed into history.[10]

Storm Clouds

The dollar's troubles, however, persisted. Closing the gold window did provide some temporary relief, by taking pressure off the US gold stock. But it could not take pressure off the dollar itself—at least not so long as external debt continued to grow. The only difference was how a flight from the dollar might now manifest itself. Under the gold-exchange standard, crisis meant an increased demand for America's gold, threatening a depreciation of the greenback in terms of the yellow metal. With gold convertibility ended, crisis would instead take the form of an increased demand for foreign currencies, threatening a depreciation of the greenback in exchange markets. At any time, sentiment among America's creditors might shift. Dollar accumulations could turn into dollar sales, and modest decline could turn into a calamitous rout. Since 1971, the United States has had to live with the ever-present risk of a collapse of the dollar's exchange rate.

Indeed, as time has passed, storm clouds seemingly have only grown darker as America's debts continue to mount. Earlier, though the overall balance of payments (as formally measured) had been in deficit, the country's current account had recorded persistent surpluses, reinforcing America's position as the world's biggest net creditor. In the aggregate, the nation's claims abroad (including private-sector investments as well government assets) far exceeded foreign liabilities. As late as 1980, the US net international investment position was still a positive $360 billion. But starting in the 1970s, America's current account turned negative, gradually adding to net external debt. In 1986, the balance of international indebtedness turned negative for the first time in the post-World War II period by a modest $27 billion, and has worsened ever since. By 2000 net debt had passed $1.3 trillion. By 2013, it had reached $4.5 trillion. Who could be blamed for worrying about where all this might lead?

The situation is clearly unprecedented. For the first time in history, the world's greatest monetary power is also the world's biggest debtor. A run on the dollar, should it occur, would force the Federal Reserve to hike interest rates sharply, which might destabilize financial markets around the globe. The greenback is the linchpin of the system. Bond prices could collapse, exposing hidden weaknesses among banks and other financial institutions. Worse, real economic growth could be stalled as monetary conditions tighten. To compensate for the depreciation of their dollar revenues, foreign governments might feel compelled to resort to protectionist import barriers, capital controls, or even debt default. At a minimum, we might find ourselves mired in a morass of stagnation and inflation. At worst, events could conspire to make the Great Depression of the 1930s look like a genteel garden party.

Risks can be exaggerated, of course. In the most recent period, current-account deficits have been on a steep downward trend, from as high as $800 billion in 2006 (the equivalent of 6.2 percent of GDP) to half that amount in 2013 (equal to just 2.4 percent of GDP). And a net debt of $4.5 trillion, while hardly trivial, is still only the equivalent of a little more than a quarter of US GDP. In gross terms, the United States holds some $22 trillion of claims on the outside world—by far, an amount of overseas wealth far greater than that of any other nation. There is still a lot of money in the till to reassure nervous creditors.

But neither can the risks be denied. Voices expressing concern have only grown louder as the years go by. Typical is Kirshner, who contends that "cracks are increasingly visible. . . . There is no good reason to believe that the US can sustain ever-widening deficits indefinitely. . . . If there was a spark, somewhere . . . a tidal wave of dollars could flood the market."[11] Echoes Alan Wheatley, an economic commentator: "How much more debt can the US accrue without undermining . . . the very confidence in the dollar that makes those securities so appealing in the first place?"[12] During his tenure as chairman of the Joint Chiefs of Staff, Admiral Mike Mullen repeatedly said that America's looming foreign debt was the greatest threat to the country's national security. Fears of a dollar collapse are clearly not going away. The respite enjoyed by the greenback in the aftermath of the 2008 financial crisis is seen as no more than a temporary reprieve. Over the longer term, the forecast is for more stormy weather ahead.

US Policy

The question, of course, is what can be done—if anything—to avert a damaging collapse. For many dollar pessimists, the onus falls squarely on the United States. That is said to be where the real problem lies. In effect, America for decades has been living beyond its means, relying too heavily on its undoubted power to delay. The fault arguably lies with US policy makers, who have exploited the borrowing capacity afforded by the greenback's worldwide acceptability to postpone adjustments indefinitely. As Eichengreen puts it, "the plausible scenario for a dollar crash is not one in which confidence collapses on the whims of investors . . . but rather because of problems with America's own economic policies."[13] The fate of the dollar rests on what happens in Washington, not elsewhere.

What should Washington do? It does not take a Nobel Prize econo-mist to think of suitable remedies. The place to begin is with broad fiscal policy. Nothing would reassure outsiders more than a determined effort to get the government's budget deficits under lasting control. Recent years have seen a dramatic drop in the federal deficit, from above $1.4 trillion in 2009 to under $500 billion in 2014. But few doubt that the deficit will soon begin to grow again under the pressure of rising costs for entitlement programs like Social Security (old-age pensions) and health care. Coping with that grim prospect would not be impossible. It was done once before, after all. That was in the 1990s, during the Clinton administration, when for a time determined tax increases and spending controls produced what Alan Greenspan, then chief of the Federal Reserve, described as "surpluses as far as the eye can see." As a practical matter, it could surely be done again. In addition, more precisely targeted export promotion measures could be strengthened to help accelerate the recent decline of the nation's current-account deficit, thus slowing the growth of foreign debt; and re-cent financial regulatory reforms could be reinforced to sustain confidence in US capital-market institutions. In principle, we know what to do.

The problem, however, is getting from Here to There: gaining the req-uisite political consensus to put needed remedies in place. That is obvi-ously easier said than done. In the current climate in Washington, action is stymied by a deep polarization of politics. Republicans and Democrats today find it difficult to agree even on something as simple as the weather, let alone how to reform the budget or manage the balance of payments. More fundamentally, across the country, the necessary motivation seems to be lacking. Most Americans appear to share the cynical view of John Connally who, shortly after taking office in 1971 as Richard Nixon's secretary of the treasury, told a group of European finance officials that the dollar "is our currency, but your problem."

After decades of dollar supremacy, dollar pessimists suggest, the United States has come to take its exorbitant privilege for granted. Seem-ingly, policy autonomy is now assumed to be something of a birthright. Only rarely do politicians or voters ever pay attention to the external accounts when thinking about fiscal or monetary policy. As David Calleo has ruefully commented, "Americans, it appears, have grown deeply ha-bituated to our exorbitant postwar privileges. . . . Instead of consuming less and exporting more, we prefer exporting more dollars."[14] Old habits are hard to break.

In effect, therefore, the United States appears to have fallen victim to Gallarotti's "power curse," underestimating accumulating vulnerabilities. We are reminded of an old adage about a frog thrown into a pot of water. If the water is boiling the frog can be expected to jump back out again, the equivalent of responding to an urgent crisis. But if the fire under the pot is turned up only incrementally—the equivalent of a gradually growing dollar overhang—the frog is more likely just to sit there until it is boiled to death. For dollar pessimists, the real danger is what used to be called "benign neglect"—essentially, a policy of inaction that simply allows storm clouds to continue to gather. No one has articulated the threat better than Jacob Frenkel, former head of the Bank of Israel, who has long despaired of Washington's approach. "I am concerned with the U.S. current-account deficit," he said in 2005, "not because it cannot be dealt with but because of the way it is not being dealt with."[15] A decade later the risk is still not being dealt with.

STORE OF VALUE

Dollar pessimism is plainly not without foundation. The likes of Mike Mullen and Jacob Frenkel cannot be accused of thoughtless hysteria. Yet after more than half a century of repeated alarms about the impending demise of the dollar, we might be justified in asking why the greenback is still out there, alive and kicking. Dollar pessimists, it turns out, are like members of one of those cults that predict the end of the world at noon tomorrow. How do we explain, the day after, why we are all still here?

At its most fundamental, the question is: Why, despite America's ever-growing debt, do outsiders continue to invest in the dollar? The answer lies, above all, in the greenback's unique advantages as an international store of value. There may be risk, but there is also great reward. The United States offers an extraordinarily well-developed set of financial markets, promising unparalleled liquidity and safety. There is no seriously competitive alternative for investors or central banks. The dollar truly is, echoing Madeleine Albright, the world's indispensable currency.

Attractions

The attractions of America's financial sector are unmistakable. Institutionalized exchanges are available not only for conventional stocks and bonds but also for swaps, options, forward and futures contracts, derivatives, and all sorts of other exotic financial instruments. Markets are broad, deep, and resilient and open to all. The range of services is wide, transactions costs are low, and property rights are well protected. Outsiders, whether private investors or public agencies, know that they can count on an exceptionally high degree of exchange convenience and capital certainty when they do business in dollar-denominated claims.

Some other countries also offer many of these same attractions, but by no means on the same scale. The euro zone, combining the financial sectors of all its members, was initially expected to pose a serious competitive challenge to the dollar. But, as indicated, its early promise has remained largely unrealized, and after a fast early start has even regressed under the pressure of Europe's sovereign debt crisis. Since the global crisis exploded in 2008, European banking and capital markets have actually fragmented, with many financial sectors retreating once again behind national frontiers. Any claim to breadth or depth has been lost. Elsewhere, such as in London or Switzerland, markets are efficient but in no way able to offer the range of investment opportunities available in the United States. Neither the British nor the Swiss can provide financial assets in the volume required by the global system. Japan's capital market is large but even after the Big Bang reforms of the 1990s remains uncompetitive with America or Europe. And China, of course, is still only at the earliest stage of financial development.

In reality, the US financial sector stands alone, at the strategic center of the global network of currency and capital markets. As one source puts it, America "has come to function as a sort of central processing core through which funds are routed."[16] In a careful analysis of links in the international financial system, Thomas Oatley and colleagues find that while most countries are strongly connected to the United States, direct ties to nodes elsewhere are much weaker.[17] The structure is clearly hierarchical and, in the absence of suitable alternatives, unavoidably dependent on America's markets. If something like the US financial sector did not exist, it would have to be invented.

Whatever the risks of America's looming debt, therefore, there are compensating advantages for outsiders to sustain the greenback's appeal. The evidence can be easily seen in the ample seigniorage that the United States is still able to enjoy at the expense of the rest of the world. As noted back in chapter 1, foreign accumulations of dollar-denominated claims appears to generate a substantial interest-rate subsidy for Americans, whether measured by the saving on borrowing costs or by the difference between net rates of return on inward and outward investments. In effect, outsiders collectively seem prepared to pay a considerable price for their right to make use of the greenback. One source refers to this as a kind of "saver's curse" in international finance.[18]

Is it rational for outsiders to tolerate the saver's curse? In terms of economic theory, the outcome would not seem unreasonable. In effect, the price reflects an implicit trade-off—a "liquidity premium" paid in return for the dollar's promise of operational and valuation efficiency.[19] Particularly relevant is the market for US government debt, which includes everything from three-month Treasury bills to much longer-term notes and bonds along with so-called agency securities—bonds issued by quasi-governmental agencies like the Federal Home Loan Mortgage Corporation ("Freddie Mac") and Federal National Mortgage Association ("Fannie Mae"). Federal debt is a popular investment medium for private actors around the globe; it is also the principal form in which central banks hold their dollar reserves. Overall, Treasury obligations and agency securities in general circulation exceed $8 trillion. With a turnover of some $500 billion daily, the government debt market offers a degree of liquidity that is difficult to match. Nothing in the world comes close to the US Treasury bill—commonly referred to simply as the T-bill—for transactional ease or assurance of value.

In political terms, an additional consideration is safety—a trade-off for the promise of a safe haven for investments or reserves; in other words, a "security premium." For many analysts today, the single most important role that an international currency can play is that of a safe haven: providing a range of assets that is as free of risk as possible. Properly understood, insists one commentary, the essential feature of a dominant money is that it "delivers a secure financial asset that facilitates the functioning of financial markets."[20] Much has been written lately about the dangers of a growing shortage of high-quality claims around the world, relative to demand.[21] Since the start of the global financial crisis, a consensus has coalesced around the view that the United States is presently the only source capable of supplying safe and liquid investment-grade assets on anything like the scale required. "There are now few genuinely safe assets," declares a prominent British journalist.[22] In the absence of alternatives, he says, the greenback "has become ultra-attractive because of bountiful supply." More bluntly, in the words of a New York investment strategist, "When people are worried, all roads lead to Treasuries."[23]

Nothing better illustrates the point than the global response to the bursting of the US real-estate bubble in 2007 and the grinding financial crisis that ensued. No one doubted that the epicenter of the crisis was the United States; America could be fairly blamed for the near-collapse of the global economy. Yet remarkably, as events unfolded, a tidal wave of capital flowed into US markets, not outward as might have been expected. In the last three months of 2008 alone, at the height of the crisis, net purchases of US assets topped half a trillion dollars—three times what had come in during the preceding nine months. The greenback appreciated rather than depreciated, and the T-bill market stood out as one of the few financial sectors anywhere able to remain liquid and to continue operating smoothly. Even when Standard and Poor's, a leading credit rating agency, downgraded its rating of Treasury securities in mid-summer 2011 following a brief shut-down of the government, outsiders continued to acquire dollars. The shutdown was triggered by a standoff between President Barack Obama and congressional Republicans over a proposed increase of the legal ceiling on US public debt.

Some of the buildup of dollar claims, we know, reflected the fact that many foreign banks and institutional investors needed greenbacks to cover their funding needs at a time when interbank and other wholesale short-term markets had suddenly frozen tight. Here the Federal Reserve played a vital role, from December 2007 onward, in effect stepping in as a global lender of last resort. Dramatically, new dollar swaps were quickly arranged with some fourteen foreign central banks. In return for reciprocal currency pledges, the Fed supplied greenbacks that could then be lent onward by each central bank to its dollar-hungry constituents. At their peak, in December 2008, credits outstanding under these arrangements totaled $580 billion. In addition, more quietly, some $500 billion or more was additionally provided under a variety of programs in direct support of private banks abroad. One source has described the Fed's operations as "the biggest United States government bailout that most people do not know anything about."[24] There is little doubt that the global crisis would have been a lot worse had America's central bank not risen to the occasion.

But funding need was hardly the only reason why outsiders piled into the dollar on such a large scale. It was also evident that much of the demand for greenbacks could be attributed to sheer fear. Who knew how bad things might get? As Helleiner summarizes, "investors also perceived the dollar to be a safe haven currency because it was backed by the world's dominant power."[25]

A Dollar Trap?

As a practical matter neither trade-off, whether for liquidity or security, seems irrational. Indeed, in an uncertain world both would seem inevitable—a kind of unspoken bargain with benefits for each side. In the absence of a global money, some national currency or currencies must be available to function as an international store of value. Where would investors and central banks look if the dollar were not there to offer an adequate degree of convenience and safety?

Not everyone agrees, however. For many, the bargain is unbalanced and perhaps even pernicious. Representative is Eswar Prasad, a former IMF economist, who in a recent book described the bargain as little more than a "con game."[26] The title of his book, *The Dollar Trap*, says it all. Like a good number of other observers,[27] he is persuaded that America's creditors are caught in a "dollar trap."

Of course, Prasad recognizes the greenback's unique advantages, particularly for international investors. The dollar is the world's "foremost store of value," he acknowledges. "Financial assets denominated in U.S. dollars, especially U.S. government securities, are still the preferred destination for investors interested in the safekeeping of their investments."[28] Moreover, he joins the consensus view that a growing shortage of high-quality claims is leaving market actors with few alternatives. "After the crisis, the price of safety has gone up in tandem with the higher demand and lower supply of safe assets."[29] But for him the price is simply too high—a snare for the unwary.

Why? In Prasad's view, there is little doubt that over time the value of the greenback must fall. "Fundamental forces," he contends, "point to a long-term depreciation of the dollar."[30] Echoing dollar pessimists going as far back as Triffin and Kindleberger, Prasad is persuaded that the day will come when the United States will no longer feel able to honor its commitments. In anticipation, he suggests, US policy makers will be sorely tempted to try to inflate their way out of their troubles. Politics might lead them to promote price increases at home in order to drive down the greenback in exchange markets and hence reduce the burden of debt abroad. In his words, it would be "a tempting proposition for the U.S. to cut its debt obligations simply by printing more dollars, thus reducing the value of that debt and implicitly reneging on part of the obligations to its foreign investors."[31] It is all, therefore, a "trillion dollar con game." Foreign investors and central banks are lured into buying US claims and then will be taken to the cleaners.

Prasad's fears cannot be dismissed out of hand. Indeed, they are shared by many. Illustrative is the oft-cited response of Luo Ping, a senior Chinese official, when asked back in 2009 whether China would continue to buy US Treasury bonds. "We hate you guys," he said. "Except for Treasuries, what can you hold? . . . US Treasuries are the safe haven. For everyone, including China, it is the only option. . . . Once you start issuing $1 trillion–$2 trillion . . . we know the dollar is going to depreciate, so we hate you guys but there is nothing much we can do."[32] Outsiders may appreciate the attractions of a dollar-based system, but that does not mean that they must like it. The late Ronald McKinnon was not far off when he called it the "unloved dollar standard."[33]

But is the bargain really so unlovable? Prasad paints a picture here that is surely a sensationalist worst-case scenario. It is true that an inflation-induced depreciation of the greenback is possible. Debtor default is a risk in any financial market, and the United States clearly does have the means to erode the dollar's value. But there is also good cause to doubt that US policy makers would ever be seriously tempted to make use of its capacity for mischief. This is a stark illustration of the potential power problem discussed back in chapter 2. Basic force is one thing; force activation, quite another. Prasad's script may be regarded as implausible for two reasons.

In the first place, there is the issue of domestic politics. Admittedly, the Federal Reserve, which is responsible for money creation, is among the most independent of central banks; political imperatives are unlikely to predominate in its decisions. But neither are politics ever apt to be entirely absent from its deliberations. Realistically speaking, any attempt to turn up the printing presses at the expense of creditors abroad could be expected to run into stiff resistance from key constituencies at home—particularly, large institutional investors. As Prasad himself admits, "the profile of domestic holders of U.S. Treasury debt renders it politically difficult to use inflation to pay down the debt. High inflation would not be politically acceptable in the U.S."[34]

Second, we need to keep broader geopolitical considerations in mind. US policy makers are not unaware of the largely positive impact of the dollar's international standing on American state power. Betraying foreign creditors would come at a high cost, surely eroding if not destroying the country's ability to run "deficits without tears" in the future. Could Washington really be expected to risk jeopardizing its ability to project authority abroad?

Moreover, to label the risk of depreciation a "con game" is to fundamentally misrepresent the nature of creditor-debtor relationships of any kind. All lending, ultimately, can be understood as an act of faith—an expression of trust in the good intentions of the borrower. Time consistency problems can surely arise: changing circumstances might drive debtors to seek relief in some form. But that does not mean that such relationships should therefore be seen as little more than a trap for creditors. Confidence is central to the story, but that does not make it a con.

OTHER STRENGTHS

America's advanced level of financial development clearly promotes the international standing of the dollar, particularly in the currency's role as an investment medium or reserve asset. But that is not the only power resource that helps to keep the greenback competitive. Additional support comes from America's still broad network externalities in trade, wide range of political ties, and vast military reach. The dollar is backed by the complete package of factors that would appear to be associated with top currency status. No other money can say the same.

Trade

Everyone knows that the United States is no longer quite the export powerhouse that it once was. For much of the twentieth century, America was by far the world's leading exporter. Even as late as the 1990s, one-eighth of all traded goods came from the United States. But since the start of the new millennium America's share of global exports has dropped by nearly a third, from above 12 percent to under 8.5 percent. Much of the decline appears to be related to the falling share of the United States in total world output.[35] In nominal terms, US GDP has trended downward from a peak above 32 percent of world output in 2001 to under 24 percent more recently. Recalculated on a purchasing power parity basis, the drop has been from 23 percent to 19 percent. The biggest gainer has of course been China, which is now the world's top exporter with a global share above 12 percent. China's GDP is expected to surpass America's within the next decade.

Yet for all that, the gravitational pull of the US economy remains exceptionally strong, still offering broad network externalities. Most informed observers agree that America's longer-term growth prospects are still bright, powered inter alia by a dynamic high-tech sector, relatively favorable demographics, a sophisticated financial sector, and flexible labor markets. Particularly influential is the energy revolution that has spread across the country as a result of the development of new methods for extracting oil and natural gas from previously inaccessible sites (hydraulic fracturing—for short, "fracking"). In just a few years, the United States has emerged as the world's largest energy producer—bigger even than Russia or Saudi Arabia—pumping massive amounts of dependable and low-cost fuel to US industry. By 2020 the economy is expected to be fully energy independent. Joel Kurtzman, a former *New York Times* business editor, lists the energy revolution as one of four major "forces" that can be counted upon to sustain American economic leadership for a long time to come.[36] The others are high levels of creativity, "gigantic" amounts of capital, and unrivaled manufacturing depth. Decades ago, US publisher Henry Luce dubbed the twentieth century the "American Century." Kurtzman is by no means alone in predicting that the present era could be remembered as the "Second American Century."

In fact, the evidence of America's staying power is impressive. As of this writing (early 2015), the greenback was trading at a four-year high, propelled upward by renewed confidence in the country's economic promise. "The increasing push by investors into the dollar," said the *New York Times*, "can be seen as a favorable report card on the United States economy, highlighting good performance in crucial benchmarks such as growth and fiscal responsibility, and an increasingly competitive position abroad because of a boom in energy exports."[37]

Once again we see the limitations of focusing too heavily on GDP as a measure of state capability in the tradition of the old-fashioned elements-of-power approach. The share of world output originating within the borders of the United States may have declined. But that fails to take into account many other critical vital signs—in particular, the share of output accounted for by US multinational corporations *outside* America's frontiers. As many knowledgeable observers have emphasized, GDP alone is no longer an especially accurate gauge of America's global economic weight.[38] A large part of the production of US companies now originates abroad via myriad foreign branches and subsidiaries. As many as 25,000 American-controlled enterprises are dispersed around the world, with sales amounting to more than three times the size of US exports.

In effect, American enterprises sit at the center of a global transactional network defined by complex supply chains and direct investment flows, greatly expanding the US economy's effective reach. No other country comes close to matching the scale of America's far-flung corporate domain. According to Sean Starrs, American companies dominate in as many as 18 of 25 broad sectors of the world economy.[39] "We live in an age of globalization," he declares. "But we also continue to live in an age of American economic dominance. . . . American economic power has not declined—it has globalized."[40] One source refers to this as America's "command capacity."[41] A more familiar term would be structural power. The United States continues to enjoy enormous influence as a result of its central position in the structure of world trade.

The most direct effect of this dimension of US power is of course on the dollar's role in import and export markets. That is suggested by the analysis in chapter 5. No other international currency function is as impacted by the size of a transactional network. So what does the future hold? If the gravitational pull of America's economy, however impressive, is weakening in relative terms, should the greenback's trade role be expected to wither away as well?

Dollar pessimists think so. As Eichengreen puts it: "It is not obvious why the dollar, the currency of an economy that no longer accounts for a majority of the world's industrial production, should be used to invoice and settle a majority of the world's international transactions."[42] And indeed, the logic of that view is unassailable. We know that roughly half of all world exports today are invoiced and settled in greenbacks—some two to three times the share of the euro, the next most widely used trading currency. It is not at all unreasonable to suspect that, in time, all that could change. Assuming continued growth in China and other emerging market economies, the dollar's structural dominance in trade will almost certainly be eroded. Prasad may be unduly skeptical concerning the greenback's future as a store of value. But he is undoubtedly right when he suggests that "the dollar is likely to become less important as a medium of exchange for intermediating international transactions."[43] Likewise, as the markets for other currencies expand, there will be less need to rely on the greenback as a vehicle for wholesale business in the global exchange market. More trading and hedging of foreign-exchange risk might be done directly in bilateral currency pairs that exclude the dollar.

However, the logic of dollar pessimists must also be qualified. Change may well come, but at worst it can be expected to be rather marginal and gradual in nature. The reason is the inertia caused by incumbency. As emphasized previously, international currency use is highly path dependent. Once a money becomes established, as the former chief of Britain's Financial Services Authority has ruefully noted, "you are embedded in a lot of contracts all over the world. It is very difficult for this suddenly to flip."[44] Network externalities are especially critical in trade markets. There is bound to be much hesitation while each market actor waits to see what other participants decide to do—particularly in global markets for reference-priced and organized exchange-traded commodities, where the greenback is still the universal currency of choice. If there is to be a shrinkage in the dollar's trade role, it is unlikely to be either sizable or swift.

In any event, shrinkage of the role would have only a limited impact on the United States in geopolitical terms. That is suggested by the analysis in chapter 4. The main effects of a trade role tend to be economic rather than political. If the greenback is used less for invoicing or as a vehicle currency, there could be some increase of transactions costs for Americans or a loss of denomination rents. But impacts on America's policy autonomy or influence would be minimal. For a money just beginning to move up the Currency Pyramid, the trade role is important for its potential influence on central-bank preferences. But that is hardly a concern for the dollar, which is already the preferred reserve medium for most of the world. Even if there is some switching away from greenback in export or exchange markets, US currency power would not be seriously threatened.

Political Factors

Finally, we must also acknowledge America's unparalleled advantages in terms of foreign-policy ties and military reach. Ever since World War II, the United States has been acknowledged as the world's most powerful nation. During the Cold War, America was the "leader of the Free World." After the breakup of the Soviet Union, the country was relabeled "the world's last superpower." French commentators spoke of US *hyperpuissance* (hyperpower). Madeleine Albright came up with the term "indispensable nation." Even today the United States has more formal or informal alliance relationships around the globe than any other nation. The US military has as many as 900 bases or installations in some 130 countries. Washington's defense budget accounts for close to half of all arms spending in the world.

Among IR scholars, a lively debate rages over whether American geopolitical supremacy is in decline. For some, the rise of China and other regional powers, as well as the revival of Vladimir Putin's Russia, inevitably spells the end of US primacy in the global order. Declares the noted historian Paul Kennedy, "the United States is slowly and naturally losing its abnormal status in the international system and returning to being one of the most prominent players in the small club of great powers."[45] Similarly, the foreign policy specialist Leslie Gelb concludes that "the United States is declining as a nation and a world power."[46] But others disagree, insisting that "declinists" are simply too gloomy. Declinists discount America's deep underlying strengths, both economic and political. Representative of this alternative perspective is Robert Lieber, who stresses above all America's remarkable ability to change and innovate, especially in response to crisis. "A fundamental characteristic of the United States," he writes, is "its unique flexibility and adaptability. . . . It is this capacity that provides a basis for optimism in assessing America's future."[47] Carla Norrlof, on a parallel track, emphasizes the synergies that derive from America's many power resources:

While the United States certainly does face a number of challenges, an analysis of the linkages between trade, money, and security shows that American power is robust. . . . The size of the American market, the role of the dollar, and American military power interact to . . . buffer the United States from the extreme consequences that a sustained deficit policy would otherwise have.[48]

At some point, of course, the declinists will undoubtedly be vindicated. No superpower has remained on top forever. In the long run US geopolitical dominance is bound to fade. The system built on America's extensive alliance networks and capacity for power projection will be replaced by something else and history will move on. But as John Maynard Keynes famously reminded us, in the long run we are all dead. Over a shorter time horizon more relevant to decision makers, measured in years or decades rather than generations, it is a good bet that US primacy will endure, if only because the margin of superiority is still so great. As Stephen Brooks and Willam Wohlforth observe: "No system of sovereign states has ever contained one state with comparable material preponderance."[49] For the foreseeable future, we can safely assume that the United States will remain number one in geopolitical terms.

In turn, that suggests a still bright future for the dollar as well. Preservation of America's widespread political ties around the globe will certainly encourage continued allegiance to the greenback by allies and other friendly governments. This will be especially so for smaller states with a more clientilistic relationship with Washington. Likewise, preservation of America's extensive military reach should help sustain the dollar's appeal as a safe haven. These factors too must be regarded as key power resources backing the greenback's still elevated standing.

A Negotiated Currency?

Given all these strengths—financial development, network externalities, foreign-policy ties, and military reach—it should be no surprise that the dollar still clings to its perch at the peak of the Currency Pyramid. Without these power resources behind it, the greenback would surely be far less competitive in the Darwinian struggle for market share. But is that the whole story? Is the dollar's dominance due entirely to the preferences of currency users? Or do the policies of the US government also play a role in sustaining the greenback's appeal? Put differently, is the dollar's endurance demand driven or is it the result of deliberate influence attempts by its supplier?

The issue, once more, may be expressed in terms of Strange's distinction between a top currency and a negotiated currency. For all intents and purposes, the dollar would appear to be a genuine top currency, popular because of America's inherent economic and political qualities. But yet again, not everyone agrees. For many, the greenback seems to endure only because of determined efforts by US policy makers to sustain and promote its use. The perception is widespread. Increasingly, it is said, the dollar is becoming a negotiated currency, more and more dependent on inducements from Washington—in effect, slipping inexorably from top standing to one or two rungs down in the Currency Pyramid. "Questions about the role of foreign political support in sustaining the dollar's international position have grown," notes Helleiner, suggesting that the greenback can by now be considered to have at least "partial negotiated status."[50] Financial elites in key emerging market economies seem overwhelmingly persuaded that "the dollar is increasingly sliding from top to negotiated international currency."[51]

Is that perception accurate? Recall that, broadly speaking, two classes of strategy are available to a government in this context—proactive policies that may be either *informal* or *formal* (chapter 5). An informal strategy aims to enhance the market appeal of a currency, targeting all users whether at the private or official level. The idea would be to encourage demand for the dollar by explicitly *catering* to the preferences of outsiders. A formal strategy, by contrast, is aimed at governments and would rely more on traditional instruments of statecraft—carrots and sticks—to *alter* existing preferences in favor of the dollar. Is there evidence that either type of strategy is actually being applied by Washington?

The answer is No. Certainly there seems to be no informal strategy at work to burnish the greenback brand. No nation wishing to promote or sustain demand for its currency would abuse its exorbitant privilege as much as has the United States. I have already indicated some of the actions that US policy makers might take to avoid abandonment of the dollar—including deficit reduction, export promotion, and reinforced financial regulatory reform. And surely more could be done to overcome the dysfunctional polarization of politics in Washington that has already led to one downgrade of America's credit rating and could lead to more. Yet little has actually been accomplished. The American political system does not appear to treat the reputation of the dollar as a high priority.

Nor does there appear to be much evidence of a more formal strategy to defend the greenback. Indeed, if anything, the trend seems to be the other way—away from, not toward, overt currency interventions. Back in the era of the gold-exchange standard, the first face of power was clearly visible. Washington rarely hesitated to make use of its ample political resources to twist the arms of allies or client states on the dollar's behalf. Francis Gavin has exhaustively documented the extent to which Washington actively manipulated its military deployments and defense commitments to convince other governments to help support the greenback, gaining commitments not to convert new dollar accumulations to gold.[52] The exercise of leverage was most obvious in West Germany and Japan, the two biggest dollar holders at the time. Eager to remain sheltered under the US security umbrella, both were vulnerable to coercion from their friends on the Potomac. In one famous incident, in 1967, West Germany's Bundesbank was persuaded to submit a formal letter to its American counterpart, the Federal Reserve, officially pledging not to seek conversion of any portion of the Federal Republic's dollar reserves. Although in fact the so-called Blessing letter—named after Karl Blessing, Bundesbank president at the time—merely confirmed a policy that had already been in force for years, the pressure from Washington was deeply resented.[53]

Likewise, less than a decade later, following the first global oil shock in 1973, Washington moved quickly to exploit its military reach to persuade Saudi Arabia to avoid any actions that might trigger a flight from the dollar. As the biggest oil exporter in the world, Saudi Arabia might have been tempted to use its newfound riches as an instrument of linkage to pressure the United States on Middle Eastern political issues. In principle, the threat of a "money weapon" seemed plausible. At the time, the Saudis were thought to account for as much as one-half to three-quarters of all Arab holdings of greenbacks.[54] In practice, however, accommodations were quickly found. In return for crucial concessions from Washington—including, in particular, informal security guarantees against possible threats from enemies within or without—the Saudis gave assurances of continued support for the greenback. The Kingdom was promised top-secret confidentiality for its holdings and was even provided a separate "add-on" facility to handle its purchases of Treasury securities outside the normal auction process.[55]

By contrast, in the most recent period one searches in vain for any comparable example. As Helleiner concedes, "scholars have produced little evidence so far of any explicit deals between the US and dollar supporting countries."[56] Benign neglect appears to prevail. Of course, Helleiner quickly adds, "this is not to say that implicit understandings are not in play."[57] He cites, for instance, the heavy reliance of large dollar holders like Japan and South Korea on the US market for their exports. Their loyalty to the greenback, he suggests, may be a quid pro quo for Washington's commitment to keep its market open to their products. But is that "negotiation," or is it simply confirmation of the structural power that the United States enjoys as a result of its still massive GDP? In reality, there seem to be no influence attempts at all. The perception that the greenback is becoming a negotiated currency may be widespread, but it is not supported by the available evidence.

DOWNSIDES

In short, to paraphrase a one-time advertising slogan for a US investment firm, the dollar has sustained its dominance the old-fashioned way: it has *earned* it. Despite anxieties about a looming foreign debt, the greenback has held its top market share due to America's many underlying strengths. The causal arrow running from state power to currency choice has clearly worked to the dollar's advantage. But what about the casual arrow that runs the other way, from currency choice to state power? Does the greenback's endurance necessarily work to America's advantage?

For many, there is no question. A popular currency must add to the power of the state that issues it. That is the conventional wisdom that we explored back in chapter 4. But as that chapter demonstrated, currency internationalization is better understood as a double-edged sword that can cut either way. High standing in the Currency Pyramid is no guarantee of net gain for the issuer. Just ask any Briton who lived through sterling's long and painful decline after World War II.

For the United States today, of course, we know there are substantial benefits. Apart from denomination rents and reduced transactions costs, these include a substantial amount of seigniorage and the exorbitant privilege of macroeconomic flexibility as well as added capacity for direct leverage (a form of hard power) and a fillip to America's reputation as a great nation (a form of soft power). Though difficult to measure empirically, these are all clearly upsides from the US point of view. But it is evident that there are downsides as well—limits to the exercise of American power—which ought not to be ignored. At least five costs or risks can be identified.

First, and most obvious, is the risk of a sudden loss of investor confidence that could cause a run on the dollar, as feared by dollar pessimists. I have offered reasons why anxieties about America's debt overhang seem excessive. These include both the attractions of the US financial sector and the lack of adequate alternatives. But I have also acknowledged that such anxieties are not without foundation. Though the probability would appear to be low, there is no doubt that at some point a tipping point could indeed be reached, leading to self-reinforcing decline. The possibility cannot be denied, and if it becomes a reality it would definitely hurt. The gain of macroeconomic flexibility derived from the dollar's investment role would be supplanted by a growing external constraint on monetary and fiscal policy, just as it was for the British.

Second, closely related, is the risk of a sudden sell-off by foreign governments and central banks—a challenge to the dollar's reserve role, which would also result in a heightened external constraint. Here too the danger can be exaggerated. Policy makers abroad are all too aware that any large-scale sales of greenbacks would simply threaten the value of their remaining reserves, causing substantial capital losses. That is precisely why the dollar standard is so "unloved."[58] But here too we must acknowledge that concern about the danger is not without foundation, not least because of who now have become the biggest dollar holders. Back when the biggest part of dollar reserves was held by countries with close security ties to the United States, Washington could count on a certain amount of self-interested restraint. Today, however, the largest dollar holders include China and Russia, nations whose geopolitical relationship with the United States is far more fraught—at best "frenemies"; at worst, strategic adversaries. As Kirshner writes: "In future monetary negotiations and during currency crises, included in prominent seats at the table will be states that are military adversaries of the US (in particular,

China) . . . wary of aspects of American power, foreign policy and unilateralism."[59] Can they too be counted upon to act with restraint? We just do not know.

Third, also closely related, is the possible damage to America's global reputation so long as the country's liabilities continue to climb. The United States has already become history's biggest debtor nation. Unless present trends can be reversed, the dollar brand could suffer, diminishing America's soft power in the world. If the greenback is no longer seen as "great," a potent symbol of international primacy, how long would it be before the "greatness" of the United States itself comes to be questioned as well, with incalculable consequences for America's ability to shape the preferences of others? Already we see some hint of cognitive change in the growing perception of the dollar as a negotiated currency. I have suggested that the facts do not appear to support that impression. But what matters here is not empirical reality but what people *believe* to be reality. Once reputation begins to slide, the momentum is hard to stop.

Fourth, as noted back in chapter 4, is the loss of a degree of control over the dollar's exchange rate that comes from the currency's role as an exchange-rate anchor. The United States occupies the position of Stackelberg leader, a form of structural power, but it is the followers that get to decide whether or how to react. John Williamson sees this as a quid pro quo for the seigniorage benefit that Americans enjoy.[60] In his words, "the Dollar Standard involves a bargain whereby the United States gains cheap finance in return for other countries having full freedom to manage their exchange rates."[61] In other words, currency internationalization does not come without a price.

Finally, we should not forget the contingent political claim that tends to go with monetary leadership—the potential "exorbitant duty" that the United States might have to bear as a counterpoint to its exorbitant privilege. This too is evidence that internationalization does not come without a price. In time of crisis, Washington may be called upon to take extraordinary—and potentially expensive—actions to help out its friends, as the Federal Reserve did with the program of swap arrangements that it launched during the crisis in 2008. In that case, as it happens, the program succeeded without any net cost to US taxpayers. Indeed, all the swaps were repaid with interest, actually earning the Fed a tidy profit. But such a happy outcome cannot always be guaranteed. It is a fair bet that in future crises Washington will be called upon again. But it would be a fool's bet to assume that other rescues will be equally cost-free.

None of these risks or costs is easy to quantify, of course. Empirical measurement is as difficult on this side of the equation as it is for the benefits of internationalization. Hence we have no way of knowing precisely how, on balance, downsides and upsides compare. But it is clear that on a net basis, benefits for the United States are not as great as many might think. The sword is powerful, but we cannot forget that it cuts two ways.

Conclusion

Despite that final qualification, the overall conclusion is clear. Contrary to the warnings of dollar pessimists, the greenback is anything but "finished." Chapter 6 suggested that decades after Triffin and Kindleberger first started writing the dollar's obituary, America's money remains at the peak of the Currency Pyramid. This chapter has explained why, even after the devastating impact of the global financial crisis of 2008, the greenback endures—its power undiminished.

First and foremost, as indicated, is the appeal of the US capital market, which gives the dollar a unique advantage as a store of value. No other currency can match the greenback in terms of either liquidity or safety. And that attraction, in turn, is amplified by the other strengths that the United States brings to the table, including still broad network externalities in trade, a wide range of political ties, and vast military reach. Evidence is lacking to back the increasingly popular perception that the greenback is becoming a negotiated currency; little help is required from the US government. The dollar remains the one major pole in the system because, alone among national moneys, it is backed by the complete package of power resources associated with top international standing. It is the world's indispensable currency.

8

The Euro: Power Unrealized

Le petit euro deviendra grand.
—Jacques Delors (1925–)

It is difficult to make forecasts, especially about the future.
—attributed to Samuel Goldwyn (1879–1974)

At the time of its birth in 1999, a rosy future was forecast for the euro. Like dollar pessimists today, euro enthusiasts then were everywhere. Typical was Robert Mundell, who expressed no doubt that the euro "will challenge the status of the dollar and alter the power configuration of the system."[1] Similarly, Daniel Gros and Niels Thygesen, two prominent European economists, asserted that "the most visible effect of EMU at the global level will be the emergence of a second global currency."[2] Despite the reservations of some,[3] the mainstream view was clear. America's greenback would face a potent rival. In the oft-quoted words of Jacques Delors, former head of the European Commission, "the little euro will become big."

In fact, the only questions seemed to be: How great a rival would the euro become, and how soon? For Fred Bergsten, the answer was: Very great and very soon.[4] Because of the inherent strengths of the European economy, Bergsten confidently predicted, the euro would achieve "full parity" with the dollar in as little as five to ten years. And that happy forecast was echoed by many others, such as economists George Alogoskoufis and Richard Portes, who contended that "the fundamentals point toward a potentially large shift in favor of the euro. . . . The dollar would immediately lose its importance as a vehicle currency."[5] Menzie Chinn and Jeffrey Frankel, rashly, even put a precise date to their prediction.[6] The euro would surpass the greenback by as early as 2015. Polls taken in late 2008, just ahead of the euro's tenth birthday, indicated that a majority of Europeans expected their money to overtake the dollar within as little as five years. A destiny of shared currency leadership with America's greenback—perhaps even global dominance—seemed imminent, shimmering brightly on the horizon.[7]

Euro enthusiasm was by no means unjustified. Indeed, as previously noted, the new currency's credentials were excellent; its future value and usability seemed secure. There seemed every reason to believe in the Economic and Monetary Union's glowing promise. But that was before the great crisis that struck the world economy in 2008, just as Europeans were preparing to celebrate completion of their joint money's first decade. Since then, a rash of sovereign debt problems around the euro zone's periphery has shaken confidence severely. The bright shimmer on the horizon turned out to be something of a mirage. After a steep takeoff, internationalization quickly reached a ceiling. By the mid-2000s, cross-border use had already leveled off and, most recently, has even slipped back a bit. Moreover, it is well known that while the greenback continues to circulate virtually everywhere, the euro's domain remains confined mostly to a limited number of economies with close geographical and/or institutional links to the European Union. As we saw in chapter 6, the global currency system is nowhere near the duopoly that so many had anticipated. In the words of the *Economist*: "Bombastic talk of the euro rivaling the dollar is gone. The aim now is simply to arrest the decline."[8] The power of the euro remains unrealized.

This chapter explains why none of that should have come as a surprise. The story was told in brief in chapter 5. Here, as promised, we will go into more detail. First and foremost, the problem begins with the design of the monetary union's governance mechanisms. As an incomplete merger of sovereign states, EMU was flawed from the start, doomed to operate in a messy netherworld of considerable inefficiency and uncertainty. The euro suffers from a critical structural defect. And that flaw, in turn, exacerbates other weaknesses that constrain the currency's competitiveness. The gravitational pull of the European economy is diluted; Europe's financial institutions are unable to match the liquidity and safety of the global dollar market; European governments cannot compete with the United States in projecting political or military power; and public policy is incapable of mounting any kind of proactive strategy in support of internationalization. The wonder is that these crippling liabilities were not anticipated from the start.

An Imperfect Construct

Governance, at its most fundamental, is about the formulation, implementation, and enforcement of rules for behavior. The basic question is: Who is in charge? For the euro, regrettably, the answer has never been clear. From the start, uncertainty has reigned concerning the delegation of authority within EMU among national governments and EU institutions. At the heart of the monetary union are ambiguities that do little to enhance either managerial efficiency or user trust.

The issue is straightforward. The euro is a currency without a country. Its members are a club of sovereign states. Unlike the dollar or other currencies, which are created and managed by a single sovereign power, Europe's money is the product of a multistate agreement—the Maastricht Treaty, EMU's founding document. Hence a fundamental mismatch prevails between the domain of the euro zone and the legal jurisdictions of its participating governments, making decision-making problematic at best. The challenges of monetary management must be resolved by diplomatic negotiation, which is notorious for its tendency toward obfuscation and ambiguity to resolve knotty questions. In lieu of efficient governance, backed by an unquestioned political authority, EMU is condemned to operate in what the *Economist* has referred to as a vague "spirit of shoddy compromise."[9] Equivocal and messy trade-offs are the norm.

That does not mean that a monetary union like EMU is necessarily condemned to outright failure. There are, after all, several common currencies of long standing to be found around the globe. Most notably, these include the CFA franc zone in Africa, with fourteen members, and the East Caribbean Currency Union (ECCU) in the Western Hemisphere, with eight participants. Both have managed for decades to function effectively without undue ruckus.

But neither does it mean that EMU can ever be expected to completely overcome its disabilities—at least not so long as it remains short of a genuine political federation (which no one expects any time soon, if ever). The CFA franc zone and ECCU offer little precedent for EMU. Each was a product of colonial relationships; its members, all small and poor, had never managed a currency of their own. None had been asked to make any new sacrifice for the sake of a common currency. EMU, by contrast, not only encompasses some of the biggest and most advanced economies in the world. More importantly, its members all had long enjoyed monetary independence before agreeing to a currency merger. For them, the benefits of a joint money must be constantly weighed against its potential disadvantages, and further encroachments on their policy autonomy are bound to be resisted to the extent possible. Shoddy compromises are the inevitable result.

For some commentators the implication is that, sooner or later, EMU will collapse. Representative is the economist Martin Feldstein, who calls the monetary union "an experiment that failed." The euro is "the little currency that couldn't."[10] Likewise, Nouriel Roubini, well known for his accurate prediction of the 2008 financial crisis, has likened the euro to "a broken marriage that requires a break-up."[11] For others, conversely, the implication is the reverse—that EMU will learn from its mistakes and become ever stronger. "Europe is well on its way to completing the original concept of a comprehensive economic and monetary union," declares Bergsten, ever the euro enthusiast, together with a colleague. Europe will "rewrite the euro area rule book and complete the half-built euro house."[12]

Reality, however, is most likely to remain somewhere in between—in the gray area between abject failure and glowing success. Radical predictions, whether for failure or success, are simply not persuasive, and for the same reason. Their logic suffers from what philosophers call the Fallacy of the Excluded Middle—a sense that outcomes must be black or white, one extreme or the other. Their argument, in effect, is that a half-built house cannot stand: either it must be completed, or it will collapse. But as a practical matter, nothing could be further from the truth. In the real world shades of gray predominate, and even if they are distinctly suboptimal they may prove to be remarkably hardy. The euro house, for all its rickety defects, has proved durable through years of stormy weather, relying on one messy trade-off after another. The house may sag in places, the floor boards may be warped, and the roof may leak. But for all that, there is no reason to believe that it cannot long remain habitable. It just will not be very comfortable—a sadly imperfect construct.

MANAGING IMBALANCES

Nothing better illustrates the hazards of EMU's spirit of shoddy compromise than its repeated efforts to deal with the risk of imbalances within the club. No issue is more central to the governance of a monetary union. In committing to a common currency, a state surrenders not only control of its own monetary policy but also many of the other instruments traditionally available to governments to cope with payments imbalances, including two of the three *D*'s—devaluation or direct controls. How, then, should internal imbalances be managed? EMU's answer has been feeble at best.

The Challenge

It is no secret that EMU has had its share of troubles in recent years. Many reasons have been offered for the sovereign debt problems that first erupted in 2010: fiscal profligacy, banking excesses, asymmetrical shocks, or the global crisis triggered by the collapse of America's housing market, among other causes. But at the bottom of them all lies a basic mismatch between EMU's rules for monetary policy and fiscal policy. While national currencies are merged under one central bank, public budgets remain almost entirely in the hands of individual governments. The challenge has been to find some way to reconcile institutional arrangements for the two realms of policy.

The challenge was foreseen from the start. How could a monetary union manage the risk of fiscal imbalances among its members? As early as 1989, an influential report of the European Commission—the celebrated Delors Report[13]—argued that a European common currency would need fiscal shock absorbers to cope with the possibility of asymmetric disturbances to member states. And over the course of the 1990s, as planning proceeded for the birth of the euro in 1999, there were many voices calling for some kind of mutual insurance mechanism—a form of institutionalized risk-sharing—to provide help to states in distress. What might that mechanism have looked like?

Europe could have turned to the United States for inspiration. America has been living with the same risk of internal imbalances ever since the Union was founded, with its separate states and single dollar. For policy purposes the United States can be considered as the equivalent of a monetary union comparable to EMU, facing the same fundamental challenge. America's solution, building on the early reforms of Alexander Hamilton, George Washington's secretary of the Treasury, was to create a transfer union based on the principle of automatic risk-sharing. In practice, however, European policy makers chose otherwise.

The US system is hardly a perfect model. Like Rome, it took much more than a day to build—nearly a century and a half, in fact. Moreover, financing of imbalances within the United States is far from comprehensive, in part because the process of adjustment is eased considerably by a degree of wage flexibility and labour mobility between the states that remains higher than in today's European Union. But there is no reason why Europe could not have learned from America's experience, and there was certainly no reason why Europeans should have to wait a century and a half to find their own solution. In practice, however, governments temporized. Members were determined to retain for themselves as many budgetary rights and privileges as possible. In such a structure a permanent transfer union never had a chance, and no adequate substitute has yet been found.

The American Approach

The American approach, arrived at experimentally over many decades, combines three critical features: (1) transfers between the federal government and the fifty states; (2) limitations on the deficits of individual states; and (3) an absence of federal bailouts for states in difficulty.[14] Together, this trio of features operates to minimize stresses that might otherwise emerge from payments imbalances within the Union. They are like the three legs of a stool, all necessary to keep things stable.

Of course, the risk of crisis is by no means eliminated, as anyone from California—which just a few short years ago appeared to be teetering on the edge of bankruptcy—can easily attest. But the chance of a systemic crisis within the US monetary union is certainly lowered to a considerable degree from what it might otherwise be in such a heterogeneous collection of units. Through the operation of so-called automatic stabilizers, the system works to ease tensions when troubles do erupt. States in deficit automatically benefit from increased transfers from the center—in the form of unemployment benefits, welfare assistance, and similar expenditures—as well as from reduced tax payments to Washington. Effectively, the money comes from states in surplus, whose net transfers to the center correspondingly increase. Studies suggest that federal fiscal stabilizers act to offset asymmetric shocks in the United States by anywhere from 10 to 40 percent.[15]

The origins of the American approach go back to the so-called debt assumption plan of 1789, devised by Alexander Hamilton, the country's first Treasury secretary under the newly ratified Constitution. Under the earlier Articles of Confederation, some of the original thirteen colonies had engaged in extensive borrowing, resulting in unbearably high level of debt. Under Hamilton's plan, salvation lay in a once-and-for-all debt mutualization. All state liabilities were consolidated and assumed by the federal government, which in turn was granted new powers to raise taxes as well as the sole right to issue currency. Outstanding obligations were converted to long-term bonds and mechanisms were created to both service and amortize the collective debt. The core idea of the "Hamiltonian moment" was to stabilize the public finances and firmly establish the fiscal authority of the center.

The next step came in the 1840s, following a new period of large-scale borrowing by the states. When crisis struck with the financial panic of 1837 and subsequent recession in 1839–1843, numerous states again sought bailouts from the federal government, recalling the precedent of the Hamiltonian moment. There had also been a second takeover of state debts after the War of 1812. But this time Congress refused to comply, forcing some eight states (plus Florida, then still a territory) into default. At issue was the problem of "moral hazard"—the risk that states might repeatedly engage in excessive borrowing precisely because of an implied commitment of support from the center. Washington was determined to send a costly but clear signal that states could no longer rely on the federal government to dig them out of their own holes. A new no-bailout norm was to be established.

In effect, Congress was invoking what an old jest calls the First Law of Holes: When you find yourself in one, stop digging. States, in turn, apparently got the message. In subsequent years, most states eventually adopted what today would be called "debt brakes"—balanced-budget amendments to their constitutions or equivalent provisions in state law requiring balanced budgets. The principle of limitations on state deficits also became an accepted norm.

The final step came during the Great Depression of the 1930s, when Franklin Roosevelt's New Deal programs greatly expanded Washington's role in the national economy. Though many states again found themselves in trouble (and one state, Arkansas, did in fact default in 1933), no new federal bailouts were provided. The no-bailout norm held. But much help did begin to come instead in the form of conditional or unconditional transfers for such purposes as unemployment compensation or welfare relief. From that point on, automatic stabilizers became an integral part of the federal system, a form of risk-sharing that is so familiar today that it is rarely even noticed—hidden in plain view, as it were. The third leg of the stool was now set in place.

The European Approach

With its three-legged stool, the US transfer union operates with reasonable effectiveness to cope with imbalances among the states. The system is hardly perfect. From time to time states do still get into trouble, sometimes quite deeply. But since the Great Depression not a single one of the fifty states of the Union has actually been forced into bankruptcy. Because transfers occur more or less automatically, overt controversy is eliminated. Effectively the process is *depoliticized*, barely noticed and rarely questioned. Compare that with the recent turmoil in EMU members like Greece or Cyprus, both of which actually defaulted on parts of their debt. In their cases, political conflict could not be avoided either domestically or in relations with creditors.

Regrettably, Europe has not chosen to learn from America's experience. EMU's architects were not unaware of the US precedent, but they were unprepared to replicate it. The opportunity was missed. Only two legs of the stool were ever attempted—a no-bailout norm and limitations on budget deficits—and neither has proved to be particularly supportive.

The third leg—automatic fiscal transfers—has never even been seriously contemplated.

Throughout the planning for EMU, it was clear that member governments were determined to keep fiscal policy in their own hands. But it was also understood that some kind of discipline would have to be enforced to limit the risk of excessive borrowing. That was the clear message of the Delors report. Hence two carefully crafted safeguards were written into the Maastricht Treaty (formally known as the Treaty on European Union), which was signed in 1992 and came into effect in 1993. One provision banned bailouts of states in difficulty. The other, called the *excessive deficit procedure* (EDP), set limits on permissible deficits and debt.

The ban on bailouts was quite explicit. In the treaty's words (Article 104b), "The Community should not be liable for or assume the commitments of central governments, regional, local or other public authorities, other bodies governed by public law, or public undertakings of any Member State." But the force of the ban was vitiated by a giant loophole spelled out elsewhere in the treaty (Article 103a), which allows that "Where a Member State is in difficulties or is seriously threatened with severe difficulties . . . the Council may . . . grant, under certain conditions, Community financial assistance to the Member State concerned." In effect, the ban holds only until it is tested, and then it may be preempted. Essentially, it is a dead letter and has not prevented rescues of several governments since EMU's troubles erupted in 2010. These have included Portugal, Ireland, Greece, and Spain—the derisively labeled PIGS—plus, most recently, Cyprus. Italy is also sometimes included in this porcine grouping (leading some to refer to the PIIGS rather than PIGS) but has never actually received a formal bailout.

In similar fashion, the excessive deficits procedure was spelled out in considerable detail in the treaty (Article 104c) and an accompanying protocol. Budget deficits were not to exceed 3 percent of gross domestic product; government debt was not to exceed 60 percent of GDP; and should either of these limits be violated, penalties might be imposed, including "fines of an appropriate size." Further detail was added in the so-called Stability and Growth Pact (SGP) agreed in 1997, clarifying provisions both for surveillance of individual government performance (the "preventive arm") and for imposition of sanctions (the "dissuasive arm").

Here too, however, the force of the safeguards turned out to be considerably less than intended, to widespread disappointment. In actual practice, the EDP and SGP proved to have little real "bite." The first major test came in the early 2000s, when both Germany and France found themselves with deficits in excess of the 3 percent limit. Enforcing penalties on EMU's two largest members simply was not feasible. So instead, in the name of greater flexibility, Berlin and Paris pushed through a reform of the rules in 2005 that allowed them to receive a waiver of their violations, setting a precedent for others to follow.

That does not mean that the arrangement thus became absolutely toothless. Empirical evidence suggests that, at least in its early years, the SGP did in fact manage to exercise some measure of discipline, with an especially strong impact on EMU's smaller members.[16] But it is significant that to date not a single government has ever been formally penalized for missing prescribed budget or debt limits. In practice, the SGP did nothing to prevent the development of a major credit boom.

Crisis

And then came the global financial crisis, which was bound to put EMU's design to the test. It quickly became clear that Europe's wobbly two-legged stool was no place to sit.

At first, Europeans were inclined to breathe a sigh of relief. Monetary union, they felt, had actually reduced their vulnerability to the kind of financial tsunami that was engulfing nations elsewhere. In the past, a crisis like this one might have triggered waves of speculation against the EU's weaker currencies, creating a maelstrom of monetary instability. But now, with a single joint money having replaced a gaggle of national currencies, members no longer had to fear the risk of exchange-rate disturbances inside their bloc. As the *Economist* commented at the time: "Being part of a big club has made a currency run far less likely."[17] For a continent long plagued by monetary instability, that seemed no small accomplishment. Europeans could be forgiven for thinking that, for them at least, the worst had been averted.

It soon became apparent, however, that they were wrong. Speculative tensions had not been eliminated. They were merely *diverted*—from the currency market to the market for government bonds. Prior to the global tsunami, investors had barely distinguished among the securities of different governments in the euro zone; spreads over the key ten-year German "bund" remained remarkably narrow, rarely going even as high as one-half of one percent (50 basis points). But by 2009 the climate had shifted. Instead of gambling on exchange rates, investors began to bet on sovereign debt, with the greatest attention focused on weaker members at the periphery of EMU. That meant in particular the notorious PIGS, with their massive liabilities and gaping budget deficits. For the four PIGS plus a few unfortunate others like Italy and Cyprus, credit ratings were downgraded and spreads soon started to widen dramatically—at times, to as much as 500 basis points or more. After "a brief moment in the sun," as the *Economist* put it, EMU found itself increasingly threatened by looming storm clouds of potential default.[18] By 2010, it was plain that Europe faced an acute internal payments problem.

Response

How should Europe have responded? For some, it was time at last to take the American precedent seriously. "Oh, for an Alexander Hamilton to save Europe!" lamented Ronald McKinnon.[19] EMU, he declared, needed its own Hamiltonian moment. And many in Europe agreed, including the European Commission, which issued a policy paper—known as the blueprint report—calling for a full fiscal union within as little as five years.[20] Key, said the Commission, would be "an autonomous euro area budget providing for a fiscal capacity for the euro area to support Member States in the absorption of shocks"—in other words, the missing third leg of the stool. But once more the opportunity was missed. Yet again, Europe's response was two-legged, leaving the stool as unsteady as ever. The third leg is still missing.

To begin, the Maastricht Treaty's bailout ban—already effectively a dead letter—has now been formally abandoned. Following an initial rescue package for Greece in March 2010 (two additional rescues had to be organized later), policy makers moved in May 2010 to create a more regularized safety net for troubled debtors. Alongside an already existing Commission lending window of some €60 billion, available to all EU countries, a new European Financial Stability Facility (EFSF) was set up as a temporary backstop for EMU. The EFSF was established for a period of three years with total resources advertised at €440 billion. Together with a parallel pledge from the International Monetary Fund of an additional €250 billion if needed, this meant a total of some €750 billion (close to one trillion dollars) might now be available to sustain investor confidence. The hope was to calm the financial waters with what would be seen as an overwhelming show of force—a strategy of "shock and awe," as it were, to forestall any further spread of default concerns across Europe.

The impact, however, was short-lived. Observers were quick to note critical weaknesses—most importantly, the fact that no money was actually being provided up front. The EFSF was not a fund. Rather, EMU governments merely committed to backing a borrowing mechanism, a so-called "special purpose vehicle," that would be authorized to raise money by issuing debt should a member country find itself in trouble. Moreover, not all of the €440 billion would actually be available for lending, since some of the cash raised would have to be held in reserve to protect the EFSF's triple-A credit rating, and all euro-zone governments would have to agree to the loan. In practice, not more than €250 billion might have been truly usable in the event of an emergency. The general sense was that the Europeans were still far from a real solution to their problems. In the words of the *Economist*, "the rescue plan has a patched-together feel. . . . The package, impressive though its scale and speed may be, only buys time for troubled governments."[21]

Within months, therefore, Europe's leaders were forced back to the drawing board, to try again to calm the waters. In November 2010, simultaneous with a rescue mounted for Ireland (the second of the PIGS to get help), agreement was reached to create a permanent new lending arrangement for EMU. That was the European Stability Mechanism (ESM), which began life in 2012 and formally succeeded the EFSF at the end of the temporary facility's three-year life in 2013. Unlike the EFSF, the ESM is a genuine intergovernmental organization with paid-in capital of €80 billion and an effective lending capacity of €500 billion. Loans from the ESM are meant to be available on an ongoing basis to deal with any future asymmetric shocks within the bloc. From now on the euro zone would have a formal safety net for governments. The message was clear. Member states were no longer on their own. The ban on bailouts was now officially renounced.

But what, then, about the moral hazard problem? What might now stop member governments from digging new holes for themselves? It was clear that once the ESM backstop was put in place, more effective safeguards would also be needed to curb the risk of renewed fiscal profligacy. So even while weakening the no-bailout leg of the stool, policy makers sought to strengthen the second leg, aiming to further limit budget deficits and debt. Under pressure from Germany, the euro zone's paymaster, a twofold strategy was devised. To deal with immediate threats, tough policy conditions would be imposed on even the most deeply troubled debtors. Austerity (the *D* of deflation) was the price to be paid for a bailout, even if it meant prolonged stagnation or worse. To deal with the longer term a tighter version of the Stability and Growth Pact would be implemented, giving real teeth to EMU's debt brakes. Discipline would be hard-wired into the management of EMU. There could be no more Greek tragedies.

Thus, after vigorous lobbying by Berlin, the European Fiscal Compact was born—an updated version of the SGP. Agreed in March 2012 by twenty-five of the twenty-seven countries that were then EU members (all but Britain and the Czech Republic; Croatia joined the EU later), the Compact called for formal balanced-budget rules to be written into national law or constitutions within one year. At the heart of the Compact is a new "golden rule" limiting primary budget deficits (that is, deficits before interest payments) to no more than 0.5 percent of GDP over the full economic cycle, with a maximum annual deficit of no more than 3 percent. In addition, both the preventive arm and the dissuasive arm of the SGP were given new muscle. Budget projections must now be submitted to the Commission every year for its approval; fiscal outcomes are supposed to be carefully monitored on a regular basis; and unless voted down by a weighted majority, costly sanctions are mandated for governments that breach the SGP's deficit limit of 3 percent of GDP. Access to the ESM safety net was not meant to be easy.

A Wobbly Stool

Would all this be enough? Key officials expressed little doubt. "A widespread lack of trust in public finances weighs heavily on growth," noted Bundesbank president Jens Weidmann when the Fiscal Compact was agreed.[22] In those circumstances, he optimistically maintained, a firm golden rule should "inspire confidence and actually help the economy to grow." But was such optimism justified? One is reminded of the jocular definition of second marriage: the triumph of hope over experience.

In reality, the stool is as wobbly as ever, still resting on just two legs: the European Stability Mechanism plus the Fiscal Compact. Neither support is especially reliable, and the critical third leg—some sort of mutual insurance mechanism to complete the transfer union—is still missing.

At least two questions hover over the ESM. First is whether the planned lending capacity of the fund, at €500 billion, will actually be enough should serious shocks simultaneously hit one or two of EMU's larger members, such as Spain or Italy. With financial-market contagion an ever-present threat, spreading pressures from country to country, the credibility of the safety net could quickly wither. In anticipation, EMU members have pledged additional capital, if needed, to raise lending capacity by another €200 billion, but many worry whether even that amount would suffice in the event of a real emergency.

The second question is whether governments would be prepared to accept the tough policy conditions that are supposed to be tied to any financial assistance. There is nothing automatic to the ESM's operations. The model is IMF conditional lending, not the US transfer union. To qualify for help, a participating state must first agree to the terms of a strict adjustment program, featuring above all fiscal "consolidation" (a polite synonym for austerity). Governments are well aware of the high price some of EMU's troubled members were forced to pay, in terms of lost growth and high unemployment. They can also see how difficult it was for countries like Greece or Cyprus, once bailed out, to get out from under the tutelage of their creditors. Few will want to be put through the same kind of wringer. For some, default may begin to seem a more attractive option.

Likewise, a major question hovers over the Fiscal Compact: Can it be enforced? We know what happened to the Stability and Growth Pact. When push came to shove, members shrank from the drastic step of enforcing formal sanctions. The dissuasive arm proved feeble. So why should any greater sense of resolve have been expected under the new rules? As the proposed regime was being negotiated, observers could be forgiven for thinking that the new Compact might turn out to have little more bite than the old SGP. Simon Tilford, chief economist at the Centre for European Reform in London, probably put it best when he described the Compact as "little more than a stability pact with lipstick."[23]

As matters have turned out, Tilford was right. For all of the Compact's insistence on formal debt brakes, the same risk of hesitation remains. Very quickly, for obvious political reasons, the terms of the Compact were eased. In 2013, the Compact's first year of operation, as many as six countries—including major players like France, the Netherlands, and Spain—were all given extra time to bring their budget deficits down below the magic 3 percent limit. And a year later further extensions were given to France and Italy when each claimed it could not meet the Compact's target on time. At the first whiff of resistance from key members, the Commission buckled. No offending state has yet been penalized for missing its goal, and pressures for greater "flexibility" in the enforcement of the rules continue to mount.

Clearly, EMU would be better off with American-style automatic transfers to balance the other two legs of Europe's stool. Even the normally circumspect IMF concurs that "some system of temporary transfers . . . to increase fiscal risk sharing" would seem "essential."[24] A formal shock absorber would not be a magic bullet, solving all ills. Perfection is too much to hope for. But without something of the kind to help cope with imbalances within the group, the stool will remain forever wobbly. The defect is built into the monetary union's governance structure.

The Reason

The reason for the defect is clear. Despite all the troubles of recent years, the basic mismatch between EMU's rules for monetary policy and fiscal policy is still firmly in place. Member governments, ultimately, remain in charge of their own budgets; and that in turn is due to a European political culture that remains stubbornly resistant to a final surrender of the last shreds of national sovereignty. As one acute observer summarizes: "The basic problem is that the EU is not a true union but more a collection of states that have not in any real sense ceded decision-making power to a central authority. The result is chaos fed by conflicting national objectives."[25]

In practice, EMU's structural defect could be remedied in any number of ways. Closest to optimal would be a full fiscal union as recommended by the European Commission in its blueprint report, modeled on (though not necessarily identical with) the historical American approach.[26] In the words of a more recent report by three influential European think tanks: "The euro area needs a single central fiscal authority with its own source of revenues . . . and the capacity to make ongoing fiscal transfers within the euro area."[27] A recent study suggests that introduction of a European transfer union replacing just one-third of national tax regimes would serve to offset up to 15 percent of regional asymmetric shocks.[28] But, sadly, a system of automatic stabilizers working through a large budget at the center seems beyond reach. The Commission's proposal was firmly rejected at a summit of EU leaders in December 2012.

More realistic might be some form of limited risk sharing that would not be strictly conditional, as suggested by the IMF.[29] One possibility would be a partial mutualization of sovereign debt through the issue of joint bonds—"Eurobonds," in the jargon. Another might be a system of collective bank-deposit guarantees, to help share the burden of sudden banking crises, or a common scheme for unemployment insurance. And yet another might be common dedicated "rainy day" fund authorized to make transfers to members experiencing negative shocks. Options such as these may be "second-best," but they would surely be better than nothing.

As a practical matter, however, not even any second-best choice seems feasible in today's Europe. In late 2013 Pierre Moscovici, then France's Finance Minister, proposed a form of mutualization through creation of a shared unemployment insurance system. But his idea was immediately shot down by German chancellor Angela Merkel in remarks during Germany's parliamentary election campaign. "I oppose mutualizing things . . . as proposed by other parties," she declared. "When at the end the stronger countries also get weak, everybody will be weak and this mustn't happen to Europe."[30] For the same reason Merkel remains adamantly opposed to Eurobonds, which she sees as a backdoor route to German taxpayer money. As the IMF commented dryly, "political backing . . . remains elusive."[31]

Therein, down deep, lies the most critical difference between the European and American approaches. The pieces of America's transfer union began to fall into place only once the original Articles of Confederation were replaced with the hallowed US Constitution, providing the space for what we now remember as the Hamiltonian moment. Thirteen fractious former colonies were merged into one federal state, with ultimate authority over fiscal policy now shifted to the center. Europe, by contrast, remains at the Articles of Confederation stage—still far from anything that might be described as a genuine political federation. Policy makers as yet are unprepared to countenance seriously any kind of automatic transfers within their group. As a result, EMU's structural defect persists. Europe is still trying to perch on a stool with only two legs—an uncomfortable prospect at best.

The Price

Europeans are entitled to their political culture, of course. If they prefer to remain at the Articles of Confederation stage, that is their choice. But they should also be aware of the material price they are forced to pay for their resistance to some form of genuine risk-sharing. The cost of a wobbly stool, in terms of real economic performance, is lamentably high.

The dilemma can be simply put. Begin with the irrefutable fact that occasional payments problems are a virtual certainty in a group of states as heterogeneous as the membership of EMU. Any country can unexpectedly find itself in trouble. We may recall Germany at the time of the euro's birth, then labeled by some the "sick man" of Europe. Or think of one-time high flyers like Ireland or Spain, brought down by banking crises not of their own making. In the absence of a permanent and automatic transfer union, every instance of serious imbalance must be negotiated anew; and since as a practical matter terms are invariably set by creditors, that means that pressures to adjust tend to be fatally skewed, falling mainly on debtors. As John Maynard Keynes wrote about the classical gold standard: "The process of adjustment is *compulsory* for the debtor and *voluntary* for the creditor."[32] While healthier countries can afford to be relatively passive, distressed states have little choice but to respond more proactively. But what can they do? Trade or capital controls are ruled out by their membership in the EU. Likewise, an independent monetary policy or exchange-rate devaluation is ruled out by their membership of EMU. Effectively, all that is left to them is the D of deflation, politely called "internal devaluation"—another synonym for austerity. An *anti-growth bias* is created.

Not everyone would agree with this interpretation, which is essentially Keynesian in nature. There is also a respectable alternative line of argument represented by Bundesbank president Weidmann and others, variously labeled "Austrian school" or "ordoliberalism." According to this line of argument, austerity is precisely what is needed to promote growth, by restoring trust in public finances. But after a half decade of exceedingly disappointing performance, it is hard to accord much credence to that sanguine point of view. In mid-2014, industrial production in the euro area was still 13 percent below its peak in April 2008; overall GDP was stagnant; and unemployment remained stuck above 11 percent. Fiscal consolidation has generated not growth but repeated recessions and massive job losses. In the words of the *Economist*: "What started more than four years ago as a banking and sovereign-debt crisis has decayed into a growth crisis."[33] An anti-growth bias seems undeniable.

Paul Krugman provides an apt illustration.[34] Compare the recent experiences of Florida and Spain, he suggests. In the early to mid-2000s each experienced a huge housing boom, followed by a spectacular bust once the global financial crisis began. Both were thrown into recession. But then their paths diverged, owing in large part to the differences between the US and European fiscal systems. In Krugman's words:

> In Florida's case, most of the fiscal burden of the slump fell not on the local government but on Washington. . . . Florida received large-scale aid in its time of distress. Spain, by contrast, bore all the costs of the housing bust on its own. The result was a fiscal crisis. . . . Spanish borrowing costs soared, and the government was forced into brutal austerity measures. The result was a horrific depression.

Europe's anti-growth bias is nowhere to be found in the charter of the ESM or the fine print of the Fiscal Compact. De facto, however, it is plainly there for all to see. In effect, EMU has succeeded in resurrecting at the regional level the nineteenth-century rules of the game, when exchange rates were rigidly fixed, capital controls were *verboten*, and the preferred method of adjustment was domestic contraction—an updated version of the gold standard without gold. "You shall not crucify mankind upon a cross of gold," declared William Jennings Bryan in 1896. Today Europe's economic fortunes are being crucified upon a "cross of euros."[35]

OTHER WEAKNESSES

Is it any wonder, then, that the power of the euro remains unrealized? A structural defect as unsettling as EMU's wobbly stool is hardly likely to engender confidence in the currency's future value and usability. For outsiders, the euro can be considered only as good as the political agreement underlying it. The experience of recent years has demonstrated that the requisite cohesion is tenuous at best. Rather than the clarity of a single sovereign power, we find discord and a spirit of shoddy compromise. How could user trust not be compromised? As one source summarizes:

> In the absence of a central authority, eurozone countries' cooperative management of the crisis has been clumsy, damaging the credibility of eurozone governance and accordingly market confidence in the euro.[36]

In turn, other weaknesses are exacerbated that further limit the euro's appeal. The dollar, I suggested in chapter 7, is backed by the complete package of factors that seem associated with top currency status. For the euro, those factors are most conspicuous by their absence.

Trade

Begin with economic size. Although not all of the twenty-eight EU countries are members of the euro zone, the relevant unit for comparative purposes would seem to be the European Union as a whole—the entire economic community that has been laboriously put together since the original Rome Treaty in 1955. With the conspicuous exceptions of Britain and Denmark, which have negotiated opt-outs, every noneuro country is formally enrolled in EMU with a "derogation." Sooner or later, they are all legally obligated to adopt the currency. And even if Britain and Denmark never follow suit, the pair are nonetheless closely tied to the rest through the myriad institutions of the "European project." To limit attention to EMU alone would be to underestimate Europe's true actual or potential impact, unfairly biasing analysis. For outsiders, what matters is not just the euro zone alone but the broader common market in which the euro is embedded.

Given the aggregate size of the EU, it is not surprising that outsiders might feel a considerable gravitational pull. Collectively, the twenty-eight members constitute an economy roughly equivalent to that of the United States, with a per-capita income above €25,000 ($35,000) for its 500 million consumers. The EU is also the biggest trading bloc in the world, with a 16 percent share of global exports (excluding intra-EU trade), nearly twice America's share. Germany alone sells as much around the globe as does the United States.

But can that gravitational pull be sustained? Prospects are not bright. The EU's share of world output has been shrinking for some time, from as much as 25 percent in the 1990s (calculated on a purchasing power parity basis) to little more than 18 percent recently; and projections into the future suggest a continuation, if not an acceleration, of the same grim trend. Observers point to three critical issues. One is the frailty of the region's demographics—a rapidly aging population with an overall growth rate under 0.2 percent—that will soon translate into a significant decline in the available labor force. A second is the low rate of productivity growth in Europe due to a paucity of investment in research and development. And a third is an expected erosion of human capital due to the prolonged unemployment since 2008. All three suggest a significantly reduced growth potential. In the words of one recent study, projecting Europe's outlook out to the year 2030: "The combination of such factors will deliver a weak GDP growth in Europe. . . . The weakness of European growth does not allow a sufficient rate of job creation to ensure a rapid decrease in the unemployment rate."[37] From a pace of some 2.6 percent during the decade before the crisis, annual growth in the EU is expected to average at best no more than 1.5 percent in coming years.

Not everyone agrees, of course. Some observers are more hopeful, predicting instead a new post-crisis era of healthy restructuring and revival. Dismal projections of long-term stagnation, it is argued, are just what the doctor ordered—just what is needed to trigger the kinds of reforms that could renew economic progress. In particular, these might include supply-side measures in product and labor markets to boost productivity and investment and reduce unemployment. Writes a former high US Treasury official, "Europe could defy conventional wisdom and again lead growth in the world economy."[38] But such optimism requires a prodigious act of faith—a belief in the EU's ability to overcome entrenched resistance to change—that would not seem justified by recent history. The fundamentals, most experts concur, point to continued weakness in Europe's economic future.[39]

And that weakness, in turn, is only amplified by the anti-growth bias created by EMU's cruel "cross of euros." Austrian-school economics, with its emphasis on austerity, merely adds more drag to Europe's recovery from its debt problems. "The most likely trajectory," summarizes one informed observer, "is a long period of slow growth, low inflation, and a constant threat of insolvency."[40] Echoes the *Economist*, even more bluntly: "Europe will be under a shadow for years to come. The cost will be measured in disillusion, blighted communities and wasted lives."[41] For members of the monetary union, the outlook could be dark indeed.

In such unpromising circumstances, is it reasonable to look for the euro to be more widely adopted by outsiders for invoicing trade or as a vehicle in currency markets? The currency does already play a substantial trade role in economies with close geographical and/or institutional links to the EU. But that was only to be expected. These are EMU's traditional hinterland—"the euro's turf," as economist Charles Wyplosz once put it.[42] For countries within the EU's orbit, the euro's gravitational pull naturally remains strong. But beyond that limited domain the currency's appeal rapidly fades. Outside of what the ECB has referred to as the "European time zone," use of the euro for trade with EMU economies remains limited; in transactions between third countries, where neither counterparty is an EMU member, it is practically nonexistent. Europe's shrinking role in the world economy is most apt to be matched by a gradual atrophy of the euro's function as a medium of exchange as well. Wider use in global trade or the foreign exchange market does not seem to be in the cards.

Finance

What about the euro's store-of-value function, as an investment currency and reserve asset? Back when EMU started, it certainly appeared reasonable to look for expansion of the euro's role in financial markets. The anticipated process of monetary integration promised to create the largest single-currency capital market in the world, with a huge pool of savings and a high degree of liquidity. Savings previously lodged outside the EU, it seemed likely, would naturally be attracted by the financial sector's new depth, enhancing the euro's global standing.

True to form, expansion was immediately evident, especially in bond markets. In short order costs for euro-denominated corporate and government issues narrowed (as measured by bid-ask spreads), becoming commensurate with those for the dollar. The result was a dramatic increase in the use of Europe's new money for international bond sales. Indeed, the euro soon actually surpassed the greenback as the world's most important currency of issue, with net bond sales rising faster than for any other denomination. By mid-decade, euro issues accounted for roughly one-third of the outstanding stock of international bonds, up from just 19 percent in 1999. Over the same period, the greenback's share fell from around 50 percent to 43 percent. The euro seemed on its way.

But the effect did not last. After peaking in 2005 at just below 34 percent, the euro's share of bond inventory dwindled again, falling to little more than a quarter in more recent years. That compares with a dollar share now back above 50 percent. Moreover, here too it is clear that the euro's domain, in terms of both borrowers and investors, has tended to remain confined more or less to the EU and its hinterland. On the supply side, where the euro performs a financing function (a medium for borrowing), most new issues tends to come from neighboring countries like Britain, Denmark, and Sweden. Borrowers farther afield, in Latin America or Asia, continue to contract more in dollars. Likewise, on the demand side, where the euro performs a store-of-value function (an investment medium), the largest part of new euro-denominated issues tends to be taken up by investors within EMU itself, making them effectively "domestic," while much of the rest goes to the nearby European region. Elsewhere, available data indicate that the greenback still dominates in holdings of bonds as foreign assets.

A major reason for the dollar's continued dominance is the absence of a universal financial instrument in Europe to rival the US T-bill for liquidity and convenience. This is a deficiency that will remain difficult, if not impossible, to rectify so long as EMU, with its separate sovereign members, lacks a counterpart to the federal government in Washington. There is no single market for public debt in EMU as there is in the United States. Rather, there are separate and distinct markets for the national issues of each individual participant—German *bunds*, French *bons du tresoir*, and so on. Full consolidation of the euro zone's government debt market is stymied by the persistence of differential credit and liquidity risk premiums among member countries as well as by variations in legal traditions, procedures, issuance calendars, and primary dealer systems. Eurobonds might have made a start toward creation of a more potent rival to America's Treasury bond market but, as indicated, have been firmly rejected by Germany and others.

Worse, once Europe's sovereign debt problems erupted, EU financial markets actually began to fragment, reversing the anticipated process of integration. As indicated in the previous chapter, many sectors have now retreated once again behind national frontiers, reducing both exchange convenience and capital certainty. In effect, Europe's capital market has become balkanized.

The retreat is particularly evident in the banking sector, where links previously cultivated through wholesale short-term markets have practically disappeared. After the global crisis began in 2008, worries about the solvency of European banks multiplied. At first, the issue was their massive exposure to questionable assets based on US mortgages. The bursting of America's housing bubble badly damaged balance sheets. But once the region's sovereign debt problems took center stage, attention shifted to the banking sector's large holdings of European public debt. Europe found itself in what has been described as a "doom loop" between weak sovereigns and fragile banks. During the previous credit boom, governments had encouraged banks to load up on their bonds. When those debts then came under a cloud, those same governments then had to come to the rescue of their banks, which only added to their own fiscal strains and further impaired the quality of their liabilities, thus weakening local banks even more. No one knew where the next bankruptcy might come from. Hence interbank lending soon ground to a halt, leaving each country's banking sector to its own devices. Lending shrank sharply and interest rates began to diverge widely.

It was this breakdown of the banking market that finally prompted Mario Draghi, president of the ECB, to intervene in July 2012 in a now celebrated speech to the London financial community. The ECB, he pledged, would do "whatever it takes to preserve the euro," adding "believe me, it will be enough."[43] Specifically the ECB would now begin, under certain conditions, to buy up some of the debt of troubled sovereigns under a new program given the label of *outright monetary transactions* (OMT). Although in fact no such purchases have yet been made, the immediate impact of OMT was positive, easing some of the sense of panic that had taken hold in Europe's financial markets. But beyond that OMT accomplished little, since it did nothing to address the euro's underlying structural defect. The doom loop was largely untouched.

Could the loop be broken? The needed remedies were well understood.[44] On the one hand, to break the link running from bank problems to sovereign stress, a common deposit-insurance scheme might have helped to ensure that individual governments would not be overwhelmed by the needs of their banks. On the other, to break the link running from sovereign stress to bank problems, a common debt instrument—in a word, Eurobonds—might have worked to ensure that banks would no longer be overwhelmed by the needs of their respective governments. But of course neither option proved feasible given Europe's prevailing political culture.

Instead, the world was treated to yet another depressing demonstration of EMU's spirit of shoddy compromise. Though a consensus soon developed that a "banking union" of some kind was needed, results were uncertain at best. In principle, an effective banking union would require two elements: a single supervisor to keep banks on the straight and narrow; and a single resolution authority with sufficient resources both to deal with the needs of troubled banks and to guarantee bank deposits. In practice, however, neither element has been clearly provided. On the one hand, the ECB has been given formal responsibility for supervision of the largest banks in the euro zone (those with assets worth more than €30 billion or 20 percent of their country's GDP—perhaps 200 banks in all). But that still leaves several thousand smaller lenders under the tutelage of their respective governments, as before. On the other hand, a small resolution authority has been established, based on industry levies. But should the authority run short of funds, national governments would still have primary responsibility for their own local banks. No euro-wide deposit insurance scheme has even been contemplated. Once again, in lieu of clarity, the Europeans have settled for equivocal and messy trade-offs that, in the end, might do more harm than good. As the *Economist* warns, "a half-baked, piecemeal banking union could be worse than none."[45]

Together, these unhappy developments can hardly be expected to enhance the euro's appeal as a store of value. Quite the opposite, in fact—particularly for investors or central banks beyond EMU's immediate neighborhood. Wider use of the euro as an investment medium or reserve asset seems no more likely than wider use as a trade currency. The early promise of a grand new capital market remains unfulfilled. Europe is still far from matching the prowess of America's financial sector.

Political Factors

Nor, last, can Europe match America's unparalleled advantages in terms of foreign policy ties and military reach. The dollar benefits greatly from the central position of the United States in the geopolitical order. By contrast, no one has ever described EMU as the "indispensable nation."

Admittedly, Europe is not without political resources. Two of the EU's members, Britain and France, are nuclear states with militaries capable of projecting power well beyond their own borders. In 2000 Britain intervened successfully in its former colony of Sierra Leone to halt a vicious and destructive civil war. Likewise, thirteen years later, France twice sent troops to Africa—first to Mali, to block a threatened takeover by Islamist insurgents; and then to the Central African Republic, to curb ethno-religious warfare. Both Britain and France maintain close ties with many of their old imperial dependencies. Each, however, acts largely on its own in pursuit of its own national interests. Apart from a very small "rapid reaction force," which exists mainly on paper, the EU has never been able to build any kind of unified armed units. Defense remains primarily the domain of individual sovereign states whose military links run mostly through the North Atlantic Treaty Organization (NATO) rather than the EU.

Some effort has been made to achieve more cohesion in foreign policy. In 2009 the position of High Representative for Foreign Affairs and Security Policy was created—in effect, an EU foreign minister—with responsibility for coordinating Europe's external diplomatic and political relations. The first high representative was Britain's Catherine Ashton, succeeded in 2014 after a five-year term by Federica Mogherini of Italy. In principle, the idea was to elevate the profile of the EU as an international actor. In practice, the effect has been mainly cosmetic, since the high representative can speak for Europe only when all twenty-eight members agree. As might be imagined, consensus in such a diverse group is difficult to achieve on any but the most innocuous of issues.

In reality, Europe is a long way from being able to challenge America's incumbency advantages in the security realm. Quite the reverse, in fact. Since World War II Europeans have tended to rely on the military prowess of the United States and NATO for most of their defense needs, and that in turn tends to further dim the putative appeal of the euro. In the words of one source, "the EU's dependence on the United States for its security precludes the EU from having the kind of political leverage to support the euro that the United States has with the dollar."[46] More bluntly, a senior official of the European Commission concedes, speaking anonymously: "We're a political dwarf." Given a choice, few governments outside the European time zone would opt for the EU as a patron in preference to the United States; few investors would see EMU as a safer haven than the greenback. As a practical matter, Europe's political capabilities are simply too limited. Here too, therefore, weakness limits the competitiveness of Europe's currency. Concludes Adam Posen, "foreign policy and national security ties . . . continue to favor the dollar's global use."[47]

Managed Internationalization?

With all these crippling liabilities, Europe's money is bound to lack a certain amount of market appeal. To be blunt, the euro brand is tarnished. But what about the supply side? The analysis to this point takes account of just the demand side of the picture: the preferences of currency users. As in the previous chapter, it is also necessary to consider the preferences of the euro's issuers. Could cross-border use of the euro be promoted by deliberate influence attempts? Could internationalization be "managed?"

Certainly more proactive policies are feasible. Again, we may recall that two classes of strategy are possible—either informal measures designed to cater to the preferences of outsiders; or formal measures aiming directly to alter existing preferences. In principle, both type of strategy are available to EMU governments.

Informally, more could be done to enhance the euro brand by reinvigorating economic growth or reintegrating financial markets. At the macroeconomic level EMU's anti-growth bias could be neutralized by adding a firm third leg to EMU's wobbly stool, easing restraints on fiscal policy. At the microeconomic level supply-side reforms could be promoted to increase competition and lower hiring costs. And in the financial sector the balkanization of markets could be reversed by returning to the drawing board to create a clearer and more efficient banking union. All of these initiatives would be desirable even apart from the issue of euro internationalization. But as already noted, recent history gives little reason to believe that we are likely to see anything along those lines anytime soon, if ever.

Formally, more could conceivably be done to encourage wider use of the euro by foreign governments. A prime target might be the Middle East, with its concentration of wealthy oil exporters. The region, as I have suggested elsewhere, could be tempting to the Europeans for three reasons.[48] First is the sheer scale of monetary riches controlled directly or indirectly by local regimes. What these governments decide to do with their money can have a major impact on the relative fortunes of international currencies. Second is the increasing instability of political alignments in the Middle East, which creates an opportunity for a more active European role. With significant and long-standing economic and cultural ties in the area, European states have an incentive to continue playing an important part in regional affairs.

And third is the seeming contradiction between the region's commercial ties with the outside world and its financial relations. Foreign trade is dominated by Europe, which is by far the biggest market for the Middle East's oil as well as the largest source of its imports. Yet financial relations are dominated by the United States and its dollar. America's currency is not only the standard for invoicing and payments in world energy markets. It also accounts for the vast majority of central bank reserves and government-held investments in the region and is the anchor, de jure or de facto, for most local currencies. In the eyes of many Europeans the disjunction seems anomalous, even irrational. Often, the question is asked: Would it not make more sense to do business with the area's biggest trading partner, Europe, in Europe's own currency rather than the greenback? And if so, would it not then make sense to switch to the euro as a reserve currency and monetary anchor as well?

But would Middle Eastern governments be receptive to any kind of overture from Europe? The probability is low. At present, most regimes in the area find it more prudent to accept US patronage and even US troops to maintain any semblance of stability in the region. Few, if any, are likely to see Europe as a better guarantor of security. And in any event Europeans know that any initiative on their part would almost certainly provoke determined opposition from the United States, which clearly prefers to keep the region's door as firmly shut to the euro as possible. However tempting the area might be, Europe has no wish to provoke a direct confrontation with Washington.

The reality is that EMU has shown little interest in either informal or formal measures to promote euro internationalization. Quite the contrary, in fact. From the beginning, as noted in chapter 5, proactive policies have been insistently eschewed. Behind the scenes, it is known, there are many Europeans who might favor a more proactive stance, if possible. But until now at least, they have had little impact on official policy. On this issue, as on so many others in the EU, it is Germany's attitude that matters most, and here German views have not changed since the heyday of the Deutsche mark.[49] Germans still fear that internationalization could weaken control of monetary policy or generate exchange-rate volatility and uncertainty. The potential costs, they worry, would simply be too high. Hence resistance to any overt influence attempt on behalf of the euro remains strong. So long as that remains the case, the future of the currency is most likely to be left to the logic of market competition. Internationalization will not be "managed."

CONCLUSION

So the euro's future has not turned out so rosy after all. Contrary to the expectations of enthusiasts, Europe's money has failed to surpass, or even approach, the dominant dollar. After a fast start, the euro's ascent stalled and in recent years has even begun a modest retreat. The little currency has not become big; its power is still unrealized. Indeed, its best days may already be behind it.

The central problem is a structural defect at the heart of EMU—an incomplete merger of sovereign states that leaves the euro prone to a debilitating spirit of shoddy compromise. Governance is inherently flawed, an imperfect construct; and that in turn amplifies other liabilities that sap the currency's appeal. Dismal growth prospects inhibit wider use for trade or as a vehicle in exchange markets. Fragmented financial markets make the euro less attractive as a store of value. And so long as the United States remains the indispensable nation in geopolitics, few investors or governments will be tempted to switch their allegiance to the money of a political dwarf. EMU's power resources are simply no match for those behind the greenback.

9

The Yuan: Power Unstoppable?

Stop spend borrowed money!
US dollar, here today. . . . Yuan tomorrow.
—*sign on a bank in Franklin, North Carolina, July 2011*

If not the euro, why not the renminbi? For many, including one small bank in rural North Carolina, it is the yuan, not Europe's joint money, that is the real currency of tomorrow—the challenger that will finally topple the dollar from its place at the top of the Currency Pyramid. Where once euro enthusiasts seemed to be everywhere, today we have innumerable yuan enthusiasts. Internationalization, it is said, is the RMB's manifest destiny, an unstoppable by-product of China's remarkable economic success.

Time and again, the word *inevitable* is heard. Many agree with Arvind Subramanian, who confidently predicts that "China's growing size and economic dominance are likely to translate into currency dominance. . . . The renminbi could surpass the dollar as the premier reserve currency well before the middle of the next decade."[1] Echoes business economist Patrick Zweifel, "The era of the renminbi is upon us."[2] The euphoric mood is captured best by one London investment manager, who declares that "I'll eat my hat if the renminbi isn't the strongest currency on the planet over the next 10 years."[3]

What makes the rise of the yuan seem so unstoppable? We know that China has emerged as an industrial and trading dynamo. Few doubt that, as a result, the country will have a major impact on the international monetary order in the years ahead.[4] But the Chinese economy is only part of the explanation. Equally important is the role of politics—specifically, the strong backing of China's government, which seems determined to use all its capabilities to promote the RMB's role as an international currency. After long hesitation, Beijing appears to have made internationalization of the "people's currency" an official policy goal, and a concerted strategy is now being implemented with that lofty ambition in mind. The yuan has embarked on a Long March toward global status, reminiscent of the Long March that was so pivotal in the Communist Party's victory in China's civil war. This is clearly a purposeful act—a deliberate influence attempt. Power resources are being employed instrumentally to widen foreign use of the RMB; wider use of the RMB, in turn, is expected to enhance Chinese influence and prestige.

In this respect, the "redback" stands in sharp contrast to antecedents like the DM, yen, and euro. In none of those previous instances, as we know, was much support provided by issuing authorities. Proactive policies were rare, whether informal or formal. Internationalization, if it was to occur at all, was to be determined solely by preferences on the demand side of the market. But that is not the prevailing attitude in Beijing, where there seems little doubt that an international currency can be "manufactured" by well designed efforts on the supply side. Internationalization can be "managed."

Is such confidence warranted? To all appearances, Beijing's ambition would not seem unreasonable. Plainly, China has restored its role as a "great" power. Why should it not also have a "great" currency? As the world's second largest economy and leader in global exports, the proverbial Middle Kingdom already offers the foundation of a broad transactional network—a significant source of power. Why should Beijing not be able to build on that foundation to enhance the yuan's appeal for various cross-border purposes?

Appearances, however, can be misleading. As a practical matter, the challenge that China faces is extraordinarily daunting. Success in manufacturing an international currency is by no means guaranteed, as I noted back in chapter 5. For the Middle Kingdom, the ascent up the greased pole is apt to prove especially difficult. Beijing's broad capabilities are obviously impressive; there is no question that China is once again a powerful nation. But as David Shambaugh suggests, it is a "partial power" at best.[5] Whether the country has the means needed to translate its generic capabilities into effective action in this specific context is actually quite doubtful. Like the DM, yen, and euro before it, the RMB seems destined to fall considerably short of expectations. The aim of this chapter is to explain why.

At issue are two critical questions. First is the question of *strategic design*. That is a matter of China's intentions. What are the government's goals for the yuan, and is the Long March properly conceived to achieve them? Second is the question of Beijing's choice of *means*. That is a matter of China's statecraft. Have the authorities chosen the right tools and instruments? Are the country's power resources sufficient for the task at hand? Analysis suggests that while China's internationalization strategy is soundly conceived, its chosen means will almost certainly prove inadequate owing to a range of practical limitations. A ceiling is likely to be reached well short of top currency status.

THE STRATEGY

No precise date can be identified when Beijing first leaned toward the goal of internationalization. Discussions began as early as 2002. A key turning point came in 2006 with publication of a report on "The Timing, Path, and Strategies of RMB Internationalization" by a study group set up by the People's Bank of China (PBOC), China's central bank. "The time has come for promotion of the internationalization of the yuan," the study group argued. Internationalization "can enhance China's international status and competitiveness significantly [and] will increase its influence in the international economy." China will "have a greater say" and will enjoy "a rise in power standing." We "should take advantage of the opportunity," the report concluded. Internationalization is "an inevitable choice."[6]

Many in China's leadership evidently agreed. Within government and party circles a distinct shift of attitude soon became apparent, spurred in particular by the 2008 global financial crisis. With its vast hoard of dollar reserves, Beijing had every reason to feel vulnerable to a sudden shift of exchange rates. Internationalization of the yuan might provide a useful means to reduce dependence on America's greenback.

Chinese elite opinion is by no means unanimous. In fact, divisions over the issue have been evident in Beijing for some time.[7] On the one side are factions led by the PBOC who see internationalization as a means to push forward with liberal financial reforms. On the other side are a range of producer interests fearful that wider use of the yuan might drive up its price, eroding export competitiveness, along with banks and state-owned enterprises that have long benefited from the government's firm controls over interest rates and credit allocation. Domestic cleavages are probably the reason why, to this day, there has never been a formal declaration anointing internationalization as official Chinese policy. Judging from Beijing's actions, however, it seems quite clear which way the prevailing wind is blowing. By late 2009, as one observer has put it, "The Chinese Government obviously changed its mind and became enthusiastic about RMB internationalization."[8] By 2011, according to an influential advisor to the PBOC, internationalization had assumed a place "at the heart of China's financial strategy."[9]

But how is the goal to be achieved? Up to the time of the PBOC's Study Group report, China had one of the most tightly controlled currencies in the world, hemmed in by all manner of exchange restrictions and capital controls. How could cross-border use of the RMB be promoted if the money was not readily convertible? Moreover, the country's leadership knew that there was no successful model in recent history for manufacturing an international currency. They had no road map to help guide their actions. Not surprisingly, therefore, the government's approach has been noticeably cautious, a careful choreography stressing gradualism above all. Following Deng Xiaoping's dictum to "cross the river by feeling the stones," strategy has developed incrementally in multiple small steps. China's ruling Communist Party is no stranger to the idea of a Long March.

Effectively, managed internationalization has been pursued along two interrelated tracks.[10] One track focuses on cultivating use of the RMB in foreign trade. At the official level, currency swap agreements with foreign central banks have been initiated facilitating use of the RMB as a means of payment. At the private level, regulations have been gradually eased to permit more trade transactions to be invoiced and settled in yuan, bypassing traditional invoicing currencies like the dollar. The other track focuses on use of the RMB in international finance. Emphasis has been placed on the development of active markets for yuan deposits and yuan-denominated bonds, mainly "offshore" in Hong Kong, the former British crown colony that is now a "special administrative region" of China. Along both tracks, initiatives have been implemented patiently in finely calibrated phases. To date, the trade track has seen much more progress than the finance track.

Trade Track

On the trade track the yuan's Long March began in late 2008, when the PBOC set out to negotiate a series of local currency swap agreements designed to provide RMB funding to other central banks, when needed, for use in trade with China. Six years later pacts had been signed with some 26 economies, including major players like Argentina, Australia, Brazil, Britain, Indonesia, Russia, Singapore, South Korea, Switzerland, and the United Arab Emirates. The size of individual swaps varies greatly, from as little as 700 million yuan (roughly $110 million) for Uzbekistan and two billion yuan ($322 million) for Albania to as much as 360 billion yuan ($58 billion) for South Korea and 400 billion yuan ($65 billion) for Hong Kong. Total facilities amount to some 2.7 trillion yuan ($435 billion).

Ostensibly, the aim of the swap agreements is to insure against the kind of risks that could come with another global financial crisis. The availability of RMB funding on an emergency basis would offer China's trading partners a useful hedge against any future liquidity crunch. But the facilities are also designed to supply yuan, when desired, for use in bilateral trade on a more regular basis—in effect, to provide indirect encouragement for commercial use of the Chinese currency.

More directly, beginning in 2009, Beijing has gradually widened the range of trade transactions that may be settled in yuan, further promoting the currency's use by nonresidents. Informally, the RMB has long been accepted as a settlement currency in border trade with neighboring countries such as Laos, Mongolia, Myanmar, Nepal, North Korea, and Vietnam, resulting in a substantial growth in the volume of yuan bank notes circulating beyond China's borders. Although overall estimates vary widely and are of questionable reliability, it is clear that the numbers are no longer trivial. In Mongolia, according to the *Economist*, as much as 60 percent of cash in circulation may now be RMB.[11]

Formal authorization of yuan trade settlement, which began with a limited pilot scheme in 2009, was extended to all Chinese enterprises by early 2012. Additionally, since September 2010, foreign enterprises have been allowed to open cross-border yuan settlement accounts at locally registered banks in China, further expanding opportunities for use of the RMB on a regular basis. And along the way the PBOC has been busily constructing a new China International Payment System, a vital piece of technical infrastructure to facilitate cross-border invoicing and payments. Agreements have been negotiated to introduce direct trading between the yuan and local currencies in a number of foreign financial centers, including London, Paris, Frankfurt, Luxembourg, Singapore, and Taiwan. In each location a single clearing bank has been designated for RMB-denominated transactions.

The results of all these initiatives have been impressive. By the end of 2014 some 20 percent of Chinese trade was being settled in yuan, up from essentially zero five years earlier. Until now, use has been mostly local. As much as 80 percent of the trade settled in yuan has been between Mainland China and Hong Kong, reflecting processing trade.[12] But RMB invoicing is gradually spreading, and further substantial increases in the currency's use for trade purposes are confidently expected in the years ahead.

Finance Track

Results on the finance track, by contrast, while not insignificant, have been less impressive. For the most part Beijing has proceeded cautiously, relying heavily on the special status of Hong Kong as a special administrative region. With its own currency and financial markets, Hong Kong offers a useful offshore laboratory for experimenting with innovations that the leadership is not yet prepared to introduce "onshore" on the Mainland. As frequently noted, this is, to say the least, an unusual pattern.[13] Never before has any government sought deliberately to develop an offshore market for its currency while still maintaining strict financial control at home. In effect, Beijing is drawing up its own road map, depending on the Hong Kong Monetary Authority (HKMA)—de facto, Hong Kong's central bank and chief financial regulator—to act as its faithful proxy.

As early as 2004 the HKMA launched the RMB Business Scheme, allowing banks in Hong Kong to open yuan deposit accounts for individuals and some enterprises. But the offshore deposit market, informally known as the CNH market, did not really begin to take off until mid-2010, when new rules were issued relaxing restrictions on the yuan activities of Hong Kong banks. (The designation CNH for offshore yuan deposits is in contrast to CNY, the designation for onshore yuan.) Daily trading of the RMB on the Hong Kong foreign-exchange market was authorized, and local financial institutions for the first time were allowed to open yuan accounts of their own, clearing the way for creation of a wider range of marketable financial products, including exchange traded funds and derivatives of various kinds. The result was a swift but still limited growth in the total value of CNH deposits, from less than 65 billion yuan ($10 billion) in December 2009 to some 860 billion yuan ($140 billion) at the end of 2013. Though nearly 150 authorized Hong Kong institutions now take part in the CNH market,[14] the amounts involved to date remain minuscule by international standards.

Development of an offshore market for yuan-denominated bonds began in 2007, when selected Mainland banks were permitted for the first time to raise funds by issuing RMB bonds in Hong Kong. The first so-called dim sum bond was issued by the China Development Bank in July 2007. Progress in the market, however, was slow until 2010, when permission was extended first to Chinese nonfinancial firms and then to foreign multinationals doing business in China. Among the first non-Chinese companies to enter, in June 2010, were Hong Kong and Shanghai Banking Corporation (HSBC) and the Bank of East Asia, followed later by such big names as McDonald's, Caterpillar, Volkswagen, and Unilever. Over the next three years the market more than tripled in size, with a value of new issues up from just 40 billion yuan ($6.3 billion) in 2010 and a cumulative total of only 22 billion yuan ($3.3 billion) previously. In all, by end-2013, more than 360 dim sum bonds had been issued. The net outstanding volume in circulation (new issues less redemptions) was up to some 572 billion yuan ($92 billion)—hardly a trivial amount, but also minuscule by international standards. In early 2014 the International Finance Corporation, a branch of the World Bank, sold a one billion yuan bond ($163 million) in London, the first dim sum issue outside of Hong Kong.

Parallel to the dim sum market, a nascent onshore market for yuan-denominated bonds, centered in Shanghai, has also been cautiously cultivated. The process began in 2005, when debt sales by non-Chinese issuers—known as "panda" bonds—were authorized inside China for the first time. Here, however, progress has been especially sluggish, even after a well-publicized pledge by China's State Council in 2009 to transform

Shanghai into an international financial center by no later than 2020. Initially limited just to "eligible" multilateral development institutions, access to the panda bond market was broadened in 2009 to include locally incorporated subsidiaries of foreign multinationals. But new issues have remained few and far between and small in value—mainly for state-backed financial institutions like the Asian Development Bank, Japan Bank for International Cooperation, and International Finance Corporation. The year 2010 saw the first sale by a private banking institution, Tokyo-Mitsubishi UFJ (China) Ltd; and in March 2014, the German automaker Daimler AG became the first foreign nonfinancial corporation to sell a panda bond, for some 500 million yuan ($81 million). But these numbers are even more minuscule by international standards. Shanghai still has a long way to go to fulfill the State Council's pledge.

STRATEGIC DESIGN

Overall, there seems little doubt that yuan internationalization has indeed assumed a place at the heart of China's financial strategy. But an international currency, clearly, is not an end in itself. Rather, the yuan's Long March must be seen as a means to promote more fundamental interests and aspirations. That raises the question of *strategic design*. What are Beijing's ultimate goals in promoting a broader role for the RMB, and is the government's strategy properly conceived to achieve them?

The question of design matters because internationalization is by no means a journey with a single unique destination. Currency internationalization, we know, involves multiple roles. We have also seen that the specific effects of individual roles may vary quite considerably and that different currencies may embody diverse mixtures of roles. Hence to frame an internationalization strategy properly, a country's leaders must first know what their priorities are; and then, second, be sure to focus their attention on the combination of roles that is most likely to satisfy their ambitions. The task, needless to say, is easier said than done.

Priorities

What are China's priorities? Regrettably, given the secretive nature of Chinese politics, no one outside the ranks of the country's close-knit leadership can really know for sure. Beijing is hardly a model of transparent governance. Furthermore, over time the signals out of China have been decidedly mixed. Yet for all the mystery, it is not impossible to make some reasonable inferences based on years of policy behavior. At a minimum, it seems fair to assume that Chinese aspirations in international affairs include political as well as strictly economic considerations.

Not surprisingly, analysts have long argued about the Middle Kingdom's broad foreign-policy ambitions.[15] Are the Chinese prepared to continue working within a global system still dominated by the United States in a "Second American Century," or does Beijing aspire to replace Washington in a new "Chinese Century"? Put bluntly, is China a status quo power or a revisionist state? Do the Chinese accept the legitimacy of the existing world order? Are they willing to limit their priorities to what John Ruggie[16] called "norm-governed" changes? Or, par contre, are they looking for a more radical transformation of the international environment? Is their goal fundamental change at the level of basic principle—a new global system based more on "Chinese characteristics"?

Many analysts dismiss the risk of Chinese revisionism. According to Andrew Nathan and Andrew Scobell, for instance, the main goals of Chinese foreign policy are strictly defensive, driven by multiple and enduring security threats.[17] China, in their words, "is too bogged down in the security challenges within and around its borders to threaten the West."[18] For John Ikenberry (2013), any danger to the status quo is moderated by the very nature of the US-dominated system, which is more institutionally embedded and functionally articulated than past international orders.[19] China is constrained in two ways. "On the one hand, [the system] will provide attractions, incentives, and opportunities for China—thereby encouraging Beijing to integrate further into the existing order. On the other hand, it is a deeply rooted and expansive order that is difficult to undermine or circumvent—thereby making it difficult for Beijing to oppose it or offer a viable alternative vision of international order."[20] In short, China has every reason to limit its priorities to "norm-governed" change.

The Chinese themselves, however, seem to be of two minds, torn between conflicting goals. As one informed source suggests, there are in fact at least two Chinas—an "economic China" concentrated on economic development and modernization; and a "political China" determined, above all, "to achieve and maintain power in an asymmetric power relation to Western superpowers."[21] While economic China would be content to continue enjoying the material benefits of the prevailing system, political China would be more inclined to regain the rights and privileges that have long been regarded as the Middle Kingdom's natural due. Deeply rooted in Chinese political culture, going back to the great philosopher Confucius (Kong Qui), is the notion of *tianxia,* literally "all-under-heaven," with its sense of power centrality expressed in a traditional tributary system.

China has long felt entitled to the mantle of regional, if not global, leadership. As historian Odd Arne Westad astutely notes, "Even when the Chinese state was at its weakest, in the late 19th and early 20th centuries, its elites felt that . . . other countries in the 'Confucian zone' were simply to accept China's natural leadership."[22] To this day the Chinese still harbor deep resentment over what they perceive as a "century of humiliation" at the hands of the barbarian West; many applaud when a commentary published by the official Xinhua news agency calls for building a "de-Americanized world."[23] In a society with a very long historical memory, we cannot lightly dismiss the salience of such sentiments.

When it comes to currency internationalization, therefore, it seems unlikely that Beijing's priorities are defined solely, or even primarily, in economic terms. China may be attracted by the chance to save on transactions costs or to garner a bit of foreign seigniorage. Almost certainly the government would like to reduce the currency mismatch in the nation's international balance sheet. But from all we know about the leadership's ambitions for a "peaceful rise" to great-power status, we have to assume that, even more importantly, some measure of power is being sought as well. In the words of Di Dongsheng, a professor at Beijing's Renmin University:

> China's policies are not a function of short-term, purely economic interests; they are the result of a series of long-term political and strategic considerations that aim to protect and expand the power of the ruling party.[24]

At a minimum, the leadership's aim would involve a greater degree of autonomy for the Chinese state, to reduce a sense of vulnerability to external crises or the vagaries of the dollar. Beyond that, it seems evident that Beijing would like as well to attain a greater measure of influence in global affairs. Ultimately an internationalized yuan, we may assume, is valued because it can add to China's geopolitical capabilities.

Focus

Seen in this light, Beijing's strategic design seems right on target. Attention has focused on precisely the combination of currency roles that is most likely to fulfil the government's ambitions.

As we saw in chapter 4, three of an international money's six possible roles are of paramount importance in promoting an issuing country's power. These are the roles in financial markets, trade, and central-bank reserves. The roles in financial markets and reserves enhance the issuer's monetary autonomy, making it easier to delay or deflect adjustment costs. Autonomy in turn creates a capacity for influence, though whether that capacity can be actualized will depend on additional considerations that may vary widely over time. A currency's role in trade is important, above all, because of its impact on the reserve preferences of foreign central banks. The currency composition of central-bank reserves generally tends to reflect the pattern of currency choice in an economy's international commercial relationships. The more a money is used for each of these three roles, the greater is its contribution to the issuer's power.

It makes sense, therefore, for Beijing to choose the two tracks that it has pursued until now. The finance track is critical to establishing the appeal of the RMB as an investment medium, starting with bank deposits and bonds and then, presumably, moving on to a steadily widening range of financial products. Though the financial-market role, on its own, is not apt to add much to China's external power, it is an essential first step toward reserve-currency status, which surely promises a greater measure of influence. A given money can play an investment role even if never used as a reserve currency. The reverse, however, is unlikely ever to happen in a market-based currency system. As I argued in chapter 4, monetary history suggests that the investment role comes first and then is followed by a reserve role *in addition*. The link is the trade role, owing to the vital part that the currency denomination of trade plays in determining which among several investment currencies will emerge as well as a favored reserve asset.

In short, Beijing does seem to have framed its strategy well. The Hong Kong and Shanghai Banking Corporation summarizes succinctly: "First trade, then investment; and after that, reserve currency status. That is the road map for the renminbi in a single sentence."[25]

MEANS

But what about Beijing's choice of *means*—its statecraft? Have the authorities chosen the right tools and instruments to make their strategy succeed? Are the country's power resources sufficient for the task at hand? Here we may be permitted a greater measure of doubt.

Power Resources

Recall the challenge. Though China may aspire to global status for its currency, it cannot, for the most part, directly force outsiders to use the yuan. Some degree of compulsion might be possible in Hong Kong, formally subject to Mainland sovereignty, and perhaps also in a few client states like North Korea. In these cases the RMB might be able to function in a manner akin to what Susan Strange meant by the term master currency. But for everyone else, influence in this context must be exercised indirectly, through other pathways. One way or another, the yuan must be made to appeal to potential users. In short, it must be made competitive. The question is: Does Beijing have the power to successfully modify preferences on the demand side of the market?

Historically, as shown in chapter 5, preferences on the demand side have tended to be shaped by four essential elements of state power: economic size, financial development, foreign-policy ties, and military reach. To the extent that this package of qualities has prevailed, a money's appeal was enhanced, encouraging wide adoption.

In China's case, however, just one of these elements is manifestly in evidence—a broad transactional network. Economic size stands out as the RMB's trump card: the principal power resource that Beijing brings to the table. The Chinese economy is already a giant among nations—the second largest in the world—and could surpass the United States in as little as another decade. The country is also now the world's leader in exports and second biggest market for imports, creating a considerable potential for network externalities. More than a hundred countries now count China as their largest trading partner. There can be no doubt about the Middle Kingdom's gravitational pull in today's global commerce.

Will the trump card hold for long? The prevailing view seems to be that China's recent success is only the beginning. The giant will continue to grow, in time emerging as the world's dominant power. The new century will belong to China in the same way that the nineteenth century was said to belong to Britain or the twentieth century to the United States. As Subramanian puts it, "the economic dominance of China . . . is more imminent (it may already have begun), will be more broad-based (covering wealth, trade, external finance, and currency), and could be as large in magnitude in the next 20 years as that of the United Kingdom in the halcyon days of empire or the United States in the aftermath of World War II."[26] There will be no "Second American Century." Like it or not, the "Chinese Century" has begun.

Not everyone agrees, however. As successful as China has been until now, its shadow may not loom as large as Subramanian and others expect. Chinese GDP may soon be the largest in the world, but on a per-capita basis China is still no better than a lower middle-income country. As the saying goes, China is big but poor. As numerous observers point out, it is important not to conflate size with power. By many measures China's economy still suffers badly by comparison with the United States. Its exports are mostly low-end consumer products with poor brand presence, and its knowledge-intensive industries and financial services fall well below world standards. In the World Economic Forum's latest survey of global competitiveness, China ranked no better than 28th, far behind the United States, which was in third place surpassed only by Switzerland and Singapore.[27] In the words of political scientist Michael Beckley, "the United States has not declined; in fact, it is now wealthier, more innovative, and more militarily powerful compared to China than it was in 1991. . . . China is rising, but it is not catching up."[28]

In fact, prospects for the Middle Kingdom look increasingly clouded. As Harvard economists Lant Pritchett and Lawrence Summers point out, it is rare for any country to maintain "super-rapid" growth for as long as China has managed to do since its market reforms began in the 1980s.[29] Historical evidence shows that sooner or later there is a "regression to the mean," where expansion drops, often sharply, toward the long-run global average of about 2 percent growth per year in real GDP per person. Years ago Herbert Stein, once chair of the Council of Economic Advisors under Presidents Nixon and Ford, coined what has come to be known as Stein's Law: If something cannot go on forever, it will stop. There is little reason to believe that China's growth is immune to Stein's Law.

Quite the opposite, grave problems have accumulated that could significantly curtail the Middle Kingdom's expansion in the years ahead. These include an excessive reliance on investment and exports to generate growth, a rapidly rising level of debt in relation to GDP, widening income inequalities, rampant corruption, severe pollution, and a swiftly aging population. Economists at the International Monetary Fund suggest that China is now poised to cross the so-called Lewis Turning Point (named after Nobel Prize winning economist Arthur Lewis, a development specialist), where the country will move from a vast supply of low-cost workers to conditions of labor shortage, restraining growth potential.[30] Many observers now foresee a sharp slowdown over the longer term.[31] Some go further, predicting a "disaster . . . of historical proportions."[32] The days of double-digit growth are definitely over.

Even if expansion is curtailed, however, China's gravitational pull is bound to remain substantial. The economy will still be big and will still offer a broad transactional network. Beijing will continue to hold a strong trump card. But that is all—the only element of power in evidence. In other respects Beijing's hand is considerably weaker.

In finance, for example, China offers little appeal. For all the success of the Chinese economy, financial institutions remain rudimentary at best and the sector is still essentially closed to the outside world. Starting as early as 2002, a few international investors were granted direct access under the so-called Qualified Foreign Institutional Investor (QFII) scheme, permitting a small number of outsiders to acquire claims in the domestic capital market. And in late 2014 a new initiative was announced, the Shanghai–Hong Kong Stock Connect, allowing indirect purchases of shares on the Shanghai stock exchange through the Hong Kong market. But all investments are subject to strict quotas and administrative controls and remain very limited in total. Overall, the RMB is still largely inconvertible for residents and nonresidents alike.

As indicated, most activity on the finance track of Beijing's internationalization strategy has been promoted offshore in Hong Kong. The former crown colony is useful to Beijing as a testing ground. But even with the recent growth in the markets for CNH deposits and dim sum bonds, Hong Kong is clearly too small to carry the load on its own. A global role for the yuan will require much greater scale than can be provided by Hong Kong alone. Moreover, until now the bulk of activity in Hong Kong has been effectively local rather than truly international. Most trades of yuan deposits do little more than shuffle cash between Mainland enterprises and their own offshore subsidiaries; few transactions involve business with genuinely foreign companies.[33] Likewise, more than three-quarters of dim sum bond issues are for the benefit of Mainland and Hong Kong firms rather than enterprises farther afield. Big foreign names like Caterpillar or Volkswagen are the exception, not the rule. Even including Hong Kong, China remains something of a pygmy as compared with more traditional financial centers. As one observer has written: China's economic influence "derives primarily from its role in the international trading system, rather than its financial might."[34]

Nor, for all of China's success in restoring its great-power status, does the Middle Kingdom offer much appeal in political terms. Certainly much effort has been put into cultivating foreign-policy ties around the globe, using strategic investments and bilateral aid programs as well as a variety of regional and multilateral forums. Beijing has gone to great lengths to persuade the world that its rise is indeed "peaceful." Typical were the remarks of President Xi Jinping during a 2014 tour of Latin America:

> The Chinese people are peace-loving, and we do not carry in our blood the gene of invaders and imperialists, inasmuch as China rejects antiquated logic that equates being great with being hegemonic. Persisting in the road of peaceful development, China actively strives for a peaceful international environment.[35]

Actions, however, speak louder than words. Offsetting such soothing homilies has been the scale of China's vast military buildup, which is clearly designed to project power well beyond the country's immediate borders. Rather than volunteer formal or informal security assurances, Beijing has increasingly chosen to act more like a bully, aggressively asserting what it regards as its core national interests. That has been most notable in the East China Sea and South China Sea, where territorial claims have embroiled the country in disputes with a number of neighboring states. For many in the East Asian region, the expansion of Beijing's military reach is seen as anything but reassuring. Few neighbors share China's nostalgia for the idealized tradition of a tributary system, with the Middle Kingdom at its center. Even fewer are prepared to dismiss entirely the risk of Chinese revisionism. China's historical sense of entitlement is deeply resented.

Finally, we need to take account of the autocratic nature of China's domestic political regime, which is so different from the more democratic forms of governance that prevailed in all previous cases of currency internationalization in the modern era. In this respect, China does not inspire a high level of confidence. There is no question that Beijing has been successful in terms of macroeconomic management; inflation has not been allowed to pose a serious threat to the RMB. But in broader political terms, the Middle Kingdom's record is anything but encouraging. To date, Beijing has shown little regard for property rights or faithful enforcement of contractual obligations. The country's governance structure is not known for transparency or accountability. Quite the reverse, in fact. The ruling Communist Party has always been dictatorial in nature and often arbitrary in behavior. In its survey of global governance indicators, the World Bank ranks China in the 40th percentile for the rule of law,[36] while Transparency International places China no higher than 100th among 177 nations in its latest corruption index.[37] Indeed, over the medium term, it is not even clear whether political stability can be assured.

To their credit, China's rulers do not deny the issue. Indeed, at the annual meeting of the Communist Party's central committee in late 2014, under the leadership of President Xi Jinping, the problem was noted and a formal commitment was made to firmly establish the "rule of law" by the year 2020. In practice, however, there was less here than meets the eye. The Party clearly did not have Western-style democracy in mind. "We absolutely cannot indiscriminately copy foreign rule-of-law concepts and models," declared the Central Committee. The goal, it seemed, was to refine Party control, not dilute it. As the *Economist* commented: "Official English translations refer to the importance of the 'rule of law.' But Mr. Xi's tactics appear better suited to a different translation of the Chinese term, *yifa zhi-guo*: 'rule *by* law.' His aim is to strengthen law to make the party more powerful, not to constrain it."[38] In this light, only the most sanguine of investors or central banks would see today's China as a safe haven for their assets. In the words of one critical commentary, "China faces a credibility problem."[39]

Limits

What, then, can China do? Given the limited range of relevant power resources at its disposal, Beijing has little choice but to play the hand it has.
If it is to have any hope of successfully altering demand-side preferences
for its currency, it must exploit the Middle Kingdom's growing weight in
the world economy—its gravitational pull—to the utmost.

In practice, that would appear to be the government's intent. Beijing
is plainly counting on China's immense leverage as a trading nation to
support wider use of the yuan. Policy has been pro-active, making use of
both informal and formal tactics. By widening the range of transactions
that may be settled with RMB and by authorizing the growth of the CNH
market in Hong Kong, the currency's market appeal has been promoted.
And use has been further encouraged by the many swap agreements that
Beijing has undertaken to negotiate with foreign central banks. China is
obviously a place where many outsiders want to do business. Beijing has
not hesitated to try to exploit that advantage.

But the task will not be as easy as it might seem. The Chinese economy is of course big and will perhaps continue to grow bigger. Trade
volume alone, however, will not be enough. The *structure* of trade relations will also make a difference. The Middle Kingdom today, despite
its great weight as a trading nation, is still more like post–World War II
Japan in the small percentage of its exports denominated in its own currency. To a large extent that is due to the distinctive character of China's
foreign trade structure, which to date has been highly networked. With
its low labor costs, China made itself into the "world's workshop" by
encouraging imports of high valued-added inputs and components (for
example, computer chips) that could then be processed or assembled into
lower value-added final products for export. In such a network structure
it makes sense to "price to market," denominating all the links of the
production chain in one widely accepted international currency such as
the dollar. That is not likely to change as much as Beijing hopes unless
China can succeed with plans to move up the technological scale to more
home-grown, high value-added industrial goods, as it has already done
in areas like solar panels and wind turbines. Across the industrial world,
as noted back in chapter 5, exports of differentiated manufactured goods
typically tend to be invoiced and settled in the seller's own currency. The

more China is able to move its production structure in that direction, the easier it will be to continue to expand the RMB's role in international trade. But success in this respect is by no means guaranteed.

Whatever the outcome, Beijing can be expected to continue seeking to exploit the advantage of its central position in trade. Basically, the idea seems to be to rely, to the extent possible, on both the second and third faces of power to realize the leadership's ambitions. At one level, it appears, the aim is to reshape incentive structures through the sheer size of "economic China." That is the second face of power, involving a logic of consequences. The hope, quite obviously, is that outsiders will be induced to shift to the yuan because of the added convenience it offers for engaging with an ever more important trade partner. As one observer writes, "the Chinese market does appear to have structural power in the suggestion that diplomatic policy toward China is influenced by commercial decisions based on the need to secure competitive market access."[40] At a deeper level, the idea seems to be to remold identities and interests by way of the rise of "political China." That is the third "soft" face of power, involving a logic of appropriateness. Internationalization may spread because market actors come to be convinced of its legitimacy—in effect, a confirmation of the Middle Kingdom's renewed prominence in the community of nations. To paraphrase Mundell, outsiders may come to believe that as an emerging great power, China *should* have a great currency.

Both logics make sense. The force of the Chinese economy's gravitational pull is undeniable. Indeed, internationalization of the yuan is difficult to imagine without it. A broad transactional network is surely necessary. But is it sufficient? As a power resource, is economic size alone enough to make the RMB competitive? About that, an ample dose of skepticism is warranted.

The reason goes back to the multiplicity of roles of an international currency and the considerable differences among them. Economic size is clearly key to a money's role as a medium for commercial invoicing and payments. In that respect, it is no surprise the yuan has already begun to establish itself as a trade currency; and that role, in turn, appears to be encouraging use of the RMB as an anchor currency as well, in a manner reminiscent of the experience of the DM in the 1970s and 1980s. Experts debate just how far the process has progressed, with some sources expressing much skepticism.[41] But a variety of studies do seem to confirm that an increasing number of countries in the East Asia region now place most weight on the yuan in the management of their exchange rates, forming what amounts to a nascent "renminbi bloc."[42] These countries include such important trading nations as Indonesia, Malaysia, Philippines, Singapore, South Korea, Taiwan, and Thailand.

Economic size, however, matters much less when it comes to the other critical roles that Beijing appears to have targeted in its strategic design—use of the yuan as an investment medium and reserve currency. Those are the roles that really add value in terms of state power. But for them, other attributes matter more—not least, an advanced degree of financial development to provide the liquidity and predictability that market actors would expect of a reliable store of value. A deep and resilient capital market, sufficiently open to outsiders, is an essential prerequisite. That, plainly, Beijing still lacks.

Should we be at all surprised, therefore, to see how little progress has been made on the finance track of the yuan's Long March, in contrast to the trade track? If there is any consensus at all among informed observers, it is that reform of both domestic financial markets and external capital controls is essential if internationalization is to succeed.[43] As Jeffrey Frankel puts it: "If China is not yet ready to liberalize its domestic financial markets [and] to legalize capital inflows . . . then full internationalization is probably a long way off."[44] Certainly it looks a long way off now.

A particular sticking point is the issue of yuan convertibility. At a minimum, convertibility for current-account transactions would seem to be an absolute requirement to sustain the process of internationalization. But what about the capital account? As the stories of the DM and the yen both demonstrate (chapter 5), widespread adoption of a money for cross-border use is possible even in the presence of a substantial array of capital controls. Serious financial liberalization did not begin in either Germany or Japan until well after their currencies had already gained broad acceptance. This would seem to suggest that *full* convertibility of the RMB is by no means necessary. But it is also clear that the achievements of the DM and yen might have been even greater had full convertibility been introduced earlier. A degree of currency internationalization was sacrificed for the sake of maintaining a grip on domestic financial conditions.

China today faces the same trade-off. Some broadening of capital-account convertibility would seem called for, if interest in the yuan as an investment medium or reserve asset is to be promoted. How much convertibility, however, is a matter of choice. At a minimum, market actors and central banks would need to be given freedom to establish yuan bank accounts and to buy and sell selected classes of Chinese bonds and stocks. Few outsiders are likely to see RMB denominated claims as attractive if they cannot be acquired or sold at will. Equally important would be the right to issue new yuan debt or equity in China, in order to facilitate portfolio balancing. Internationalization on the asset side must be complemented by internationalization on the liability side. But at the same time trading in certain classes of liquid claims—especially in more speculative sectors such as options, futures, or other exotic derivatives—might well remain prohibited or tightly regulated in order to reduce the risk of destabilizing capital flows. The idea would be to encourage greater use of the yuan as a store of value while minimizing resulting vulnerabilities.

Complicating the trade-off is the fact that today many more currencies are convertible than was the case in the 1970s and 1980s, when the DM and yen were on the rise. These days, by comparison, market actors and central banks enjoy a much wider range of investment opportunities. In principle, that would seem to increase the pressure on Beijing to liberalize fully—but not entirely. Given China's great economic importance, even a partial opening of the capital account could be expected to attract wider use of the yuan. Though the availability of more accessible alternatives might slow down the RMB's Long March to elevated status, it would be unlikely to stop it altogether. In practice, some range of restrictions on more speculative market sectors could be preserved to sustain financial control at home.

Whatever the degree of convertibility permitted, however, it is evident that further financial reform at home is required to make the RMB attractive as a store of value. To date, in the all-important bond sector, progress has been painfully slow for both the dim sum and panda markets. Overall bond-market capitalization inside China is barely more than one-eighth of that in the United States, offering limited liquidity. Moreover, potential investors have been discouraged by still strict restraints over what they can do with their money, as well as by a host of other unanswered questions. Can political stability be assured? Can a government be trusted that remains so autocratic in nature? Will property rights be respected? Hesitation in the face of such uncertainties is only natural.

Economic size, therefore, does not in fact seem to be enough to make the RMB fully competitive as an international currency. As one astute observer comments: "A great currency is built on trust in the issuing state . . . and China is discovering that trust and credit cannot be boiled down to GDP."[45] Put differently, Beijing has a serious "fungibility problem." A broad transactional network cannot easily compensate for other critical inadequacies. The separate roles of an international money call for different kinds of power resources, and these resources are not necessarily interchangeable. In its choice of means—its statecraft—Beijing would seem to be relying too much on too little.

Command and Control

Of course, it is not difficult to understand why Beijing has tried to rely so much on so little. Firm control of financial activity is a central element of China's economic model, an integral part of its authoritarian system of governance. China may no longer be a command economy, but the ruling party clearly wishes to remain in charge.

Despite the remarkable changes that have taken hold in China over the last three decades, it is well understood that the country's distinctive political economy—variously labeled the "Beijing Consensus"[46] or "Sino-capitalism"[47]—remains far removed from standard Western models. First and foremost, the regime relies on a continuing role for an unchallenged central bureaucracy. As Stefan Halper describes it, the Beijing Consensus "combines market economics with traditional autocratic or semiautocratic politics. . . . The government maintains central control over a partly liberalized economy."[48] In Christopher McNally's words, Sino-capitalism "assigns the Chinese state a leading role in fostering and guiding capitalist accumulation."[49]

It is also well understood that resistance to any significant change of the regime is very strong. Institutionally, the Communist Party of China has every reason to fear a loss of authority should its reins on the economy be loosened. Personally, the fortunes of many of the country's elite—not least, the "princelings" descended from party's founding fathers—rely too much on preserving the status quo. Interests in the banking sector, state-owned enterprises, and provincial and local governments are by now deeply entrenched. In such circumstances, any serious reform is highly problematic. The incentive structure is stacked up against it.

In the context of the Chinese model, nothing is more critical to successful control than an ability to manage monetary and financial conditions. Domestically, this means direct authority over interest rates and the availability of credit, enabling the state to allocate resources to favored borrowers and to minimize its own funding costs. Authority is exercised through regulated deposit and lending rates, quantitative credit guidance, and bond market rationing. Internationally, control means a closed capital account and managed exchange rate. Financial repression, as economists call it, is a vital cog in the machinery of political autocracy.

It is not surprising, therefore, that even as China's government has adopted internationalization as a goal, it has moved so cautiously and incrementally. The hope, plainly, is to be able to encourage gradually wider use of the RMB abroad without seriously threatening financial control at home. That explains why, for example, so much of the finance track of Beijing's strategy has been carried out in Hong Kong's offshore market, which is largely insulated from onshore markets on the Mainland. It also explains why China's political leadership has long resisted pressure from the PBOC and others[50] to liberalize domestically or open the country's capital account. Of particular concern is the risk that convertibility would trigger a flood of capital outflows seeking diversification for China's large pool of domestic savings.[51] To say the least, policy makers are faced with a delicate balancing act. In effect, Beijing has tried to promote internationalization on the cheap—to make as few concessions as possible in terms of financial reform, hoping that economic size alone will manage to do the job.

In the end, however, the balancing act almost certainly will prove untenable. As many observers have noted, yuan internationalization will eventually provide means to "punch holes"[52] in China's capital controls, challenging the government's grip over money and credit at home. And of course, judging from the carefully calibrated choreography that has been followed until now, that would seem to be understood by China's leadership as well. Policy makers appear to recognize that, sooner or later, diminished command is the price they will have to pay for an internationalized RMB. But in the spirit of Saint Augustine—who prayed to the Almighty for celibacy, just "not yet"—it seems that Beijing would prefer to postpone the moment for as long as possible.

CONCLUSION

The lessons from China's experiment with managed internationalization are clear. First, there is nothing in Beijing's experience to suggest that a state *cannot* manufacture an international currency. The first steps of the yuan's Long March have indeed achieved tangible results, particularly along the trade track. Second, however, it is clear that the process is by no means unstoppable. Real success is possible only if the right power resources are available and used appropriately. Since for this purpose a capacity for direct coercion is limited, strategy must be more indirect, concentrating on enhancing the currency's international appeal. But demand-side preferences will not be favorably modified by relying on just one attribute alone. On its own, the "gravitational pull" of China's economic size will not suffice. Other factors—above all, a well-developed and open financial structure—must also come into play, and the degree of fungibility among them is low.

In the end, therefore, it is clear that there are limits to the use of power to manufacture an international currency, unless a government is willing to pay the necessary price. For China, the cost is financial liberalization and with it a significant modification of Beijing's authoritarian economic model. Currency internationalization is no cinch and cannot be had on the cheap. The yuan's tomorrow is still a long way off.

10

Summing Up

"It's complicated."
—2009 film written and directed by Nancy Meyers

What, then, can we conclude about the relationship between currency and power? Robert Mundell may be right that great powers have great currencies; certainly, China's leadership seems convinced. But both theory and praxis suggest that the connections are anything but simple. Nancy Meyers's 2009 film, *It's Complicated*, set in Santa Barbara, California, humorously shows just how complex the eternal battle of the sexes can be. The message of this book, looking at monetary rivalry, is much the same. It's complicated.

ANALYTICAL CONTRIBUTIONS

In analytical terms, this book makes three key contributions. The first is to move the political dimensions of currency internationalization to center stage. The literature on international money is enormous, going back generations. With relatively few exceptions, however, the main contributions have come from economics, not political science. Politics may lurk in the wings, but only rarely is its leading role formally acknowledged. This book provides a corrective, giving politics the top billing that it deserves.

Second, the book systematically explores the causal relationships that link currency internationalization and state power. That has never been done before in any detail. We see that there is every reason to believe that the connections between currency and power are mutually endogenous, with the causal arrow running simultaneously in both directions. Currency internationalization influences state power; state power influences currency internationalization. We also see that the relationship is not always beneficial for the issuer. In some ways, currency internationalization may actually diminish rather than augment state power. International money turns out to be a double-edged sword that can cut either way. And we see that the element of time matters in several critical ways. As the years pass the relationship may change considerably, both when internationalization and power are on the rise and when they are in decline.

Third, the book demonstrates the importance of disaggregating the concept of currency internationalization into the several separate roles that an international money may play. Individual roles have distinctly different effects on state power. Conversely, different power resources have distinctly different effects on individual currency roles. It is no accident that among the small number of moneys to be found at the peak of the Currency Pyramid, there is so much variation in terms of domain and scope.

Theory

Until now, the literature of IR and IPE has offered little formal theory to help us understand the relationship between currency and power. To remedy that deficiency, this book proceeded in three steps.

First, after a review of the essentials of currency internationalization in chapter 1, chapter 2 offered a basic primer on the study of power in world politics. The concept of state power, we saw, is highly contested among scholars. Hence it seemed necessary, at the outset, to go back to first principles to build a solid foundation for analysis. Above all, it is clear that in any power analysis we must be prepared to be pragmatic, emphasizing context above all. Four key clusters of questions dominate the agenda—questions concerning, respectively, the meaning, sources, uses, and limits of power. These questions provided the conceptual framework for all the discussion that followed.

The next step, in chapter 3, was to narrow the focus from power in general to the specifics of monetary power. In this context, the central issue is state autonomy: the ability to reduce or avoid the burden of adjustment to external imbalance. Only once monetary autonomy is established will a country, in addition, be in a position to exercise influence as well. Monetary power has two hands—the power to delay adjustment and the power to deflect adjustment costs. By adding to a country's ability to finance deficits over time, an international currency amplifies the power to delay. In effect, the state's borrowing capacity is enhanced.

The final step, making use of these building blocks, was to narrow the focus even further to explore in detail the causal relationships linking currency internationalization and state power (chapters 4 and 5). Answers were offered to four critical questions that were initially posed in the introduction.

From Power to Currency

Is state power necessary or sufficient for a currency to gain international status? Historical evidence suggests that some measure of state power is surely *necessary*. Great currencies do not spring from the loins of small or weak nations. Four elements of state power matter most. These are economic size, financial development, foreign-policy ties, and military reach. Each of these factors can be regarded as a source of power—expressions of geopolitical capability. Great weight in the world economy exercises a kind of gravitational pull by creating a potential for network externalities. An advanced financial sector enhances the appeal of a currency as an investment medium and reserve asset. Extensive political linkages and military capabilities encourage greater use both by governments and by jittery investors seeking a safe haven for their savings.

But are these power resources *sufficient*? About that there is much more uncertainty. Even were a state able to put the entire package together—all four elements of power—its currency might not gain widespread cross-border use. Much depends on the structure of currency competition prevailing at the time. The larger the number of rivals, actual or potential, the more difficult it will be to gain a foothold near the peak of the Currency Pyramid. Prospects will be limited by the incumbency advantages of already established international currencies, which benefit from the force of inertia.

Furthermore, for countries that cannot put the entire package together, the process of internationalization will be critically limited by uneven impacts across the range of a money's possible functions. Large economic size, for example, may enhance a currency's appeal as a medium of exchange but, in and of itself, offers little advantage as a store of value. Financial development, by contrast, could promote use for investment purposes but have little effect on use in trade. And political and security ties are apt to be more influential at the official level than among private market actors. The several sources of state power in this context are by no means fungible.

Can a government overcome these limits by deliberate efforts to alter demand for its currency? For states with relevant power resources, an attempt to "manufacture" an international currency—"managed internationalization"—is not at all unrealistic. Indeed, history suggests that official backing may actually be necessary to overcome market inertia; at the least, it might help. But without the complete package, even the most determined proactive policies are unlikely to suffice to develop a full-bodied international money. Given the uneven impact of different power resources, reliance on just one attribute or another will not be enough. One or two roles might be encouraged, but not others. Real success is possible only if all the right power resources are available and are used appropriately. Additional limits may also be imposed by costs of implementation or domestic politics.

From Currency to Power

Does currency internationalization add to or subtract from a state's power? Here the answer is decidedly mixed. In many respects currency internationalization does add to a state's power, as one might expect— but that is not true of all of a currency's roles and it is not necessarily true for all time.

State power is enhanced in particular by three of an international currency's several possible roles—use in financial markets, in trade, and in central-bank reserves. The investment and reserve roles both serve to enhance a country's monetary autonomy, making it easier to delay adjustment costs, and also reinforce centrality in the global financial network. The trade role plays a critical part in determining the currency preferences of central banks. The more a money dominates in these three roles, the greater is the overall impact on the issuer's power capabilities.

But state power may also be eroded by internationalization, depending on circumstances. The double-edged sword can also cut the other way.

Some roles may put the issuer in the position of a Stackelberg leader, effectively hostage to the decisions of followers. That is especially evident in the anchor currency role, where the issuer's power to manage its exchange rate is largely transferred to others. Other roles, such as the investment and reserve roles, may endow the issuer with an "exorbitant privilege" to finance "deficits without tears," but may also impose an "exorbitant duty" to come to the rescue of others when needed, possibly at considerable cost.

Furthermore, there is the element of time, which can hurt in two ways. On the one hand is the insidious effect of Gallarotti's "power curse"— the risk that over time the advantages of an international currency could lull the issuer into a false sense of security, leading it to discount growing vulnerabilities and feedbacks. On the other hand is the risk of a growing overhang of external debt that could eventually eliminate any room for macroeconomic flexibility. Contrary to the opinion of many, currency internationalization does not require an economy to run a persistent current-account deficit. But even if the process of internationalization occurs entirely through intermediation on the capital account, an accumulation of liquid liabilities is likely to weigh increasingly heavy as the years pass. Both risks—the power curse and the overhang—are inherent in the nature of currency internationalization.

In turn, this suggests why it is not unrealistic to think in terms of life cycles for international currencies—first a rise and then a fall of popularity. Early on, the benefits of internationalization will almost certainly outweigh possible costs. But sooner or later, as time passes and the effects of both the power curse and a liabilities overhang kick in, a tipping point is bound to be reached when the calculus is inverted and decline begins. First comes a "virtuous circle," when power resources promote internationalization and internationalization simultaneously promotes state power; and then comes a "vicious circle," when the reverse is true. No currency has ever dominated forever.

Loss of State Power

Does a loss of state power necessarily reduce international use of a currency? The answer here is Yes—but not right away. Once the geopolitical foundations of a currency's status start to erode, users have an incentive to look elsewhere for a more attractive alternative. Not only will this cause a loss of the benefits of internationalization. In addition, it may impose additional costs to the extent that the issuer is forced to resort to extraordinary measures to avoid a messy rush to the exits. Increasingly, terms and conditions will have to be negotiated, either via explicit bargaining or through implicit understandings. None of this, however, is apt to happen overnight. Historical evidence underscores the crucial advantages of incumbency. Owing to the highly path-dependent nature of international currency use, reflecting the potentially steep cost of switching, moneys tend to hang onto their place in the Currency Pyramid long after the onset of geopolitical decline. The lag may be quite considerable. Much depends on whether there are any talented understudies waiting in the wings, ready to step into a leading role.

Loss of Competitiveness

Does a loss of currency's competitive status diminish the power of the issuing state? Here the answer is a more unqualified Yes. A widely used currency adds to a state's power both directly and indirectly. Directly, the money itself can become an instrument of statecraft—something that the issuer is able to offer to friends or withhold from foes. Indirectly, the currency may enhance other pathways to influence by increasing state autonomy. Power is easier to project when the government does not have to worry about the balance of payments. Conversely, should a currency start to lose its popularity, these capabilities will quickly fade. Geopolitical decline will follow.

PRAXIS

Guided by these insights, we could then address the outlook for monetary rivalry in the world today. Here, in chapters 6 to 9, two questions dominated. First, what is the present state of play among the key currencies at the peak of the Currency Pyramid? Of most interest, of course, are the dollar, euro, and (potentially) the yuan—at the moment, considered to be the three top rivals for global dominance. And second, what is the prospect for each of these three moneys going forward? For now, the greenback is king. But can America's currency keep its claim to the crown, or are its days of supremacy numbered?

Analysis began in chapter 6 with a look at the evolution of competition in the international currency system in recent years. Among specialists, a broad consensus seems to have developed that the system is becoming increasingly competitive. More and more, we hear talk of an emerging multipolarity. But a closer look at the data actually shows little or no alteration in the system's competitive structure. At the peak of the Currency Pyramid, levels of concentration have shown no significant decline. The state of play today remains much as it was a quarter of a century ago. The dollar still dominates. Neither the euro nor the yuan has yet to offer a serious challenge.

Could that change? Many would say Yes. Careful analysis, however, suggests otherwise. On the evidence presented in chapters 7 to 9, neither dollar pessimism nor euro or yuan enthusiasm seems justified.

Quite noticeably, the power of the greenback remains undiminished despite America's ever-expanding overhang of foreign liabilities. The risk of a collapse of confidence in the dollar cannot be entirely dismissed; nor can we ignore the signs of a power curse at work. But neither danger trumps the unparalleled liquidity and safety of US financial markets, which together make the greenback a truly indispensable currency. Moreover, the United States is alone among nations in offering the complete package of power resources associated with top currency status. In addition to advanced financial development, these include a still broad network of trade relations, wide political ties, and vast military reach. No evidence exists to suggest that the enduring appeal of the dollar is the result of deliberate influence attempts by Washington. The dollar is not—or, at least, not yet—a negotiated currency. The time may yet come in the greenback's life cycle when the currency's popularity passes its peak and goes into decline. But there is little to indicate that such a tipping point will be reached anytime soon.

Conversely, the dollar's two rivals continue to be seriously handicapped by persistent and unforgiving deficiencies. The power of the euro remains unrealized, above all, because of structural defects in the design of its governance mechanisms. The euro is a currency without a country, an imperfect construct at best; and that flaw in turn amplifies other liabilities that limit the money's appeal. Today's Europe simply cannot compete with the United States in projecting financial, political, or military power. In similar fashion, the power of the RMB looks to be anything but unstoppable because of a range of practical constraints in the realms of both finance and politics. China has invested heavily in a two-track strategy meant to promote international use of the yuan. Its ambition to "manufacture" a top currency seems nakedly clear. But prospects for "managed internationalization" are limited by a shortage of the needed instruments of statecraft, including in particular a well developed financial sector. Beijing faces a fungibility problem. The gravitational pull of China's huge economy will not suffice on its own to propel the yuan upward.

For the moment, therefore, there seems little chance of any significant change in the system's broad competitive structure. Monetary rivalry will persist, of course, and almost certainly there will be some modest erosion of the dollar's dominance at the margins as the years pass. The euro will continue to compete in its own neighborhood; likewise, the RMB is bound to gain wider user in China's periphery. But overall, the balance of power among currencies is unlikely to shift dramatically. Well into the foreseeable future, the greenback will remain supreme.

Notes

INTRODUCTION

1. Mundell (1993).
2. As quoted in *IMF Survey* (22 January 2001: 27).
3. Cohen (1998, 2004).
4. Kindleberger (1970); Strange (1971a, 1971b); Cohen (1971a, 1977).
5. Kirshner (1995: 3).
6. Kirshner (1995); Lawton et al. (2000); Andrews (2006a).
7. Including especially Cohen (1998, 2004, 2012a).
8. Cohen and Chiu (2014).
9. Cohen (2006, 1966).
10. Cohen (2013).
11. Cohen (2014a).
12. Cohen and Benney (2014).
13. Cohen (2011, 2012b, 2015b).
14. Cohen (2012c, 2014b).

CHAPTER 1

1. Lake (2009: 2).
2. Cohen (1998).
3. Cohen (1971a).
4. Hartmann (1994: 1).
5. Cipolla (1967: chap. 2).
6. Frankel (1995: 13).
7. Sobel (2012).
8. McKinnon (2013: 6).
9. Eichengreen and Flandreau (2009, 2012).
10. Lake (2009: 3).
11. Cohen (1998).
12. Cipolla (1967); Groseclose (1976).
13. Brown (1978).
14. Strange (1971a, 1971b).
15. Cohen (1998, 2004).
16. Cohen (1971a); Schenk (2013).

17. Helleiner and Kirshner (2009); Norrlof (2010); Eichengreen (2011); Prasad (2014); Overholt et al. (2014).
18. Chinn and Frankel (2007, 2008).
19. Subramanian (2011).
20. Harris (2001: 35).
21. Swoboda (1968).
22. Swoboda (1968: 14).
23. Genberg (2010).
24. Judson (2012).
25. Norrlof (2010).
26. Wheatley (2013b).
27. Warnock and Warnock (2009); Kaminska and Zinna (2014).
28. Papaioannou and Portes (2008).
29. Gourinchas and Rey (2007); European Central Bank (2010: 45–55).
30. Frieden (1991).
31. Kirshner (1995).
32. Cohen (1998); Helleiner (2003); McNamara (2008).
33. Dobbs et al. (2009: 10).
34. Austin (2014).
35. Cohen (1971b).
36. Gourinchas et al. (2010).
37. Federal Open Market Committee (2008: 21).
38. Machlup (1958: 12).
39. Dobbs et al. (2009).
40. Dobbs et al. (2009: 9, 19).
41. Bernstein (2014).
42. Genberg (2010).
43. Bergsten (2009: 23).
44. Papaioannou and Portes (2008).
45. Hai and Yao (2010).
46. Johnson (1971: 9).

CHAPTER 2

1. Reich and Lebow (2014: 25).
2. Dowding (2011: xxiii).
3. Fels et al. (2012: vi).
4. Gilpin (1981: 13).
5. Baldwin (2013: 273).
6. Finnemore and Goldstein (2013).
7. Barnett and Duvall (2005: 40).
8. Nye (2011: xiv).
9. Dahl (1957: 202–203).
10. Baldwin (2013).
11. Baldwin (1979, 1989).
12. Carroll (1972).

13. Pansardi (2011).
14. Dahl (1984: 33).
15. Harknett and Yalcin (2012).
16. Andrews (2006b).
17. Cohen (2008a).
18. Singer et al. (1972).
19. National Intelligence Council (2012).
20. Rogers et al. (2014).
21. Shambaugh (2013).
22. Shambaugh (2013: 5–6).
23. Pillsbury (2000).
24. FNSR Group of Experts (2012).
25. Olivié et al. (2014).
26. Garrett and Tsebelis (1999); Guzzini (2009).
27. Nye (2011: 5).
28. Hirschman ([1945] 1969).
29. Keohane and Nye (1973, 1977).
30. Keohane and Nye (1973: 122).
31. Hafner-Burton et al. (2009).
32. Maoz (2011: 7).
33. Kahler (2009: 12).
34. Bachrach and Baratz (1962).
35. Strange (1988; second edition published in 1994).
36. Strange (1988: 24–25).
37. Cohen (2008b).
38. Keohane (2000: x–xi).
39. Cohen (2015a).
40. Palan (2003: 121).
41. Cohen (1977).
42. Strange (1979).
43. Helleiner (2006); Norrlof (2014a).
44. Strange (1994).
45. Lukes (1974); Dahl (1984).
46. Strange 1996).
47. Gruber (2000).
48. Gruber (2000: 7).
49. Strange (1996: 26).
50. Strange (1988: 28).
51. Guzzini (1993).
52. Breslin (2013: 137).
53. Lukes (1974).
54. Lukes (1974: 23).
55. Nye (1990).
56. Nye (2008: 29).
57. Hay (1997).
58. Barnett and Duvall (2005).

59. Krasner (2013).
60. Krasner (2013: 347).
61. Andrews (2006b).
62. Reich and Lebow (2014: 5).
63. Nye (2011: 8).
64. March (1966).
65. Baldwin (2013).
66. Putnam (1988).
67. Baldwin (2013).
68. Lasswell (1958); Baldwin (1985).
69. Baldwin (1999).
70. Gallarotti (2010).
71. Gallarotti (2010: 9).

CHAPTER 3

1. Gowa (1984).
2. Keohane (1984).
3. Milner (1993); Kirshner (2014).
4. Kirshner (1995).
5. Simmons (2001).
6. Simmons (2001: 596).
7. Helleiner (2006).
8. Norrlof (2008, 2010).
9. Kirshner (1995).   10.   McNamara (1998).
11. Helleiner (2008: 355).
12. Helleiner (2006: 89).
13. Andrews (1994); Webb (1994); Henning (1998); Kaelberer (2001, 2005); Vermeiren (2014).
14. Cohen (1977, 2000).
15. Cohen (2006).
16. Cohen (1966).
17. Cohen (1966: 3).
18. Walter (2013).
19. Walter (2013: 6).
20. Walter (2013: 116).
21. Cohen (1966).
22. Keohane and Nye (1977).
23. Cohen (1976).
24. Rueff (1972).
25. Kindleberger (1973).
26. Kindleberger (1976).
27. Chinn and Frankel (2007, 2008).
28. Subramanian (2011).
29. Norrlof (2014a).
30. Armijo et al. (2014).

CHAPTER 4

1. Baldwin (2013).
2. Strange (1971a: 222).
3. Kirshner (1995); Andrews (2006a); Armijo and Katada (2014, 2015).
4. Zimmermann (2013: 149).
5. BIS (2013).
6. Swoboda (1968).
7. Cappella (2014).
8. Oatley (2013); Stokes (2014).
9. Viotti (2014: 156).
10. Kirshner (1995: 159–166); Cohen (1998: 44–46).
11. Rajendran (2013: 93).
12. McKinnon (2013: 4); Williamson (2013: 80–81).
13. James (2009: 30).
14. McCauley and Chan (2014: 32).
15. Cohen (2012a).
16. Kelly (2009: vi).
17. Germain and Schwartz (2014: 1098).
18. Tilford (2007).
19. Lo (2010: 32).
20. Despres et al. (1966).
21. Eichengreen (2007: 136–137).
22. Gallarotti (2010).
23. Chey (2012: 57).
24. Schenk (2013).
25. Cappella (2014).
26. Kirshner (1995: 64–70).
27. Kirshner (2009: 191).
28. Layne (2012: 418).
29. Helleiner (2008, 2009).
30. Eichengreen and Flandreau (2009, 2012).
31. Krugman (1992: 173).

CHAPTER 5

1. Tavlas and Ozeki (1992: 32–34).
2. BIS (1999).
3. Thygesen (1995); McCauley (1997).
4. Frenkel and Goldstein (1999: 712–713).
5. Tavlas (1991).
6. Von Hagen and Fratianni (1990); Laopodis (2001).
7. Frenkel and Goldstein (1999: 720).
8. Bundesbank (1988: 14).
9. Bénassy-Quéré and Deusy-Fournier (1994); Frankel and Wei (1995).
10. Neumann (1986: 110).
11. Henning (1994).

12. Strange (1980: 47).
13. Frenkel and Goldstein (1999: 712–713).
14. Iwami (2000).
15. Tavlas and Ozeki (1992: 40); Kawai (1996: 319–320).
16. BIS (1999).
17. Thygesen (1995).
18. Frankel (1993); Frankel and Wei (1995).
19. Maehara (1993: 164).
20. Bénassy-Quéré and Deusy-Fournier (1994: 138).
21. Tavlas and Ozeki (1992: 9).
22. Shigehara (1991); Kawai (1996).
23. Garber (1996).
24. Kwan (1994); Hale (1995).
25. Sato (1999).
26. For example, Okina et al. (2001); Hamada and Okada (2009).
27. Grimes (2003).
28. Takagi (2012: 83).
29. Chinn and Frankel (2008); Papaioannou and Portes (2008).
30. ECB (2008: 7).
31. ECB (2010: 7).
32. ECB (2012: 7, 9).
33. Cohen (2003).
34. ECB (1999: 31, 45).
35. Posen (2008: 80).
36. Armijo et al. (2014); Norrlof (2014a).
37. Chinn and Frankel (2007); Subramanian (2011).
38. Posen (2008); Brooks et al. (2013); Stokes (2014).
39. Momani (2008: 309).
40. Q. Li (2003); Posen (2008).
41. Posen (2008: 96).
42. McCauley (2011).
43. Kirshner (2014: 108).
44. Frankel (2011).
45. Cohen (2004: 158–160).
46. Helleiner (2008).
47. Norrlof (2014b).
48. Helleiner (2008: 362).
49. Kirshner (1995).
50. Helleiner (2008: 373).
51. Cohen (1971a).
52. Helleiner (2014).
53. Kirshner (2008, 2009).
54. Cohen (1998: 30–31).
55. Kirshner (2008, 2009).
56. Lopez (1951).
57. Groseclose (1976: 49–50).
58. Gallarotti (2010).

CHAPTER 6

1. Eichengreen (2011).
2. Eichengreen (2011: 150).
3. World Bank (2011: 125–126).
4. Kirshner (2014: 16).
5. Bergsten (2011).
6. ECB (2012: 11).
7. Dailami (2011).
8. Bénassy-Quéré and Pisani-Ferry (2011).
9. Otero-Iglesias and Steinberg (2013a, 2013b).
10. Mansfield (1993).
11. For example, Norrlof (2014a).
12. Chinn and Frankel (2007, 2008).
13. Subramanian (2011).
14. Subramanian (2011: 99).
15. Chen and Peng (2010: 120–121).
16. Papaioannou and Portes (2008).
17. Prasad and Ye (2012).
18. ECB (2010: 56).
19. Thimann (2008).
20. World Bank (2011: 131–132).
21. Singer et al. (1972).
22. McKeown (1991); Mansfield (1994).
23. Hirschman (1964).
24. Mansfield (1992).
25. Schwartz (2009: 119).
26. Kamps (2006); Goldberg and Tille (2008); Auboin (2012).
27. Bracke and Bunda (2011); Cobham (2011); McCauley and Chan (2014).
28. BIS (2013).
29. For example, Auboin (2012).
30. Mansfield (1993: 113).
31. Ray and Singer (1973); Modelski (1974); Thompson (1988).
32. Zimmermann (2013: 148).
33. Cohen (2011).
34. Casarini (2012).
35. Williamson (2013: 76).
36. Kirshner (2014a: 137).
37. Bracke and Bunde (2011: 5).
38. Auboin (2012).
39. World Bank (2011).

CHAPTER 7

1. Kindleberger (1976).
2. Triffin (1960b: 230).
3. Eichengreen (2011: 121).

4. Kirshner (2014: 140).
5. Rickards (2014: 303–304).
6. Helleiner (2014: 9–10).
7. Williamson (2013: 76).
8. Rolfe and Burtle (1974).
9. Triffin (1960a).
10. Gowa (1983).
11. Kirshner (2008: 419–420).
12. Wheatley (2013a: 13).
13. Eichengreen (2011: 162).
14. Calleo (2009: 186–187).
15. Frenkel, as quoted in the *New York Times* (3 March 2005).
16. Rajendran (2013: 92).
17. Oatley et al. (2013).
18. Jeanne (2012: 3).
19. Gourinchas and Rey (2007); Kaminska and Zinna (2014).
20. Fields and Vernengo (2013: 746).
21. Chen and Imam (2012).
22. Tett (2014).
23. As quoted in the *New York Times* (13 May 2012).
24. Irwin (2014).
25. Helleiner (2014: 8).
26. Prasad (2014).
27. For example, Otero-Iglesias and Steinberg (2013a); Helleiner (2014).
28. Prasad (2014; xi).
29. Prasad (2014: 84).
30. Prasad (2014: 99).
31. Prasad (2014: xiv).
32. As quoted in *Financial Times* (12 February 2009).
33. McKinnon (2013).
34. Prasad (2014: 110).
35. Mandell (2012).
36. Kurtzman (2014).
37. Thomas (2014).
38. Quinlan and Chandler (2001); Norrlof (2010); Starrs (2013).
39. Starrs (2013).
40. Starrs (2013: 828).
41. Stokes (2014).
42. Eichengreen (2011: 121).
43. Prasad (2014: xviii).
44. As quoted in the *New York Times* (16 October 2013).
45. Kennedy (2010: 10).
46. Gelb (2009: 56).
47. Lieber (2012: 3).
48. Norrlof (2010: 2).
49. Brooks and Wohlforth (2008: 1).
50. Helleiner (2009: 76).

51. Otero-Iglesias and Steinberg (2013a: 328).
52. Gavin (2003, 2004).
53. Zimmermann (2002: 226).
54. Cohen (1986: 126).
55. Spiro (1999).
56. Helleiner (2008: 368).
57. Helleiner (2008: 368).
58. McKinnon (2013).
59. Kirshner (2008: 421).
60. Williamson (2013).
61. Williamson (2013: 80).

CHAPTER 8

1. Mundell (2000: 57).
2. Gros and Thygesen (1998: 373).
3. Feldstein (1997); Calomiris (1999); Cohen (2003).
4. Bergsten (1997).
5. Alogoskoufis and Portes (1997: 4).
6. Chinn and Frankel (2008).
7. Papaioannou and Portes (2008); De La Dehesa (2009).
8. *Economist* (25 May 2013).
9. *Economist* (2011).
10. Feldstein (2012: 105).
11. Roubini (2011).
12. Bergsten and Kirkegaard (2012: 1–2).
13. Committee for the Study of Economic and Monetary Union (1989).
14. Bordo et al. (2011); Henning and Kessler (2012).
15. Kletzer and von Hagen (2001); Mélitz and Zumer (2002); HM Treasury (2003); O'Rourke and Taylor (2013).
16. Annett (2006).
17. *Economist* (3 January 2009).
18. *Economist* (7 February 2009).
19. McKinnon (2011).
20. European Commission (2012).
21. *Economist* (15 May 2010).
22. As quoted in the *New York Times* (27 April 2012).
23. As quoted in the *New York Times* (10 December 2011).
24. Allard et al. (2013: 4).
25. Unger (2013).
26. European Commission (2012).
27. Pickford et al. (2014: ix).
28. Bargain et al. (2013).
29. Allard et al. (2013).
30. As quoted in the *Wall Street Journal* (10 September 2013).
31. Allard et al. (2013: 6).
32. As quoted by Moggridge (1980: 28); emphasis in the original).

33. *Economist* (30 August 2014).
34. Krugman (2014).
35. O'Rourke and Taylor (2013).
36. Chey (2012: 64).
37. Gros and Alcidi (2013: v).
38. Altman (2013: 13).
39. DeLong and Summers (2012); Lane (2012).
40. Münchau (2014).
41. *Economist* (25 May 2013).
42. Wyplosz (1999: 89).
43. Draghi (2012).
44. Lane (2012); J. Shambaugh (2012); Pickford et al. (2014).
45. *Economist* (14 December 2013).
46. Brooks et al. (2013: 140).
47. Posen (2008: 88).
48. Cohen (2011).
49. Zimmermann (2013).

CHAPTER 9

1. Subramanian (2011: 5).
2. Zweifel (2014).
3. As quoted in the *Financial Times* (30 September 2014).
4. Helleiner and Kirshner (2014).
5. Shambaugh (2013).
6. PBOC Study Group (2006).
7. Helleiner and Malkin (2012); Volz (2014).
8. Zhang (2009: 24).
9. As reported by Dow Jones News Service (17 February 2011).
10. Subacchi (2010).
11. *Economist* (26 April 2014).
12. European Central Bank (2013: 46).
13. Frankel (2011).
14. CME Group (2014).
15. For example, Goldstein (2005); Gurtov (2013).
16. Ruggie (1981).
17. Nathan and Scobell (2012).
18. Nathan and Scobell (2012: xi).
19. Ikenberry (2013).
20. Ikenberry (2013: 55).
21. X. Li (2010: 13).
22. Westad (2013).
23. As quoted in the *New York Times* (16 October 2013).
24. Di Dongsheng (2013: 115).
25. Hong Kong and Shanghai Banking Corporation (2011: 15).
26. Subramanian (2011: 4).

27. Schwab (2014).
28. Beckley (2011–2012: 43–44).
29. Pritchett and Summers (2014).
30. Das and N'Diaye (2013).
31. Lardy (2012); Gurtov (2013); Hoffman and Polk (2014).
32. Gorrie (2013: 6).
33. Cookson (2011).
34. Kelly (2009: 6).
35. Xi (2014).
36. World Bank (2014).
37. Transparency International (2014).
38. *Economist* (1 November 2014).
39. Lo (2013: 162).
40. Breslin (2013: 141).
41. Kawai and Pontines (2014).
42. Subramanian and Kessler (2012); Fratzscher and Mehl (2014); Henning (2014).
43. Eichengreen (2011); Helleiner (2014); Prasad (2014).
44. Frankel (2011: 13).
45. Wheatley (2013c: 68).
46. Halper (2010).
47. McNally (2012).
48. Halper (2010: 3).
49. McNally (2012: 744).
50. For example, World Bank (2012); Sheng (2012).
51. Dong et al. (2012); International Monetary Fund (2013).
52. McCauley (2011).

References

Allard, Céline, Petya Koeva Brooks, John C. Bluedorn, Fabian Bornhorst, Katherine Christopherson, Franziska Ohnsorge, Tigran Poghosyan, and an IMF Staff Team (2013), *Toward a Fiscal Union for the Euro Area* (Washington, DC: International Monetary Fund).

Alogoskoufis, George, and Richard Portes (1997), "The Euro, the Dollar, and the International Monetary System," in Paul R. Masson, Thomas H. Krueger, and Bart G. Turtelboom, eds., *EMU and the International Monetary System* (Washington, DC: International Monetary Fund), 58–78.

Altman, Roger C. (2013), "The Fall and Rise of the West: Why America and Europe Will Emerge Stronger from the Financial Crisis," *Foreign Affairs* 92:1 (January/February), 8–13.

Andrews, David M. (1994), "Capital Mobility and State Autonomy: Toward a Structural Theory of International Monetary Relations." *International Studies Quarterly* 38:2, 193–218.

——— (2006b), "Monetary Power and Monetary Statecraft," in David M. Andrews, ed., *International Monetary Power* (Ithaca, NY: Cornell University Press).

Andrews, David M., ed. (2006a), *International Monetary Power* (Ithaca, NY: Cornell University Press).

Annett, Anthony (2006), "Enforcement and the Stability and Growth Pact: How Fiscal Policy Did and Did Not Change under Europe's Fiscal Framework," Working Paper WP/06/116 (Washington, DC: International Monetary Fund).

Armijo, Leslie E., and Saori N. Katada (2015), "Theorizing the Financial Statecraft of Emerging Powers," *New Political Economy* 20:1, 42–62.

Armijo, Leslie E., and Saori N. Katada, eds. (2014), *The Financial Statecraft of Emerging Powers: Shield and Sword in Asia and Latin America* (New York: Palgrave Macmillan).

Armijo, Leslie E., Laurissa Mühlich, and Daniel C. Tirone (2014), "The Systemic Financial Importance of Emerging Powers," *Journal of Policy Modeling* 36: Supplement 1, S67–S88.

Auboin, Marc (2012), "Use of Currencies in International Trade: Any Changes in the Picture?," Staff Working Paper ERSD-2012-10 (Geneva: World Trade Organization).

Austin, Kenneth (2014), "Systemic Equilibrium in a Bretton Woods II–Type International Monetary System: The Special Roles of Reserve Issuers and Reserve Accumulators, *Journal of Post Keynesian Economics* 36:4 (Summer), 607–633.

Bachrach, Peter, and Morton S. Baratz (1962), "Two Faces of Power," *American Political Science Review* 56:4 (December), 947–952.

Baldwin, David A. (1979), "Power Analysis and World Politics: New Trends vs. Old Tendencies," *World Politics* 31:2 (April), 161–194.

—— (1985), *Economic Statecraft* (Princeton, NJ: Princeton University Press).

—— (1989), *Paradoxes of Power* (New York: Blackwell).

—— (1999), "Force, Fungibility, and Influence," *Security Studies* 8:4 (Summer), 173–183.

—— (2013), "Power and International Relations," in Walter Carlsnaes, Thomas Risse, and Beth A. Simmons, eds., *Handbook of International Relations*, 2nd ed. (Los Angeles: Sage Publications), 273–297.

Bank for International Settlements (1999), *Central Bank Survey of Foreign Exchange and Derivatives Market Activity, 1998* (Basel: Bank for International Settlements).

—— (2013), *Triennial Central Bank Survey of Foreign Exchange and Derivatives Market Activity in 2013* (Basel: Bank for International Settlements).

Bargain, Olivier, Mathias Dolls, Clemens Fuest, Dirk Neumann, Andreas Peichl, Nico Pestel, and Sebastian Siegloch (2013), "Fiscal Union in Europe? Redistributive and Stabilizing Effects of a European Tax-Benefit System and Fiscal Equalization Mechanism," *Economic Policy* 75 (July), 375–422.

Barnett, Michael, and Raymond Duvall (2005), "Power in International Politics," *International Organization* 59:1 (Winter), 39–75.

Beckley, Michael (2011/2012), "China's Century? Why America's Edge Will Endure," *International Security* 36:3 (Winter), 41–78.

Bénassy-Quéré, Agnès, and Pierre Deusy-Fournier (1994), "La concurrence pour le statut de monnaie internationale depuis 1973," *Économie Internationale* 59:3, 107–144.

—— (2011), "The Long March toward a Multipolar Monetary Regime," Lettre du CEPII 308 (Paris: Centre d'Etudes Prospectives et d'Informations Internationales).

Bergsten, C. Fred (1997), "The Impact of the Euro on Exchange Rates and International Policy Cooperation," in Paul R. Masson, Thomas H. Krueger, and Bart G. Turtelboom, eds., *EMU and the International Monetary System* (Washington, DC: International Monetary Fund), 17–48.

—— (2009), "The Dollar and the Deficits: How Washington Can Prevent the Next Crisis," *Foreign Affairs* 88:6 (November/December), 20–38.

—— (2011), "Why the World Needs Three Global Currencies," *Financial Times*, 15 February.

Bergsten, C. Fred, and Jacob F. Kirkegaard (2012), "The Coming Resolution of the European Crisis," Policy Brief PB 12-1 (Washington, DC: Peterson Institute for International Economics).

Bernstein, Jared (2014), "Dethrone 'King Dollar,'" *New York Times*, 28 August.

Bordo, Michael D., Agnieszka Markiewicz, and Lars Jonung (2011), "A Fiscal Union for the Euro: Some Lessons from History," Working Paper 17380 (Cambridge, MA: National Bureau of Economic Research).

Bracke, Thierry, and Irina Bunda (2011), "Exchange Rate Anchoring: Is There Still a De Facto US Dollar Standard?," Working Paper 1353 (Frankfurt, Germany: European Central Bank).

Breslin, Shaun (2013), *China and the Global Political Economy* (London: Palgrave Macmillan).

Brooks, Stephen G., G. John Ikenberry, and William C. Wohlforth (2013), "Lean Forward: In Defense of American Engagement," *Foreign Affairs* 92:1 (January/February), 130–142.

Brooks, Stephen G., and William C. Wohlforth (2008), *World Out of Balance: International Relations and the Challenge of American Primacy* (Princeton, NJ: Princeton University Press).

Brown, Brendan (1978), *Money Hard and Soft: On the International Currency Markets* (New York: Wiley).

Bundesbank (1988), "Forty Years of the Deutsche Mark," *Monthly Report* 40 (May), 13–23.

Calleo, David (2009), "Twenty-First Century Geopolitics and the Erosion of the Dollar Order," in Eric Helleiner and Jonathan Kirshner, eds., *The Future of the Dollar* (Ithaca, NY: Cornell University Press), 164–190.

Calomiris, Charles W. (1999), "The Impending Collapse of the European Monetary Union," *Cato Journal* 18:3 (Winter), 445–452.

Cappella, Rosella (2014), "Economic Statecraft and Power Redistribution during Wartime: Lessons from the Sterling Era and the Future of America's Military Might" (Boston University), unpublished.

Carroll, Berenice A. (1972), "Peace Research: The Cult of Power," *Journal of Conflict Resolution* 16:4 (December), 585–616.

Casarini, Nicola (2012), "For China, the Euro Is a Safer Bet than the Dollar," ISS Analysis (Paris: European Union Institute for Security Studies).

Chen, Hongyi, and Wensheng Peng (2010), "The Potential of the Renminbi as an International Currency," in Wensheng Peng and Chang Shu, eds., *Currency Internationalization: Global Experiences and Implications for the Renminbi* (New York: Palgrave Macmillan), 115–138.

Chen, Jiaqian, and Patrick Imam (2012), "Consequences of Asset Shortages in Emerging Markets," Working Paper WP/12/102 (Washington, DC: International Monetary Fund).

Chey, Hyoung-Kyu (2102), "Theories of International Currencies and the Future of the World Monetary Order," *International Studies Review* 14:1 (March), 51–77.

Chinn, Menzie, and Jeffrey Frankel (2007), "Will the Euro Eventually Surpass the Dollar as Leading International Reserve Currency?," in Richard H. Clarida, ed., *G7 Current Account Imbalances: Sustainability and Adjustment* (Chicago, IL: University of Chicago Press), 283–335.

——— (2008), "Why the Euro Will Rival the Dollar," *International Finance* 11:1 (Spring), 49–73.

Cipolla, Carlo M. (1967), *Money, Prices and Civilization in the Mediterranean World: Fifth to Seventeenth Century* (New York: Gordian).

CME Group (2014), "Offshore Chinese Renminbi Market (CNH)," 4 March (Chicago, IL: CME Group).

Cobham, David (2011), "Currency Alignments and the Crisis: How Has the Use of Anchor Currencies Changed?" (Heriot-Watt University, Edinburgh, UK), unpublished.

Cohen, Benjamin J. (1966), *Adjustment Costs and the Distribution of New Reserves*, Princeton Studies in International Finance 18 (Princeton, NJ: International Finance Section).

—— (1971a), *The Future of Sterling as an International Currency* (London: Macmillan).

—— (1971b), "The Seigniorage Gain of an International Currency: An Empirical Test," *Quarterly Journal of Economics* 85:3 (August), 494–507.

—— (1976), "Mixing Oil and Money," in J. C. Hurewitz, ed., *Oil, the Arab-Israel Dispute, and the Industrial World: Horizons of Crisis* (Boulder, CO: Westview Press), 195–211.

—— (1977), *Organizing the World's Money* (New York: Basic Books).

—— (1986), *In Whose Interest? International Banking and American Foreign Policy* (New Haven, CT: Yale University Press).

—— (1998), *The Geography of Money* (Ithaca, NY: Cornell University Press).

—— (2000), "Money and Power in World Politics," in Thomas C. Lawton, James N. Rosenau, and Amy C. Verdun, eds., *Strange Power: Shaping the Parameters of International Relations and International Political Economy* (Aldershot, UK: Ashgate), 91–113.

—— (2003), "Global Currency Rivalry: Can the Euro Ever Challenge the Dollar?," *Journal of Common Market Studies* 41:4 (September), 575–595.

—— (2004), *The Future of Money* (Princeton, NJ: Princeton University Press).

—— (2006), "The Macrofoundations of Monetary Power," in David M. Andrews, ed., *International Monetary Power* (Ithaca, NY: Cornell University Press), 31–50.

—— (2008a), "The International Monetary System: Diffusion and Ambiguity," *International Affairs* 84:3 (May), 455–470.

—— (2008b), *International Political Economy: An Intellectual History* (Princeton, NJ: Princeton University Press).

—— (2011), *The Future of Global Currency: The Euro versus the Dollar* (London: Routledge).

—— (2012a), "The Benefits and Costs of an International Currency: Getting the Calculus Right," *Open Economies Review* 23, 13–31.

—— (2012b), "The Future of the Euro: Let's Get Real," *Review of International Political Economy*, 19:4 (October), 689–700.

—— (2012c), "The Yuan Tomorrow? Evaluating China's Currency Internationalization Strategy," *New Political Economy*, 17:3 (July 2012), 361–371.

—— (2013), "Currency and State Power," in Martha Finnemore and Judith Goldstein, eds., *Back to Basics: State Power in a Contemporary World* (New York: Oxford University Press), 159–176.

—— (2014a), "Will History Repeat Itself? Lessons for the Yuan," Working Paper 453 (Tokyo: Asian Development Bank Institute).

——— (2014b), "The Yuan's Long March," in Benjamin J. Cohen and Eric M. P. Chiu, eds., *Power in a Changing World Economy: Lessons from East Asia* (London: Routledge Publishers, 2014), 144–159.

——— (2015a), ""Money, Power, Authority," unpublished.

——— (2015b), "Why Can't Europe Save Itself? A Brief Note on a Structural Failure," unpublished.

Cohen, Benjamin J., and Tabitha M. Benney (2014), "What Does the International Currency System Really Look Like?," *Review of International Political Economy* 21:5 (October), 1017–1041.

Cohen, Benjamin J., and Eric M. P. Chiu (2014), "Introduction," in Benjamin J. Cohen and Eric M.P. Chiu, eds., *Power in a Changing World Economy: Lessons from East Asia* (London: Routledge), 1–20.

Committee for the Study of Economic and Monetary Union (1989), *Report on Economic and Monetary Union in the European Community* (Brussels: European Commission).

Cookson, Robert (2011), "Renminbi Threat to Dollar Could Be Stalling," *Financial Times*, 23 November.

Dahl, Robert A. (1957), "The Concept of Power," *Behavioral Science* 2, 201–215.

——— (1984), *Modern Political Analysis*, 4th ed. (Englewood Cliffs, NJ: Prentice-Hall).

Dailami, Mansoor (2011), "The New Triumvirate," *Foreign Policy*, 7 September. Available at http://foreignpolicy.com/2011/09/07/the-new-triumvirate (accessed 28 January 2015).

Das, Mitali, and Papa N'Diaye (2013), "Chronicle of a Decline Foretold: Has China Reached the Lewis Turning Point?," Working Paper WP/13/26 (Washington, DC: International Monetary Fund).

De La Dehesa, Guillermo (2009), "Will the Euro Ever Replace the US Dollar as the Dominant Global Currency?," Working Paper 54/2009 (Madrid: Real Instituto Elcano).

DeLong, J. Bradford, and Lawrence H. Summers (2012), "Fiscal Policy in a Depressed Economy," *Brookings Papers on Economic Activity* (Spring), 233–274.

Despres, Emile, Charles P. Kindleberger, and Walter S. Salant (1966), *The Dollar and World Liquidity: A Minority View* (Washington, DC: Brookings Institution).

Di, Dongsheng (2013), "The Renminbi's Rise and Chinese Politics," in Alan Wheatley, ed., *The Power of Currencies and Currencies of Power* (London: International Institute for Strategic Studies), 115–125.

Dobbs, Richard, David Skilling, Wayne Hu, Susan Lund, James Manyika, and Charles Roxburgh (2009), *An Exorbitant Privilege? Implications of Reserve Currencies for Competitiveness* (Washington, DC: McKinsey Global Institute).

Dong, He, Lillian Cheung, Wenlang Zhang, and Tommy Wu (2012), "How Would Capital Account Liberalization Affect China's Capital Flows and the Renminbi Real Exchange Rate?," *China and World Economy* 20:6 (November–December), 29–54.

Dowding, Keith (2011), "Introduction," in Keith Dowding, ed., *Encyclopedia of Power* (Los Angeles: Sage Publications), xxiii–xxvi.

Draghi, Mario (2012), "Speech by Mario Draghi, President of the European Central Bank, at the Global Investment Conference in London" (Frankfurt: European Central Bank), 26 July.

Economist (2011), "Staring into the Abyss," Special Report, 12 November.

Eichengreen, Barry (2007), *Global Imbalances and the Lessons of Bretton Woods* (Cambridge, MA: MIT Press).

——— (2011), *Exorbitant Privilege: The Rise and Fall of the Dollar and the Future of the International Monetary System* (New York: Oxford University Press).

Eichengreen, Barry, and Marc Flandreau (2009), "The Rise and Fall of the Dollar (or When Did the Dollar Replace Sterling as the Leading Reserve Currency?)," *European Review of Economic History* 13:3 (December), 377–411.

——— (2012), "The Federal Reserve, the Bank of England and the Rise of the Dollar as an International Currency, 1914–1939," *Open Economies Review* 23:1 (February), 57–87.

European Central Bank (1999), "International Role of the Euro," *Monthly Bulletin*, August, 31–53.

——— (2008), *Review of the International Role of the Euro* (Frankfurt: European Central Bank).

——— (2010), *The International Role of the Euro* (Frankfurt: European Central Bank).

——— (2012), *The International Role of the Euro* (Frankfurt: European Central Bank).

——— (2013), *The International Role of the Euro* (Frankfurt: European Central Bank).

European Commission (2012), *A Blueprint for a Deep and Genuine Economic and Monetary Union: Launching a European Debate* (Brussels: European Commission).

Federal Open Market Committee (2008), "Meeting of the Federal Open Market Committee on October 28–29, 2008" (Washington, DC: Federal Reserve Board of Governors).

Feldstein, Martin (1997), "EMU and International Conflict," *Foreign Affairs* 76:6 (November–December), 60–73.

——— (2012), "The Failure of the Euro: The Little Currency That Couldn't," *Foreign Affairs* 91:1 (January–February), 105–116.

Fels, Enrico, Jan-Frederik Kremer, and Katharina Kronenberg (2012), "Preface," in Enrico Fels, Jan-Frederik Kremer, and Katharina Kronenberg, eds., *Power in the 21st Century: International Security and International Political Economy in as Changing World* (Berlin: Springer), v–xiii.

Fields, David, and Matías Vernengo (2013), "Hegemonic Currencies during the Crisis: The Dollar versus the Euro in a Cartelist Perspective," *Review of International Political Economy* 20:4 (August), 740–759.

Finnemore, Martha, and Judith Goldstein (2013), "Puzzles about Power," in Martha Finnemore and Judith Goldstein, eds., *Back to Basics: State Power in a Contemporary World* (New York: Oxford University Press), 3–17.

FNSR Group of Experts (2012), *National Power Index 2012* (New Delhi: Foundation for National Security Research).

Frankel, Jeffrey A. (1993), "Is Japan Creating a Yen Bloc in East Asia and the Pacific?," in Jeffrey A. Frankel and Miles Kahler, eds., *Regionalism and Rivalry: Japan and the United States in Pacific Asia* (Chicago: University of Chicago Press), 53–85.

―――― (1995), "Still the Lingua Franca: The Exaggerated Death of the Dollar," *Foreign Affairs* 74:4 (July/August), 9–16.

―――― (2011), "Historical Precedents for Internationalization of the RMB" (New York: Council on Foreign Relations).

Frankel, Jeffrey A., and Shang-Jin Wei (1995), "Emerging Currency Blocs," in Hans Genberg, ed., *The International Monetary System: Its Institutions and Future* (New York: Springer-Verlag), 111–143.

Fratzscher, Marcel, and Arnaud Mehl (2014), "China's Dominance Hypothesis and the Emergence of a Tri-Polar Global Currency System," *Economic Journal* 124 (December), 1343–1370.

Frenkel, Jacob A., and Morris Goldstein (1999), "The International Role of the Deutsche Mark," in Deutsche Bundesbank, ed., *Fifty Years of the Deutsche Mark: Central Bank and the Currency in Germany Since 1948* (Oxford: Oxford University Press), 685–729.

Frieden, Jeffry A. (1991), "Invested Interests: The Politics of National Economic Policies in a World of Global Finance," *International Organization* 45:4 (Autumn), 425–451.

Gallarotti, Giulio M. (2010), *The Power Curse: Influence and Illusion in World Politics* (Boulder, CO: Lynne Rienner).

Garber, Peter M. (1996), "The Use of the Yen as a Reserve Currency," *Bank of Japan Monetary and Economic Studies* 14 (December), 1–21.

Garrett, Geoffrey, and George Tsebelis (1999), "Why Resist the Temptation to Apply Power Indices to the European Union?," *Journal of Theoretical Politics* 11:3, 291–308.

Gavin, Francis (2003), "Ideas, Power, and the Politics of U.S. International Monetary Policy during the 1960s," in Jonathan Kirshner, ed., *Monetary Orders: Ambiguous Economics, Ubiquitous Politics* (Ithaca, NY: Cornell University Press), 195–217.

―――― (2004), *Gold, Dollars, and Power: The Politics of International Monetary Relations, 1958–1971* (Chapel Hill, NC: University of North Carolina Press).

Gelb, Leslie H. (2009), "Necessity, Choice, and Common Sense," *Foreign Affairs* 88:3 (May–June), 56–72.

Genberg, Hans (2010), "The Calculus of International Currency Use," *Central Banking* 20:3, 63–68.

Germain, Randall, and Herman Schwartz (2014), "The Political Economy of Failure: The Euro as an International Currency," *Review of International Political Economy* 21:5 (October), 1095–1122.

Gilpin, Robert (1981), *War and Change in World Politics* (New York: Cambridge University Press).

Goldberg, Linda S., and Cedric Tille (2008), "Vehicle Currency Use in International Trade," *Journal of International Economics* 76:2, 177–192.

Goldstein, Avery (2005), *Rising to the Challenge: China's Grand Strategy and International Security* (Stanford, CA: Stanford University Press).

Gorrie, James R. (2013), *The China Crisis: How China's Economic Collapse Will Lead to a Global Depression* (Hoboken, NJ: Wiley).

Gourinchas, Pierre-Olivier, and Hélène Rey (2007), "From World Banker to World Venture Capitalist: US External Adjustment and the Exorbitant Privilege," in Richard Clarida, ed., *G7 Current Account Imbalances: Sustainability and Adjustment* (Chicago: University of Chicago Press), 11–55.

Gourinchas, Pierre-Olivier, Hélène Rey, and Nicolas Govillot (2010), "Exorbitant Privilege and Exorbitant Duty," Discussion Paper 10-E-20 (Tokyo: Institute for Monetary and Economic Studies, Bank of Japan).

Gowa, Joanne (1983), *Closing the Gold Window: Domestic Politics and the End of Bretton Woods* (Ithaca, NY: Cornell University Press).

—— (1984), "Hegemons, IOs, and Markets: The Case of the Substitution Account," *International Organization* 38:4 (Autumn), 661–683.

Grimes, William W. (2003), "Internationalization of the Yen and the New Politics of Monetary Insulation," in Jonathan Kirshner, ed., *Monetary Orders: Ambiguous Economics, Ubiquitous Politics* (Ithaca, NY: Cornell University Press), 172–194.

Gros, Daniel, and Cinzia Alcidi (2013), *The Global Economy in 2030: Trends and Strategies for Europe* (Brussels: Centre for European Policy Studies).

Gros, Daniel, and Niels Thygesen (1998), *European Monetary Integration: From the European Monetary System to European Monetary Union*, 2nd ed. (London: Longman).

Groseclose, Elgin E. (1976), *Money and Man: A Survey of Monetary Experience*, 4th ed. (Norman: Oklahoma University Press).

Gruber, Lloyd (2000), *Ruling the World: Power Politics and the Rise of Supranational Institutions* (Princeton, NJ: Princeton University Press).

Gurtov, Mel (2013), *Will This Be China's Century? A Skeptic's View* (Boulder, CO: Lynne Rienner).

Guzzini, Stefano (1993), "Structural Power: The Limits of Neorealist Power Analysis," *International Organization* 47:3 (Summer), 443–478.

—— (2009), "On the Measurement of Power and the Power of Measure in International Relations," Working Paper 2009:28 (Copenhagen: Danish Institute for International Studies).

Hafner-Burton, Emilie M., Miles Kahler, and Alexander H. Montgomery (2009), "Network Analysis for International Relations," *International Organization* 63:3 (Summer), 559–592.

Hai, Wen, and Hongxin Yao (2010), "Pros and Cons of International Use of the RMB for China," in Wensheng Peng and Chang Shu, eds., *Currency Internationalization: Global Experiences and Implications for the Renminbi* (New York: Palgrave Macmillan), 139–166.

Hale, David D. (1995), "Is It a Yen or a Dollar Crisis in the Currency Market?," *Washington Quarterly* 18:4 (Autumn), 145–171.

Halper, Stefan (2010), *The Beijing Consensus: How China's Authoritarian Model Will Dominate the Twenty-First Century* (New York: Basic Books).

Hamada, Koichi, and Yasushi Okada (2009), "Monetary and International Factors behind Japan's Lost Decade," *Journal of the Japanese and International Economies* 23:2 (June), 200–219.

Harknett, Richard J., and Hasan B. Yalcin (2012), "The Struggle for Autonomy: A Realist Structural Theory of International Relations," *International Studies Review* 14:4 (December), 499–521.

Harris, Richard G. (2001), "Mundell and Friedman: Four Key Disagreements," *Policy Options/Options Politiques* (May), 34–36.

Hartmann, Philipp (1994), "Vehicle Currencies in the Foreign Exchange Market," Document de travail du seminaire Delta 94-13 (Paris: École Normale Superieure).

Hay, Colin (1997), "Divided by a Common Language: Political Theory and the Concept of Power," *Politics* 17:1, 45–52.

Helleiner, Eric (2003), *The Making of National Money: Territorial Currencies in Historical Perspective* (Ithaca, NY: Cornell University Press).

——— (2006), "Below the State: Micro-Level Monetary Power," in David M. Andrews, ed., *International Monetary Power* (Ithaca, NY: Cornell University Press), 72–90.

——— (2008), "Political Determinants of International Currencies: What Future for the US Dollar?," *Review of International Political Economy* 15:3 (August), 354–378.

——— (2009), "Enduring Top Currency, Fragile Negotiated Currency: Politics and the Dollar's International Role," in Eric Helleiner and Jonathan Kirshner, eds., *The Future of the Dollar* (Ithaca, NY: Cornell University Press), 69–87.

——— (2014), *The Status Quo Crisis: Global Financial Governance after the 2008 Meltdown* (New York: Oxford University Press).

Helleiner, Eric, and Anton Malkin (2012), "Sectoral Interests and Global Money: Renminbi, Dollars, and the Domestic Foundations of International Currency Policy," *Open Economies Review* 23:1 (February), 33–55.

Helleiner, Eric, and Jonathan Kirshner, eds. (2009), *The Future of the Dollar* (Ithaca, NY: Cornell University Press).

——— (2014), *The Great Wall of Money: Power and Politics in China's International Monetary Relations* (Ithaca, NY: Cornell University Press).

Henning, C. Randall (1994), *Currency and Politics in the United States, Germany, and Japan* (Washington, DC: Institute for International Economics).

——— (1998), "Systemic Conflict and Regional Monetary Integration: The Case of Europe," *International Organization* 52:3, 537–573.

——— (2014), "Choice and Coercion in East Asian Exchange-Rate Regimes," in Benjamin J. Cohen and Eric M. P. Chiu, eds., *Power in a Changing World Economy: Lessons from East Asia* (London: Routledge), 89–110.

Henning, C. Randall, and Martin Kessler (2012), "Fiscal Federalism: US History for Architects of Europe's Fiscal Union," Working Paper 12-1 (Washington, DC: Peterson Institute for International Economics).

Hirschman, Albert O. ([1945] 1969), *National Power and the Structure of Foreign Trade* (Berkeley: University of California Press).

——— (1964), "The Paternity of an Index," *American Economic Review* 54:5, 761–762.

HM Treasury (2003), *The United States as a Monetary Union* (Norwich, UK: Stationary Office).

Hoffman, David, and Andrew Polk (2014), *The Long Soft Fall in Chinese Growth: Business Realities, Risks and Opportunities*, Research Report R-1563-14-RR (New York: Conference Board).

Hong Kong and Shanghai Banking Corporation (2011), "A Currency Revolution: The Rise of the RMB," *Week in China*, 4 November.

Ikenberry, G. John (2013), "The Rise of China, the United States, and the Future of the Liberal International Order," in David Shambaugh, ed., *Tangled Titans: The United States and China* (New York: Rowman and Littlefield), 53–74.

International Monetary Fund (2013), "People's Republic of China: 2013 Article IV Consultation," Staff Report (Washington, DC: International Monetary Fund).

Irwin, Neil (2014), "Fed's Aid in 2008 Crisis Stretched Worldwide," *New York Times*, 24 February.

Iwami, Toru (2000), "A Vulnerable Power in the World Economy: Japan's Economic Diplomacy and the Yen," Discussion Paper (Faculty of Economics, University of Tokyo).

James, Harold (2009), "The Enduring International Preeminence of the Dollar," in Eric Helleiner and Jonathan Kirshner, eds., *The Future of the Dollar* (Ithaca, NY: Cornell University Press), 24–44.

Jeanne, Olivier (2012), "The Dollar and Its Discontents," Working Paper WP 12-10 (Washington, DC: Peterson Institute for International Economics).

Johnson, Harry G. (1971), "The Keynesian Revolution and the Monetarist Counter-Revolution," *American Economic Review* 61: 2 (May), 1–14.

Judson, Ruth (2012), "Crisis and Calm: Demand for U.S. Currency at Home and Abroad from the Fall of the Berlin Wall to 2011," International Finance Discussion Paper IFDP 1058 (Washington, DC: Federal Reserve Board of Governors).

Kaelberer, Matthias (2001), *Money and Power in Europe: The Political Economy of European Monetary Cooperation* (Albany: State University of New York Press).

——— (2005), "Structural Power and the Politics of International Monetary Relations," *Journal of Social, Political, and Economic Studies* 30:3 (Fall), 333–359.

Kahler, Miles (2009), "Networked Politics: Agency, Power, and Governance," in Miles Kahler, ed., *Networked Politics: Agency, Power, and Governance* (Ithaca, NY: Cornell University Press), 1–20.

Kaminska, Iryna, and Gabriele Zinna (2014), "Official Demand for U.S. Debt: Implications for U.S. Real Interest Rates," Working Paper WP/14/66 (Washington, DC: International Monetary Fund).

Kamps, Annette (2006), "The Euro as Invoicing Currency in International Trade," Working Paper 665 (Frankfurt: European Central Bank).

Kawai, Masahiro (1996), "The Japanese Yen as an International Currency: Performance and Prospects," in Ryuzo Sato, Rama Ramachandran, and Hajime Hori, eds., *Organization, Performance, and Equity: Perspectives on the Japanese Economy* (Boston: Kluwer Academic Publishers), 305–355.

Kawai, Masahiro, and Victor Pontines (2014), "Is There Really a Renminbi Bloc in Asia?," Working Paper 467 (Tokyo: Asian Development Bank Institute).

Kelly, Brendan (2009), "China's Challenge to the International Monetary System: Incremental Steps and Long-Term Prospects for Internationalization of the Renminbi," *Issues and Insights* 9:11 (Honolulu: Pacific Forum CSIS).

Kennedy, Paul (2010), "Back to Normalcy," *New Republic*, 30 December, 10–11.

Keohane, Robert O. (1984), *After Hegemony: Cooperation and Discord in the World Political Economy* (Princeton, NJ: Princeton University Press).

—— (2000), "Foreword," in Thomas C. Lawton, James N. Rosenau, and Amy C. Verdun, eds., *Strange Power: Shaping the Parameters of International Relations and International Political Economy* (Aldershot, UK: Ashgate), ix–xvi.

Keohane, Robert O., and Joseph S. Nye, Jr. (1973), "World Politics and the International Economic System," in C. Fred Bergsten, ed., *The Future of the International Economic Order: An Agenda for Research* (Lexington, MA: D.C. Heath), 115–179.

—— (1977), *Power and Interdependence: World Politics in Transition* (Boston: Little, Brown).

Kindleberger, Charles P. (1970), *Power and Money* (New York: Basic Books).

—— (1973), *The World in Depression* (Berkeley: University of California Press).

—— (1976), "Systems of International Economic Organization," in David P. Calleo, ed., *Money and the Coming World Order* (New York: New York University Press), 15–39.

Kirshner, Jonathan (1995), *Currency and Coercion: The Political Economy of International Monetary Power* (Princeton, NJ: Princeton University Press).

—— (2008), "Dollar Primacy and American Power: What's at Stake?," *Review of International Political Economy* 15:3 (August), 418–438.

—— (2009), "After the (Relative) Fall: Dollar Diminution and the Consequences for American Power," in Eric Helleiner and Jonathan Kirshner, eds., *The Future of the Dollar* (Ithaca, NY: Cornell University Press), 191–215.

—— (2014), *American Power after the Financial Crisis* (Ithaca, NY: Cornell University Press).

Kletzer, Kenneth, and Jürgen von Hagen (2001), "Monetary Union and Fiscal Federalism," in Charles Wyplosz, ed., *The Impact of EMU on Europe and the Developing Countries* (New York: Oxford University Press), 17–39.

Krasner, Stephen D. (2013), "New Terrains: Sovereignty and Alternative Conceptions of Power," in Martha Finnemore and Judith Goldstein, eds., *Back to Basics: State Power in a Contemporary World* (New York: Oxford University Press), 339–358.

Krugman, Paul (1992), *Currencies and Crises* (Cambridge, MA: MIT Press).

—— (2014), "Scots, What the Heck?," *New York Times*, 8 September.

Kurtzman, Joel (2014), *Unleashing the Second American Century: Four Forces for Economic Dominance* (New York: PublicAffairs).

Kwan, C. H. (1994), *Economic Interdependence in the Asia-Pacific Region: Towards a Yen Bloc* (London: Routledge).

Lake, David A.(2009), *Hierarchy in International Relations* (Ithaca, NY: Cornell University Press).

Lane, Philip R. (2012), "The European Sovereign Debt Crisis," *Journal of Economic Perspectives* 26:3 (Summer), 49–68.

Laopodis, Nikiforos T. (2001), "International Interest-Rate Transmission and the 'German Dominance Hypothesis' within EMS," *Open Economies Review* 12:4 (October), 347–377.

Lardy, Nicholas R. (2012), *Sustaining China's Economic Growth after the Global Financial Crisis* (Washington, DC: Peterson Institute for International Economics).

Lasswell, Harold D. (1958), *Politics: Who Gets What, When, How* (New York: Meridian Books).

Lawton, Thomas C., James N. Rosenau, and Amy C. Verdun, eds. (2000), *Strange Power: Shaping the Parameters of International Relations and International Political Economy* (Aldershot, UK: Ashgate).

Layne, Christopher (2012), "US Decline," in Michael Cox and Doug Stokes, eds., *US Foreign Policy*, 2nd ed. (New York: Oxford University Press), 410–421.

Li, Quan (2003), "The Effect of Security Alliances on Exchange-Rate Regime Choices," *International Interactions* 29:2, 159–193.

Li, Xing (2010), "The Rise of China and the Capitalist World Order: The 'Four-China' Nexus," in Li Xing, ed., *The Rise of China and the Capitalist World Order* (Burlington, VT: Ashgate), 1–24.

Lieber, Robert J. (2012), *Power and Willpower in the American Future: Why the United States Is Not Destined to Decline* (New York: Cambridge University Press).

Lo, Chi (2010), "The Myth of the Internationalization of the Chinese Yuan," *International Economy* (Fall), 30–33.

––––– (2013), *The Renminbi Rises: Myths, Hypes and Realities of RMB Internationalisation and Reforms in the Post-Crisis World* (London: Palgrave Macmillan).

Lopez, Robert S. (1951), "The Dollar of the Middle Ages," *Journal of Economic History* 11:3 (Summer), 209–234.

Lukes, Steven (1974), *Power: A Radical View* (London: Macmillan).

Machlup, Fritz (1958), "Equilibrium and Disequilibrium: Misplaced Concreteness and Disguised Politics," *Economic Journal* 68 (March), 1–24.

Maehara, Yasuhiro (1993), "The Internationalization of the Yen and Its Role as a Key Currency," *Journal of Asian Economics* 4:1 (Summer), 153–170.

Mandel, Benjamin R. (2012), "Why Is the U.S. Share of World Merchandise Exports Shrinking?," *Current Issues in Economics and Finance* 18:1, 1–8.

Mansfield, Edward D. (1992), "The Concentration of Capabilities and the Onset of War," *Journal of Conflict Resolution* 36:3, 3–24.

––––– (1993), "Concentration, Polarity, and the Distribution of Power," *International Studies Quarterly* 37:1, 105–128.

––––– (1994), *Power, Trade, and War* (Princeton, NJ: Princeton University Press).

Maoz, Zeev (2011), *Networks of Nations: The Evolution, Structure, and Impact of International Networks, 1816–2001* (New York: Cambridge University Press).

March, James G. (1966), "The Power of Power," in David Easton, ed., *Varieties of Political Theory* (Englewood Cliffs, NJ: Prentice-Hall), 39–70.

McCauley, Robert (1997), *The Euro and the Dollar*, Essays in International Finance 205 (Princeton, NJ: International Finance Section).

––––– (2011), "Internationalization of the Renminbi and China's Financial Development Model" (New York: Council on Foreign Relations).

McCauley, Robert, and Tracy Chan (2014), "Currency Movements Drive Reserve Composition," *BIS Quarterly Review*, December, 23–34.

McKeown, Timothy J. (1991), "A Liberal Trade Order? The Long-Run Pattern of Imports to the Advanced Capitalist States," *International Studies Quarterly* 35:2, 151–171.

McKinnon, Ronald I. (2011), "Oh, for an Alexander Hamilton to Save Europe!," *Financial Times*, 18 December.

—— (2013), *The Unloved Dollar Standard: From Bretton Woods to the Rise of China* (New York: Oxford University Press).

McNally, Christopher A. (2012), "Sino-Capitalism: China's Reemergence and the International Political Economy," *World Politics* 64:4 (October), 741–776.

McNamara, Kathleen R. (1998), *The Currency of Ideas: Monetary Politics in the European Union* (Ithaca, NY: Cornell University Press).

—— (2008), "A Rivalry in the Making? The Euro and International Monetary Power," *Review of International Political Economy* 15:3 (August), 439–459.

Mélitz, Jacques, and Frédéric Zumer (2002), "Regional Distribution and Stabilization by the Center in Canada, France, the UK and the US: A Reassessment and New Tests," *Journal of Public Economics* 86:2, 263–286.

Milner, Helen V. (1993), "American Debt and World Power," *International Journal* 48:3 (Summer), 527–560.

Modelski, George (1974), *World Power Concentrations: Typology, Data, Explanatory Framework* (Morristown, NJ: General Learning Press).

Moggridge, Donald, ed. (1980), *The Collected Writings of John Maynard Keynes* (Cambridge, UK: Cambridge University Press), vol. 25.

Momani, Bessma (2008), "Gulf Co-operation Council Oil Exporters and the Future of the Dollar," *New Political Economy* 13:3, 293–314.

Münchau, Wolfgang (2014), "Europe Faces the Horrors of Its Own House of Debt," *Financial Times*, 16 June.

Mundell, Robert A. (1993), "EMU and the International Monetary System: A Transatlantic Perspective," Working Paper 13 (Vienna: Austrian National Bank).

—— (2000), "The Euro and the Stability of the International Monetary System," in Robert A. Mundell and Armand Cleese, eds., *The Euro as a Stabilizer in the International Economic System* (Boston: Kluwer Academic), 57–84.

Nathan, Andrew J., and Andrew Scobell (2012), *China's Search for Security* (New York: Columbia University Press).

National Intelligence Council (2012), *Global Trends 2030: Alternative Worlds* (Washington, DC: National Intelligence Council).

Neumann, Manfred J. (1986), "Internationalization of German Banking and Finance," in Korea Federation of Banks, *Internationalization of Banking: Analysis and Prospects* (Seoul: Korea Federation of Banks), 67–144.

Norrlof, Carla (2008), "Strategic Debt," *Canadian Journal of Political Science* 41:2 (June), 411–435.

—— (2010), *America's Global Advantage: US Hegemony and International Cooperation* (New York: Cambridge University Press).

—— (2014a), "Dollar Hegemony: A Power Analysis," *Review of International Political Economy* 21:5 (October), 1042–1070.

—— (2014b), "States, Markets and the Dollar" (University of Toronto), unpublished.

Nye, Joseph S., Jr. (1990), "Soft Power," *Foreign Policy* 80 (Fall), 153–171.

—— (2008), *The Powers to Lead* (New York: Oxford University Press).

—— (2011), *The Future of Power* (New York: PublicAffairs).

Oatley, Thomas (2013), "The Macro-Dynamics of American Financial Power" (University of North Carolina), unpublished.

Oatley, Thomas, W. Kindred Winecoff, Andrew Pennock, and Sarah Bauerle Danzman (2013), "The Political Economy of Global Finance: A Network Model," *Perspectives on Politics* 11:1 (March), 133–153.

Okina, Kunio, Masaaki Shirakawa, and Shigenori Shiratsuka (2001), "The Asset Price Bubble and Monetary Policy: Japan's Experience in the Late 1980s and the Lessons," *Monetary and Economic Studies* 19: S-1 (February), 395–450.

Olivié, Iliana, Manuel Gracia, and Carola García-Calvo (2014), *Elcano Global Presence Report 2014* (Madrid: Royal Elcano Institute).

O'Rourke, Kevin H., and Alan M. Taylor (2013), "Cross of Euros," *Journal of Economic Perspectives* 27:3 (Summer), 167–192.

Otero-Iglesias, Miguel, and Federico Steinberg (2013a), "Is the Dollar Becoming a Negotiated Currency? Evidence from the Emerging Markets," *New Political Economy* 18:3, 309–336.

—— (2013b), "Reframing the Euro vs. Dollar Debate through the Perceptions of Financial Elites in Key Dollar-Holding Countries," *Review of International Political Economy* 20:1 (February), 180–214.

Overholt, Willam H., et al. (2014), "Will the Dollar Remain the Reserve Currency? A Symposium of Views," *International Economy*, Fall, 16–31.

Palan, Ronen P. (2003), "Pragmatism and International Relations in the Age of Banker's Capitalism: Susan Strange's Vision for a Critical International Political Economy," in Harry Bauer and Elisabetta Brighi, eds., *International Relations at LSE: A History of 75 Years* (London: Millennium Publishing Group), 117–138.

Pansardi, Pamela (2011), "Power To and Power Over," in Keith Dowding, ed., *Encyclopedia of Power* (Los Angeles: Sage Publications), 521–525.

Papaioannou, Elias, and Richard Portes (2008), *The International Role of the Euro: A Status Report* (Brussels: European Commission).

People's Bank of China Study Group (2006), "The Timing, Path, and Strategies of RMB Internationalization," *China Finance* 5, 12–13 [translated from Chinese].

Pickford, Stephen, Federico Steinberg, and Miguel Otero-Iglesias (2014), *How to Fix the Euro: Strengthening Economic Governance in Europe*, Joint Chatham House, Elcano and AREL Report (London: Chatham House).

Pillsbury, Michael (2000), *China Debates the Future Security Environment* (Washington, DC: National Defense University Press).

Posen, Adam (2008), "Why the Euro Will Not Rival the Dollar," *International Finance* 11:1 (Spring), 75–100.

Prasad, Eswar S. (2014), *The Dollar Trap: How the U.S. Dollar Tightened Its Grip on Global Finance* (Princeton, NJ: Princeton University Press).

Prasad, Eswar S., and Lei (Sandy) Ye (2012), *The Renminbi's Role in the Global Monetary System* (Washington, DC: Brookings Institution).

Pritchett, Lant, and Lawrence Summers (2014), "Asiaphoria Meet Regression to the Mean," Working Paper 20573 (Cambridge, MA: National Bureau of Economic Research).

Putnam, Robert D. (1988), "Diplomacy and Domestic Politics: The Logic of Two-Level Games," *International Organization* 42:3 (Summer), 427–460.

Quinlan, Joseph P., and Marc Chandler (2001), "The U.S. Trade Deficit: A Dangerous Obsession," *Foreign Affairs* 80:3 (May–June), 87–97.

Rajendran, Giri (2013), "Financial Blockades: Reserve Currencies as Instruments of Coercion," in Alan Wheatley, ed., *The Power of Currencies and Currencies of Power* (London; International Institute for Strategic Studies), 87–100.

Ray, J. L., and J. David Singer (1973), "Measuring the Concentration of Power in the International System," *Sociological Methods and Research* 1:4, 403–437.

Reich, Simon, and Richard Ned Lebow (2014), *Good-Bye Hegemony! Power and Influence in the Global System* (Princeton, NJ: Princeton University Press).

Rickards, James (2014), *The Death of Money: The Coming Collapse of the International Monetary System* (New York: Penguin).

Rogers, James, Daniel Fiott, and Luis Simón (2014), "European Geostrategy's 'Audit of Major Powers': The World's Fifteen Most Powerful Countries in 2014," *European Geostrategy*. Available at www.europeangeostrategy.org (accessed 28 January 2015).

Rolfe, Sidney E., and James L. Burtle (1974), *The Great Wheel: The World Monetary System—A Reinterpretation* (London: Macmillan).

Roubini, Nouriel (2011), "Greece Should Default and Abandon the Euro," *Financial Times*, 19 September.

Rueff, Jacques (1972), *The Monetary Sin of the West* (New York: Macmillan).

Ruggie, John G. (1983), "International Regimes, Transactions, and Change: Embedded Liberalism in the Postwar Economic Order," in Stephen D. Krasner, ed., *International Regimes* (Ithaca, NY: Cornell University Press), 195–231.

Sato, Kiyotaka (1999), "The International Use of the Japanese Yen: The Case of Japan's Trade with East Asia," *World Economy* 22:4 (June), 547–584.

Schenk, Catherine R. (2013), *The Decline of Sterling: Managing the Retreat of an International Currency, 1945–1992* (New York: Cambridge University Press).

Schwab, Klaus, ed. (2014), *The Global Competitiveness Report 2014–2015* (Geneva: World Economic Forum).

Schwartz, Herman M. (2009), *Subprime Nation: American Power, Global Capital, and the Housing Bubble* (Ithaca, NY: Cornell University Press).

Shambaugh, David (2013), *China Goes Global: The Partial Power* (New York: Oxford University Press).

Shambaugh, Jay C. (2012), "The Euro's Three Crises," *Brookings Papers on Economic Activity* (Spring), 157–211.

Sheng, Songcheng (2012), "The Basic Conditions Are Mature for Accelerating China's Capital Account Opening," *China Securities Journal*, 23 February.

Shigehara, Kumiharu (1991), "Japan's Experience with Use of Monetary Policy and the Process of Liberalization," *Monetary and Economic Studies* 9:1 (March), 1–21.

Simmons, Beth A. (2001), "The International Politics of Harmonization: The Case of Capital Market Regulation," *International Organization* 55:3 (Summer), 589–620.

Singer, J. David, Stuart Bremer, and John Stuckey (1972), "Capability Distribution, Uncertainty, and Major Power War, 1820–1965," in Bruce Russett, ed., *Peace, War, and Numbers* (Beverly Hills, CA: Sage), 19–48.

Sobel, Andrew C. (2012), *Birth of Hegemony: Crisis, Financial Revolution, and Emerging Global Networks* (Chicago: University of Chicago Press).

Spiro, David E. (1999), *The Hidden Hand of American Hegemony: Petrodollar Recycling and International Markets* (Ithaca, NY: Cornell University Press).

Starrs, Sean (2013), "American Economic Power Hasn't Declined—It Globalized! Summoning the Data and Taking Globalization Seriously," *International Studies Quarterly* 57:4 (December), 817–830.

Stokes, Doug (2014), "Achilles' Deal: Dollar Decline and US Grand Strategy after the Crisis," *Review of International Political Economy* 21:5 (October), 1071–1094.

Strange, Susan (1971a), "The Politics of International Currencies," *World Politics* 23:2 (January), 215–231.

—— (1971b), *Sterling and British Policy* (London: Oxford University Press).

—— (1979), "Review of *Organizing the World's Money*, by Benjamin J. Cohen," *International Affairs* 55:1 (January), 107–109.

—— (1980), "Germany and the World Monetary System," in Wilfred Kohl and Giorgio Basevi, eds., *West Germany: A European and Global Power* (Lexington, MA: Lexington Books), 45–62.

—— (1988), *States and Markets* (London: Pinter Publishers).

—— (1994), "Who Governs? Networks of Power in World Society," *Hitotsubashi Journal of Law and Politics* 22: Special Issue (June), 5–17.

—— (1996), *The Retreat of the State: The Diffusion of Power in the World Economy* (London: Cambridge University Press).

Subacchi, Paola (2010), "'One Currency, Two Systems': China's Renminbi Strategy," Chatham House Briefing Paper (London: Royal Institute of International Affairs).

Subramanian, Arvind (2011), *Eclipse: Living in the Shadow of China's Economic Dominance* (Washington, DC: Peterson Institute for International Economics).

Subramanian, Arvind, and Martin Kessler (2012), "The Renminbi Bloc Is Here: Asia Down, Rest of the World to Go?," Working Paper WP 12-19 (Washington, DC: Peterson Institute for International Economics).

Swoboda, Alexander K. (1968), *The Euro-Dollar Market: An Interpretation*, Essays in International Finance 64 (Princeton, NJ: International Finance Section).

Takagi, Shinji (2012), "Internationalizing the Yen, 1984–2003: Unfinished Agenda or Mission Impossible?," BIS Papers 61 (Basel: Bank for International Settlements).

Tavlas, George S. (1991), *On the International Use of Currencies: The Case of the Deutsche Mark*, Essays in International Finance 181 (Princeton, NJ: International Finance Section).

Tavlas, George S., and Yuzuru Ozeki (1992), *The Internationalization of Currencies: An Appraisal of the Japanese Yen*, Occasional Paper 90 (Washington, DC: International Monetary Fund).

Tett, Gillian (2014), "Why the Dollar Stays Steady as America Declines," *Financial Times*, 6 February.

Thimann, Christian (2008), "Global Role of Currencies," *International Finance* 11:3 (Winter), 211–245.

Thomas, Landon (2014), "Bouyant Dollar Recovers Its Luster, Underlining Rebound in U.S. Economy," *New York Times*, 26 September.

Thompson, William R. (1988), *On Global War: Historical-Structural Approaches to World Politics* (Columbia: University of South Carolina Press).

Thygesen, Niels (1995), *International Currency Competition and the Future Role of the Single European Currency*, Final Report of a Working Group on European Monetary Union—International Monetary System (London: Kluwer Law International).

Tilford, Simon (2007), "The Euro as the World's Reserve Currency?," posted on the blog of the Centre for European Reform. Available at http://centrefor europeanreform.blogspot.com/2007/11/euro–as–world's–reserve–currency .html (accessed 28 January 2015).

Transparency International (2014), *Corruption Perceptions Index 2014* (Berlin: Transparency International).

Triffin, Robert (1960a), *Gold and the Dollar Crisis* (New Haven, CT: Yale University Press).

——— (1960b), "Statement of Robert Triffin to the Joint Economic Committee of the Congress," December 8 (Washington, DC: Government Printing Office), 228–233.

Unger, David C. (2013), "Who Can Bring the EU to Its Senses?," *New York Times*, 31 March.

Vermeiren, Mattias (2014), *Power and Imbalances in the Global Monetary System: A Comparative Capitalism Perspective* (London: Palgrave Macmillan).

Viotti, Paul R. (2014), *The Dollar and National Security: The Monetary Component of Hard Power* (Stanford, CA: Stanford University Press).

Volz, Ulrich (2014), "All Politics Is Local: The Renminbi's Prospects as a Future Global Currency," in Leslie E. Armijo and Saori Katada, eds., *The Financial Statecraft of Emerging Powers: Shield and Sword in Asia and Latin America* (New York: Palgrave Macmillan), 103–137.

Von Hagen, Jürgen, and Michele Fratianni (1990), "German Dominance in the EMS: Evidence from Interest Rates," *Journal of International Money and Finance* 9:4 (December), 358–375.

Walter, Stefanie (2013), *Financial Crises and the Politics of Macroeconomic Adjustments* (New York: Cambridge University Press).

Warnock, Francis E., and Veronica Cacdac Warnock (2009), "International Capital Flows and U.S. Interest Rates," *Journal of International Money and Finance* 28:6 (October), 903–919.

Webb, Michael C. (1994), "Capital Mobility and the Possibilities for International Policy Coordination," *Policy Sciences* 27:4 (December), 395–423.

Westad, Odd Arne (2013), "In Asia, Ill Will Runs Deep," *New York Times*, 7 January.

Wheatley, Alan (2013a), "Introduction," in Alan Wheatley, ed., *The Power of Currencies and Currencies of Power* (London: International Institute for Strategic Studies), 9–16.

————— (2013b), "The Origins and Use of Currency Power," in Alan Wheatley, ed., *The Power of Currencies and Currencies of Power* (London: International Institute for Strategic Studies), 17–43.

————— (2013c), "The Pretenders to the Dollar's Crown," in Alan Wheatley, ed., *The Power of Currencies and Currencies of Power* (London: International Institute for Strategic Studies), 45–73.

Williamson, John (2013), "The Dollar and US Power," in Alan Wheatley, ed., *The Power of Currencies and Currencies of Power* (London: International Institute for Strategic Studies), 75–85.

World Bank (2011), *Multipolarity: The New Global Economy* (Washington, DC: World Bank).

————— (2012), *China 2030: Building a Modern, Harmonious, and Creative High-Income Society* (Washington, DC: World Bank).

————— (2014), *Worldwide Governance Indicators*. Available at www.info.world bank.org/governance (accessed 12 October 2014).

Wyplosz, Charles (1999), "An International Role for the Euro?," in Jean Dermine and Pierre Hilton, eds., *European Capital Markets with a Single Currency* (New York: Oxford University Press), 76–104.

Xi, Jinping (2014), "Long Distance Does Not Weaken Close Friendship," remarks to journalists, 15 July. Available at www.globallearning-cuba.com/xi-jinping -president-of-china.html (accessed 4 August 2014).

Zhang, Ming (2009), "China's New International Financial Strategy amid the Global Financial Crisis," *China and World Economy* 17:5 (September–October), 22–35.

Zimmermann, Hubert (2002), *Money and Security: Troops, Monetary Policy, and West Germany's Relations with the United States and Britain, 1950–1971* (New York: Cambridge University Press).

—————(2013), "Can the Euro Rival the Dollar?," in Alan W. Cafruny and Herman M. Schwartz, eds., *Exploring the Global Financial Crisis* (Boulder, CO: Lynne Rienner), 147–162.

Zweifel, Patrick (2014), "Era of Renminbi Dawns as China's Influence Grows," *Financial Times*, 6 January.

Index